THE LIFE WORTH LIVING

THE
LIFE
WORTH
LIVING

DISABILITY, PAIN, AND MORALITY

Joel Michael Reynolds

University of Minnesota Press
Minneapolis
London

Small portions of the Introduction were previously published in "'I'd Rather Be Dead than Disabled'—The Ableist Conflation and the Meanings of Disability," *Review of Communication* 17, no. 3 (2017): 149–63, and in "Merleau-Ponty, World-Creating Blindness, and the Phenomenology of Non-Normate Bodies," *Chiasmi International: Trilingual Studies Concerning the Thought of Merleau-Ponty* 19 (2017): 419–36. A minor portion of chapter 2 was previously published in "Feeding upon Death: Pain, Possibility, and Transformation in S. Kay Toombs and Kafka's 'The Vulture,'" in *Jahrbuch Litertur und Medizin,* ed. Bettina von Jagow and Florian Steger, vol. 6, 135–54 (Heidelberg: Universit.tsverlag Winter, 2014).

Published by the University of Minnesota Press
111 Third Avenue South, Suite 290
Minneapolis, MN 55401-2520
http://www.upress.umn.edu

ISBN 978-1-5179-0265-0 (hc)
ISBN 978-1-5179-0778-5 (pb)

A Cataloging-in-Publication record for this book is available from the Library of Congress.

Printed in the United States of America on acid-free paper

The University of Minnesota is an equal-opportunity educator and employer.

31 30 29 28 27 26 25 24 23 22   10 9 8 7 6 5 4 3 2 1

For Jason and Gail
And for the principal supports without
which they, and I, would not exist:
Alan, Papa Jack, and Grandma Babe

[Alyosha] "Brother, let me ask you one more thing: can it be that any man has the right to decide about the rest of mankind, who is worthy to live and who is more unworthy?"

[Ivan] "But why bring worth into it? The question is most often decided in the hearts of men not at all on the basis of worth, but for quite different reasons, much more natural ones."

—Dostoevsky, *The Brothers Karamazov*

Contents

Introduction

The Ableist Conflation

> The history of ethics shows all too clearly how much our
> thinking is shaped by what our sages omit to mention.
>
> —Mary Midgley, "Duties Concerning Islands"

> Let us discuss this, then, starting from the beginning
> [λέγωμεν οὖν ἀρξάμενοι].
>
> —Aristotle, final line of *Nicomachean Ethics*

On his death bed, awaiting the vial of hemlock that would consummate his juried execution, Socrates asks, "Is life worth living with a body that is corrupted and in a bad condition?" "In no way," replies his friend Crito (Plato, *Crito,* 47e).[1] This judgment will be repeated across cultures and epochs: the corrupted body, a body many today would call a disabled body, is so undesirable that one would rather not be than bear its existence. Here, at the canonical origins of the Western intellectual tradition, one finds certainty that some forms of life are worth less than others or not worth living at all.[2]

In the end, the Socratic deathbed hallows an otherworldly set of values. From Plato to Aquinas, Descartes to Kant and beyond, the life of the body for the "Western canon" is so often held to be worth less than that of the mind—and the lives of certain bodies and certain minds deemed worth less still. Yet, what do the actual conditions of life, the fleshy, enmeshed conditions that forever come to us with a past, present, and future, in fact tell us? What does the constitutive variability of our bodies suggest about how we ought to treat others and the worth of a life? What, to invoke the troubling insight of

Dostoevsky's Ivan, are the "much more natural" reasons than worth that in fact determine the worth of life, and who has the right to decide it?

This work is an attempt to answer these questions by investigating the claim that some lives are not worth living. This idea has enjoyed an astonishing consensus across the history of philosophy—to the point that it often functions as an *arche,* a foundation for and origin of further thought, judgment, and action.

The invariable variability of human embodiment underwrites all human values, including that of *life worthy of life.* Disability, one name for such variability, is a touchstone for both how we are and how we ought to strive to be. In arguing so, I contend that the Socratic deathbed, a millennia-spanning metaphor for unyielding commitment to both truth and justice, is not the beginning of the examined life worth living but instead an end for countless lives, examined or not. It is an end, a deathbed, and a sentence for so many because Socrates, Plato, and the many traditions that followed *failed to appreciate the meaning of disability.*

Within the canonical Western history of philosophy, disability has been understood above all as lack and privation. In an example to which I will return in greater detail in chapter 3, Aristotle (*Metaphysics,* 2:1615/1022b27–22) writes:

> Blindness *(tuphlotes)* is a privation *(steresis),* but one is not blind at any and every age, but only if one has not sight at the age at which one would naturally have it. Similarly a thing suffers privation when it has not an attribute in those circumstances, or in that respect and in that relation and in that sense, in which it would naturally have it.—The violent taking away *(biaia aphaeresis)* of anything is called privation.[3]

The idea that disabilities like blindness are defined by lack, defined by a violent, harmful taking away, is translated into policy in his *Politics*: "as for the exposure and rearing of children, let there be a law that no deformed [*peperomenon*] child shall live" (1335b20–21). For Aristotle, this conceptualization of a particular set of bodily forms—those that are *peperomenon,* "mutilated," "deformed," or "malformed"—is obvious. He neither offers a substantive definition of the term nor seems bothered to address limit cases.

In many ways agreeing with Aristotle, Kant will later claim, "infirmity of the mind [*Gebrechen des Gemüths*] is just such a crippled state [*krüppelhafter Zustand*] of mind, as infirmity of the body is a crippled state for the body. Infirmities are not hindrances of the powers [*Kräfte*] of mind, but a lack [*ein Mangel*], but the latter exists when the condition for the regular use of the powers [*regelmäßigen Gebrauchs der Kräfte*] of mind is lacking" (Kant 2012, 113/25:554). To the extent that one does not meet Kant's implicit or explicit norms for mental ability, one is lacking, and lacking fundamentally as a "human." It is telling that there are ongoing and serious scholarly arguments over whether it is possible to grant people with intellectual disability moral status within a Kantian framework, notwithstanding the fact that Kant himself didn't think it possible.

Or take Mill's famous judgment about happiness and satisfaction: "better to be Socrates dissatisfied than a fool satisfied" (Mill 2006, 212).[4] Fool, in late nineteenth-century English, typically picks out what today would be called a type of "intellectual disability." In that light, one could read Mill as in fact reiterating a variation of Socrates's rhetorical question.[5] A lack of intelligence, regardless of the outcome that lack has on overall well-being, is worse than not having that lack. Furthermore, Mill claims that if the fool judges their life in fact to be as satisfactory as the nonfool's, "it is because they only know their own side of the question. The other party to the comparison knows both sides." Does the other side know? How do they have knowledge about an experience of which they have never been privy? Assuming so is a textbook case of epistemic injustice against those with other sorts of experiences, especially intellectual disabilities with respect to which the very parameters of satisfaction may be importantly different (Dohmen 2016). This is also a paradigmatic result of what Robert McRuer calls "compulsory able-bodiedness," wherein assumptions based in able-bodied experiences shape what counts as knowledge and knowing by default (McRuer 2006). In the (ableist) philosophical imaginary, it seems there are no limits to what the *able body* can know.

These are just a few instances demonstrating how ableism shapes philosophical, not to mention other forms, of thinking. Yet, tellingly, each of these instances fails for the same core reason: it understands disability as a lack, and a lack that cannot but result in reduction of happiness—a lack, in other words, that brings about pain and suffering, as compared to an idealized able body, which is to say, the normate. One reason for philosophy's long-standing failure to reflect carefully upon disability is the absence, devaluation, or active ignornace of the testimony of people who are disabled, of those whose bodies and minds have for so long in philosophy been considered worth less or worthless. If the question of the life worth living is to move beyond ignorance and prejudice, then philosophy itself must be reexamined through the lived experiences of disability.

The Ableist Conflation

The central argument of this book can be stated simply: the canonical idea that some lives are not worth living results from the ableist conflation of disability with pain and suffering. That is to say, the reason for this entrenched, tradition-spanning idea is the habit of thought wherein one conflates experiences of pain and suffering with experiences of disability—experiences whose form, mode, matter, or style of living is considered categorically outside ableist norms.

I offer the *ableist conflation* as a concept to capture the underlying presuppositions that guide ableist discourses and practices in philosophy; ethics; politics; medicine; local, national, and international policy; and beyond. Although it can take many forms, the ableist conflation involves some variation of at least the following four claims:

1. Disability necessarily involves a lack or deprivation of a natural good.
2. Deprivation of a natural good is a harm.
3. Harm causes or is itself a form of pain and suffering.[6]
4. Given 1–3, disability comes along with or directly causes pain and suffering.

The ableist conflation functions in part by capitalizing upon the ambiguity of the array of terms it involves. *Disability, harm, pain,* and *suffering* are all uncritically underdefined, as are the relations between them. A central goal of this book is to decouple disability and pain through phenomenological investigation and, by doing so, to dismantle the ableist conflation and the uncritical assumptions behind each of its operative terms.

My description of the ableist conflation synthesizes and builds out groundbreaking claims made by disability studies scholars and, before them, disability rights activists since at least the time of the Union of the Physically Impaired against Segregation in the United Kingdom and the Independent Living Movement in the United States. These activists fought tooth and nail against both locally and globally dominant understandings of disability, namely, understandings that took disability as "something to be avoided," that confers "pain, disease, suffering, functional limitation, abnormality, dependence, social stigma, and economic disadvantage and [limits] life opportunities and quality" (Garland-Thomson 2012, 340). To combat the ableist conflation, however, it is not enough to claim that experiences of disability and pain are separate—it also requires reflection, in a rigorous and not reflexive manner, upon how they can be related in certain circumstances and contexts.

The reality is that, historically, most scholars in disability studies and philosophy of disability have avoided the problem of pain. Impaired conditions involving pain have more often than not been left to the side in discussions both theoretical and concrete. As Margaret Price (2015, 276) puts the matter, echoing earlier work by scholars like Liz Crow and Susan Wendell, "feminist disability studies, particularly in its American iteration, has not yet contended much with pain." But, if the thesis of the ableist conflation is correct, then failing to deal with the relation between disability and pain is failing to deal with one of the primary obstacles not only to disability justice but to justice writ large.

By taking the ableist conflation head-on, this project thus contributes to what is an old yet undying problem in disability studies and philosophy of disability in at least five respects: by

1. situating the ableist conflation in the context of the history of philosophy;
2. explaining its origins and demonstrating its failings in light of phenomenological analysis;
3. offering novel analyses of both pain and disability, including their contrasts and comparisons specifically as these bear upon disability theory;
4. expanding and refining existing concepts that distinguish experiences amid and across disability differences, ability transitions, and, most broadly of all, ability troubles of all sorts; and

  5. further developing a theory of ability based on the concept of access.

If one is still at this point unconvinced that a philosophical analysis centered on disability and pain—and one methodologically rooted in phenomenology—is needed, let me place this project in what I take to be its larger philosophical context. Whether based in virtue, duty, utility, or social contract, models of flourishing in the canon of the so-called Western intellectual tradition assume a general minimization of pain to be a central goal. Pain is, in turn, thought of as a sort of constraint or lack relative to potentials of purposiveness and flourishing. All such models of flourishing also assume that the corporeal variations we today categorize as "disabilities" are, on the whole, constraints or lacks relative to those potentials, whether defined in primarily physiological or psychological terms. The ableist conflation, then, names a prevalent facet not only of historical and contemporary imaginaries but of *reflective thought* undergirding multiple canons and traditions as they take up the project of human life.[7]

In a related manner to Charles Mills's (1994) damning claim that there exists "a conceptual or theoretical whiteness" that serves as a "pretheoretical intuition" for the discipline of philosophy, there exists a conceptual or theoretical *ableism* that serves as a pretheoretical intuition for the discipline of philosophy, an ableism underwritten by the framework of the ableist conflation. It is in this light that I contend that the ableist conflation is still today the most pressing and pernicious issue facing reflective thought about disabled experience and that I find ableism to be a problem that philosophy, as a whole, has yet to take as seriously as it should (Tremain 2015a).[8] The ableist conflation, despite notable political and academic victories, is an old, ingrained problem whose grip on the present, and not just the philosophical present, forcefully shapes the wider global scales of cultural, sociopolitical, legal, and philosophical judgment over lives worth living.

With minimal alteration, the ableist conflation can support eugenic discourses and practices. For example, consider the following claim, one for which people across the political spectrum typically express support: "the aim of politics and ethics is to maximize flourishing, in part by reducing harms and ameliorating pain and suffering." If claim 4 of the ableist conflation holds, then it seems to follow that individuals and the state are in certain cases justified in ending or otherwise curtailing the lives of people with disabilities. Justice Oliver Wendell Holmes Jr. articulated this eugenic form of the ableist conflation with crystal clarity in the majority opinion for the 1927 *Buck v. Bell* U.S. Supreme Court decision: "the public welfare may call upon the best citizens for their lives. It would be strange if it could not call upon those who already sap the strength of the State for these lesser sacrifices . . . in order to prevent our being swamped with incompetence. It is better for all the world, if . . . society can prevent those who are manifestly unfit from continuing their kind. . . . Three generations of imbeciles are enough." To maximize flourishing, this decision affirms that the state can forcibly call on the "unfit" not to reproduce. Their reproduction constitutes a *harm* against the state, so they can be sterilized against their will. For Justice Holmes, certain forms of disability don't just trump liberal egalitarianism; they call on a liberal society to end the reproductive futures of some of its citizens. A most illiberal inference, indeed. One might think these ideas to have died out in our supposedly "posteugenic" world, but that would, sadly, be wrong.

The Case of the Problem of Ableism in Bioethics

Bioethics, a field meant to support the ethical treatment of human and, increasingly, nonhuman animal life, is rife with examples that reveal the harmful effects of the ableist conflation. Both bioethics literature and downstream biomedical practices are still today too often structured by what disability studies scholars call the medical model of disability: disability understood merely as an individual tragedy or misfortune due to genetic or environmental insult. This interpretation persists despite decades of disability activism and critical disability studies scholarship spanning the humanities and social sciences that show this model to be problematic, if not irremediable, except in highly qualified circumstances. When bioethicists do engage alternative, nonmedical conceptions of disability, such alternatives are too often conglomerated into a mere "position." They are treated as if there were some subset of people who simply have a different view about disability and as if ethicists, after fulfilling the due diligence of mentioning that view, can go on with metaethical, normative, or applied business as usual. This type of scholarly attitude is also reflected in practical domains. For example, the extent and role of education about disability in medical education and training are still today points of contestation (McKim 2005). Given this, it is unsurprising that people with disabilities report significantly higher inadequacies than people without disabilities in patient–provider communication (Smith 2009). It is also unsurprising that people with disabilities are disproportionately impacted by medical error (Pena-Guzman and Reynolds 2019).

Wherever operative, the ableist conflation flattens communication about disability to communication about pain, suffering, hardship, undesirable experiences, morbidity, and mortality. Take the following argument, from a text still referenced today, by four prominent bioethicists, meant to address critiques from what they call the "radical disability rights advocates":

> We devalue disabilities because we value the opportunities and welfare of the people who have them. And it is because we value people, all people, that we care about limitations on their welfare and opportunities. We also know that disabilities *as such* diminish opportunities and welfare, even when they are not so severe that the lives of those who have them are not worth living, and even if those individuals do not literally suffer as a result of their disabilities. Thus there is nothing irrational, motivationally incoherent, or disingenuous in saying that we devalue the disabilities and wish to reduce their incidence while valuing existing persons with disabilities, and that we value them the same as those who do not have disabilities. (Buchanan et al. 2000, 278)

Though they don't explain how, the authors claim to *know* that "disabilities *as such* diminish opportunities and welfare" (my italics). In the hope that one is interested in arguments, not assumptions, what is the actual relationship between disability and such "diminishments"? And insofar as lives are *defined by* disability along social, narrative, political, and other dimensions, and in many cases defined so with *pride*, what would it mean to devalue disability "as such" but not the person with disabilities? Given the intersection of one's embodiment and social location with one's identity, this distinction is patently specious and betrays a fundamental misunderstanding of disability experiences and, for that matter, decades of disability theory and work on embodiment and social identity more broadly.

The use and meaning of disability in Buchanan et al.'s text varies greatly and serves as a useful example of equivocation, confusion, naïveté, or active ignorance among bioethicists or philosophers on the topic. For example, the authors regularly commit the ableist conflation by using phrases like "disease and disability" (10, 51, 105, 124, 182, 345, etc.), "harm or disability" (227), and the "great burden of disability or exclusion" (321) and by grouping "disease, disorder, impairment, or disability" (106). In other words, despite being aware of and laudably engaging at least some disability studies and activism, their indiscriminate exchange of the terms *impairment, disability,* and *disease* is inconsistent and betrays an underlying acceptance of the ableist conflation.[9]

To be clear, the situation in the field of bioethics is improving as a growing number of bioethicists seriously engage and build on disability critiques of the field (Parens and Asch 2000; Scully 2008; Garland-Thomson 2015b). In fact, if one understands "disability bioethics" as an approach to bioethics that centers the lived experiences of people with disabilities and is rooted in research from disability studies and disability experiences writ large, it is increasingly recognized in bioethics and beyond (Reynolds and Wieseler, 2022). As positive as this development is, the ableist conflation is a habit of thought that has proved quite recalcitrant, and greater clarity is needed if it is to be sufficiently overcome.

Ability Trouble

Popular discourse engaging biomedical ethics sometimes goes even further than previous examples, exhibiting the ableist conflation to such a degree that disability is taken to be essentially *no different than* pain and suffering. To take an especially egregious example, witness the actual variability of embodied conditions and how we use and experience our bodies, as well as the performances and scripts by and through which we all play, be leveled to the ableist ground by Steven Pinker in a 2015 *Boston Globe* op-ed:

> Some say that it's simple prudence to pause and consider the long-term implications of [biomedical] research before it rushes headlong into changing the human condition. But this is an illusion. . . . Slowing down research has a massive human cost. Even a one-year

delay in implementing an effective treatment could spell death, suffering, or disability for millions of people.

Setting aside the patently question-begging nature of his argument, Pinker finds that death, suffering, and disability are so similar that they can be listed together as experiences no one wants, and obviously so. Imagine making sense of one's life when one is labeled "disabled" under such circumstances. Imagine the limitations thereby placed upon communication and understanding about it from the outset. Insofar as Pinker appeals to common sense, a disabled person who disagrees with the aspiration of "eliminating disability" begins on defense about the experience of their own life.

Pinker's understanding is in step with the majority of transhumanists and posthumanists.[10] Thinkers, activists, and others who claim such a title typically seek the total eradication of "disability" from the human species as a central goal. Yet they rarely, if ever, critically reflect on their use of that term, not to mention the copious literatures that engage it, whether reflective or empirical in nature (Hall 2016). Trans- and posthumanists conflate a whole range of corporeal variabilities categorized as "disabilities" not only with pain and suffering but also with disease, illness, morbidity, and mortality. To be fair, Pinker does not explicitly claim in the foregoing quote that disability is in and of itself a type of suffering or identical to it. Yet, the rhetorical force of his series "death, suffering, or disability" could not be clearer: these phenomena are identical in that no one desires to experience them. Pinker capitalizes on this false equalization to fan the flames of urgency in countering the "threat" this triumvirate poses to progress.

In another section from the same piece, he writes:

Have you had a friend or relative who died prematurely or endured years of suffering from a physical or psychiatric disease, such as cancer, heart disease, Alzheimer's, Huntington's, Parkinson's, or schizophrenia? Of course you have: the cost of disease is felt by every living human. The Global Burden of Disease Project has tried to quantify it by estimating the number of years lost to premature death or compromised by disability. In 2010 it was 2.5 billion, which means that about a third of potential human life and flourishing goes to waste. The toll from crime, wars, and genocides does not come anywhere close.

Disease, disability, and (premature) death are treated interchangeably. In terms of its negative status for potential human life and flourishing, disability is here of a kind with death, crime, war, and genocide. Disability, as Pinker understands it, is a form of constitutive, if not consuming, pain and suffering. He not only commits the ableist conflation but then employs its logic to argue against ethical reflection that would halt or slow the future of biomedical technologies. This night in which all nonnormate bodies are bad leaves one wondering what the day must look like. Worry about risk on your own time, Pinker implies, because our globalized society must immediately continue reducing disability, disease, and death. Here the force of the ableist conflation to foreclose the lived experience and meaningfulness of disability—and, ultimately, the meaning of being human as such—is on full display. It is a bold-faced linking of disability with pain, suffering, and death that culminates in such a spectacle of ignorant, uncritical thinking about disability, embodiment, and flourishing.

Undoing the Ableist Conflation

Combating harmful ableist attitudes in philosophy, bioethics, and popular culture requires getting at the root of the ableist conflation of disability with privation, pain, suffering, and death. This project does so by providing critical phenomenological analyses of pain and of disability to see where they are distinct as well as where and how they intersect, which is to say, by critically looking to lived experience. Throughout the book, I emphasize the ways that pain and disability remain diverse and varied experiences that challenge attempts to unite them, let alone distinctively philosophical attempts to sufficiently account for them. In doing so, I show how a phenomenological understanding of disability and ability can reorient philosophy in a more genuinely ethical direction that embraces the many ways and modes of human, ever-embodied life that in fact make up our world.

In chapter 1, I analyze dominant theories of pain, detailing the meaning of pain in religious, neurobiological, humanist, existential, and biomedical theories. I show how pain functions regulatively in each of these domains: how it orients and directs one's relationship to oneself and one's life. There is a long-standing tension between theories that hold pain to be uniquely subjective—"no one can feel my pain"—and those that hold it to be deeply intersubjective, for example, group-based traumas. I argue that pain vacillates between these two poles because pain is simultaneously that which opens and closes us off to the world. Pain is paradigmatic of the porous beings we are. Most theories of pain go awry by thinking of pain as a discrete quality or feeling. On the contrary, pain—like gravity—is a force. We can measure it, feel it, alter it, study it, and even exploit it, but we still don't really know how it works, nor do we know how to hold together its many disparate meanings. At an existential level, we ultimately understand pain through knowledge of the force it exerts on our lives, for, when all is said and done, the measurer cannot disappear from the scene of measurement. In light of this conundrum, as well as that of the differential meaning of pain across its many theories, I argue that it serves a single, overarching role at the level of lived experience: pain is a command to reorient oneself.

With this thesis in mind, and following in the footsteps of recent work in critical phenomenology (Guenther 2013), I develop a phenomenology of chronic pain in chapter 2 through the case of complex regional pain syndrome. After a detailed description of living in chronic pain, I argue that chronic pain involves four general features: foreboding, beholdenness, bioreckoning, and disruption. After analyzing examples of each, I close the chapter by discussing the central problem of chronic pain and illness: though all theories of pain work to afford one a way to regain one's sense of agency, constitutive and consuming pain is fundamentally deregulative and disorienting. Such experiences are antithetical to *anyone's* sense of agency and well-being. I offer a novel set of analytic differences concerning different types of lived pain (Leder 2016; Carel 2016), and I engage wider debates over the meaning of pain, with respect to both the seminal work of Elaine Scarry and also contemporary debates in philosophy of mind (Scarry 1985; Klein 2015).

In chapter 3, I provide an overview of theories of disability. I group these according to three primary categories: personal, social, and postsocial theories. I first address the moral theory of disability by looking to its treatment in the Abrahamic traditions before turning to the much-maligned medical model, which I show to be problematically alive and well through an analysis of recent medical textbooks. I then briefly address the complex history of social models of disability, including their origins in disability activism in the United Kingdom and United States as well as the development of biopsychosocial models, largely by those working in the social sciences, in the late 1980s to 1990s. Last, I examine two leading postsocial theories: dispersive approaches angled against identity politics, such as that of Lennard J. Davis, and genealogical approaches operating under the theoretical aegis of biopolitics, such as that of Shelly Tremain. In notable contrast to theories of pain, I show how neither personal nor postsocial but only social theories of disability afford self-regulation and assist in purposive action. Unlike experiences of pain, experiences of disability do not automatically issue regulative commands. At the broadest level, I argue that the meaning of disability is instead defined by the experience of being nonnormate.

I then contrast these theories with a phenomenology of disability in chapter 4. Drawing especially upon the life and work of S. Kay Toombs, I do so through the case of a noncongenital, late-onset, and degenerative disability: multiple sclerosis (MS). I argue that, phenomenologically, MS involves three primary, general features: attentional, personal–social, and existential reconfiguration. As a whole, this phenomenology demonstrates how even in the case of a noncongenital, degenerative disability, the link between disability and constitutive or consuming pain proves false. Corporeal alteration does not entail degradation. New normals, new goods, and new senses of self arise as others fall away. Yet, the ableist conflation's connection of constitutive pain with disability leads to an interpretive aporia for disabled people, preemptively hindering one's ability to comprehend and narrate one's life lived with disability to oneself and to others and also fundamentally undercutting inclusive political goals (cf. Stramondo 2020).

In chapter 5, I bring together the conclusions of the last four chapters to defend the following argument: the ableist conflation gets experiences of disability and pain so wrong because of its implicit conception of ability—ability as personal control. This conception is indefensible. After laying out how that idea works, I then turn in chapter 6 to a phenomenology of ability. Unlike accounts of access that focus largely on the built environment (Hamraie 2017; Titchkosky 2011), on the role of normality for sociocultural knowledge, institutions, and practices (Kafer 2013; Davis 2013b), or on organism–environment relations of affordance (Gibson 1979), I offer a phenomenology that understands access and caring systems as fundamental to human being-in-the-world. This account builds on yet goes beyond recent social accounts of disability (Barnes 2016).

I conclude by recalling the stakes of ableism for philosophy in general and ethical inquiry in particular. I return to the fact that people with disabilities and people living in pain have historically been given remarkably short shrift by philosophers. While some recent social-political philosophers have worked to address this, too many see the sociopolitical stakes of disability as primarily a question of inclusion. My research, in step with many others in disability studies and philosophy of disability, suggests that the problem is much more complex. Disability has not been included in theories of justice and models of flourishing for a simple reason: it cannot be included precisely insofar as it designates an experience of pain and suffering—that for which normative theories seek redress, not support. But that designation is false. The lived experiences of disability demand of philosophical inquiry a far richer account of human flourishing and embodiment. Honoring and following more than a half-century of work by disability studies scholars and disability activists, I call for an anti-ableist future grounded in the myriad experiences of disability and actively engaged with experiential insights concerning the profound meaning and value afforded by human corporeal (body and mind) variability.

PART I

Pain

1
Theories of Pain

Though what is painful is borne for a short time, no one could continuously endure even the Good Itself if it were painful to him.

—Aristotle, *Nicomachean Ethics*

Today hurts.

The world feels different. Light—its expanse, its warmth—is an adversary. Motion—that energy breaking in and pushing out, that dynamism we equivocate as power itself—is in cuffs. Radiating tendrils of pressure and tension grip your eyes like clamps. Sight and sound turn against you, extinguishing each and every effort. Is this a "migraine headache"? The phrase seems completely insufficient for this unnamable agony. What could name this pain that destroys relations to the old, familiar world? Is there a word for that? Wouldn't that word first need to exist in the old world, the world before everything was different? Could it traverse each, going back and forth, around and back again? Can a word pirouette like that, describing an experience so disorienting that it can uproot the very possibility of meaning?

The English noun *pain* originates from the classical Latin *poena*: "penalty, punishment, satisfaction, revenge, unpleasant consequence" and in postclassical Latin also "suffering" and "affliction." The Latin root, in turn, originates from the Attic Greek *poine* (ποινή): "blood money, fine, penalty, satisfaction, reward." The Indo-European foundation of this root, appearing in multiple languages, holds the same core sense: *pain is the price one pays for something.*[1] This "for" structure is constitutive of pain's sense. Etymologically, pain is always in a dynamic relationship, one that cannot be understood in terms of its mere happening. By definition, pain has a cause, an etiology, a why.

Yet, as I argued in the introduction, ableist habits of thought repeatedly conflate disability with pain and suffering to such a degree that this conceptual confusion is a foundational problematic for critical reflection on disability. I hope to here explore the hypothesis that ableism, and the ableist conflation in particular, is predicated on a misunderstanding of pain. That is why, as a first step, the complex phenomenon of pain must be examined more carefully. How, then, is ableism connected to pain? First, a definition of ableism is in order. Definitions abound, but for the purposes at hand, I understand ableism to involve two component presumptions.[2] The first component is the presumption of a standard body. More technically, this is an ontological presumption that holds there to be psychological and physiological norms sufficient to distinguish normality from abnormality (cf. Canguilhem 1978). This presumption is indefensible in the sense that it must discount the facts of variability of bodies and minds, and it is harmful insofar as it creates a hierarchy that, whether implicitly or explicitly, disparages those outside ableist norms. The second component is the presumption that disabled ways of being are undesirable and thereby in some form or another involve pain and/ or suffering. This is an existential presumption insofar as it defines the nature and value of the *way lives are experienced* that fall on the hither side of the ontological presumption of a standard body.

Joining these two presumptions together leads to the following definition of ableism: (1) the "standard" or "normal" able body is, all other things being equal, better than nonstandard, nonnormate bodies in form, matter, manner, and prospect *by virtue of* being standard or normal, and (2) this judgment holds whether with respect to social practices, institutions, laws, kinship relations, or what have you (Reynolds 2015, 59). The idea that there is a "standard" or "normal" body—which is to say, the idea that there is some uncontroversial matter of fact about how bodies *normally are*—has, on the whole, been roundly debunked (Davis 1995; Zebrowski 2009). In short, the human body comes in many shapes, sizes, and modalities of existence, and arguments to the contrary fail the moment one does even minimal research concerning the limits of statistical knowledge or, more broadly, even minimal historical research, not to mention research in other disciplines. The focus of this chapter and the next is on how ableism specifically relegates "nonstandard," "abnormal," and "dis-abled" bodies to undesirable existences—to lives of/in pain and/or suffering.[3]

To undermine the ableist conflation of disability and pain, the following two chapters attempt to provide a more complex and nuanced account of pain, before I turn in the next two chapters to doing so with disability. I first provide a brief history of pain to trace how different theories across history and across disciplines have attempted to articulate the conditions and set of relations that give rise to, sustain, or otherwise explain the many phenomena that fall under the term *pain*. Rather than focusing only on the biomedical sciences, I turn to a variety of disciplines across the natural sciences, social sciences, and humanities that discuss pain, for it is such a fundamental human concern that one is hard-pressed to find any theory that meaningfully structures human life without taking pain's role seriously, whether via elevation, neutralization, or deflation. Given the variety of fields and disciplines that discuss pain, as well as the increasingly common histories of pain, this chapter cannot provide anything close to a comprehensive survey.[4] Instead, I focus on comparing five of the more prominent theories of pain: religious, neurobiological, humanist, existential, and medical.

My use of *theory* here warrants further explanation, especially because it is a term that seems more appropriate for neurobiological and medical approaches to pain and less relevant for religious approaches. Here I do not take *theory* to mean a formal hypothesis to be tested but instead use it in Thomas Nail's (2016, 11) sense: "the purpose of a theory or concept of [a phenomenon] is not to explain or predict every detail of empirical [phenomena of that sort]; a theory . . . aims to describe the conditions or sets of relations under which those phenomena occur." Each of the theories I discuss attempts to describe the conditions or set of relations that can explain the phenomenon of pain. For stylistic reasons, at times I speak of "models" and at other times of "theories," and the reader should take these terms to be synonymous. Because my approach focuses on the lived experience of pain, and because I understand this inquiry to be geared toward disability justice, I would modify Nail's definition in the following two ways. First, a theory aims to describe the conditions or sets of relations under which a given phenomenon is experienced as meaningful. Second, and following Sally Haslanger (2012), a theory that bears directly upon social reality should try to capture the phenomenon under consideration in a way that might *improve* the lives of those to whom it refers. That is to say, socially relevant theories should be ameliorative (Haslanger 2012). For those well acquainted with the literatures discussed herein, it will be clear that I ultimately design this chapter to offer a theory of theories concerning pain: I offer a metatheory of pain as regulative orientation. Put simply, I argue that pain is a command to reorient oneself. This chapter builds this metatheory through critical analysis, whereas the following chapter illustrates it through phenomenology.

Religious–Moral (Abrahamic)

I begin with religious theories of pain in the Abrahamic tradition. Because I am, relative to the limits of this project, working within the Western philosophical tradition, I focus on the "religious model" of pain only with respect to the Abrahamic traditions: Judaism, Christianity, and Islam. A further benefit of engaging solely the Abrahamic traditions is that it allows me to focus primarily on the Genesaic cosmogony (which the Qur'an largely follows). Given that each of these traditions begins in the Near East, not what is today ambiguously referred to as the West, there is a certain geographic irony in such a qualification. My focus, of course, must be understood in terms of a canonical socio-historico-political trajectory and thus one that is constructed and contestably, problematically so.[5]

In the Abrahamic traditions, pain is understood not as a necessary condition of being human but as a price that humans have paid due to an act of transgression. The latter act causes pain to enter into the world, for example, in the Genesaic cosmogony:[6]

> The Lord God took the man and put him in the garden of Eden to till it and keep it. And the Lord God commanded the man, "You may freely eat of every tree of the garden; but of the tree of the knowledge of good and evil you shall not eat, for in the day that you eat of it you shall die [*muth*: תָּמֻת]." (2:15–17, NRSV)[7]

The majority of scholars argue that the book of Genesis was written by multiple authors. This is part of a larger "documentary hypothesis" that understands the Pentateuch (Genesis, Exodus, Leviticus, Numbers, and Deuteronomy) to be a compilation of differing documents, each of which presupposes a unique source: the Jahwist (J), Elohist (E), Deuteronomist (D), or Priestly (P) source. For the purposes at hand, only the differences between P and J are relevant. Unlike the P account in Genesis 1, in which God[8] offers only positive directives, the first commandment in the J account, Genesis 2–3, is dual. The sole action the human[9] cannot take is contrasted with the human's relative freedom, but the *poine,* the price, of defying that injunction is death. The cosmogony of J installs power absolutely; the possibility of the anarchic, of an absolute rebellion against the *theos,* is the price, the pain, of death—an absolute injunction for an absolute insurrection.

> To the woman he said, "I will greatly increase your pangs [*itstsabon:* וְעִצְּבֹנֵךְ] in childbearing; in pain [*etseb:* בְּעֶצֶב] you shall bring forth children, yet your desire shall be for your husband, and he shall rule over you." And to the man he said, "Because you have listened to the voice of your wife, and have eaten of the tree about which I commanded you, 'You shall not eat of it,' cursed is the ground because of you; in toil [*itstsabon:* בְּעִצָּבוֹן] you shall eat of it all the days of your life; thorns and thistles it shall bring forth for you; and you shall eat the plants of the field. By the sweat of your face you shall eat bread until you return to the ground, for out of it you were taken; you are dust [*aphar:* עָפָר], and to dust you shall return." (3:16–19, NRSV)

The divine's response to transgression lays bare the logic of pain. Pain is a price one pays for a wrong one has committed and a price that is essentially experienced as to-be-avoided. There is a single root in ancient Hebrew of the words translated as "pangs," "pain," and "toil" in the preceding quote: *atsab* (עָצַב). It means "an earthen vessel; usually (painful) toil; also a pang (whether of body or mind): grievous, idol, labor, sorrow" (Strong 1996, 6093). Tellingly, the Genesaic account does not offer Adam and Eve a way to rectify their transgression. And, contra how many existentialists might be tempted to read this passage, the idea that Adam and Eve would take joy in these pains, pangs, and toils runs headstrong against the larger narrative.

Moreover, Adam and Eve only figuratively pay the ultimate price stated earlier in Genesis 2, for they do not die.[10] The dry earth or dust, *aphar* (עָפָר), out of which the human is formed is precisely conceived as a sort of vessel because the human only becomes a living creature upon receiving the breath of life into its earthen, dusty vessel (Genesis 2:7–8). They live on, but they live on in the only way nonmythic accounts of humans live on: as mortals, which is always to say, *as creatures who experience pain*. Recall that there are three impetuses for Eve's decision. (That it is taken to be *Eve's* decision, when Adam was with her the whole time, is another issue I unfortunately cannot broach here.) She chooses the tree because it offers sustenance, aesthetics, and wisdom. It is not accidental that she makes her choice only upon an understanding that the tree would *feed* her, that it would *please* her, and that it would, third and finally, make her more *wise*. I do not read the order of these functions as accidental. It is only upon the reproduction of one's life, to borrow the Marxian idiom, that the tree appeals to Eve in the first place. It is easy to forget the power of bread—or, in this case, apples. Secondarily, it is pleasuring, which one need not take as a mere matter of *aesthesis* but as a more general question of enlivening, of a flourishing beyond the exigencies of subsistence. That is to say, that the tree brings pleasure is good, but the condition of the possibility of both recognizing and enjoying that pleasure is the baseline necessity of reproducing life. It is only as the final and third consideration that Eve takes up the serpent's bait: wisdom is good, to be sure, assuming it follows upon the reproduction of the condition of the possibility of material life in combination with the joys of flourishing.

God's punishment links the creation of the human as an *atsab*[11] to its first experience of *atsab*. That is to say, the human comes to experience itself in relation to its materiality through pain. 'Adam—as being *'adamah*, as being made up of *aphar* and as an *atsab*—experiences *atsab*, experiences *itstsabon* and *etseb*. The price (death, *muth*) of transgression is to bring the human to experience itself as itself, which is to say, in its pain.[12] When the human experiences itself human*ly*, it does so through pain.[13]

That the Genesaic account does not entertain the idea that one might desire to pay this price or that this pain has a use beyond mere retribution marks a notable difference from the understanding of pain in a host of later theological accounts, whether explicitly theodical or not. It is only after this mythical, primordial, and essentially unwanted pain first occurs that pain can enter into redemptive logics. For example, the author of Luke, the gospel held by most scholars as the last of the three synoptic Gospels to be written, has the resurrected Jesus offer a soteriological–Christological interpretation of his own suffering: "Was it not necessary that the Messiah should suffer these things?" (24:26, cf. 24:46).[14] This is based on an interpretation of Isaiah 53, and this soteriology, this doctrine of salvation, requiring Jesus to suffer is a prevalent theme and argument across the Christian New Testament.[15]

To take another example, suffering often takes on an essential role in Pauline theology, marking an experience in which one ought to rejoice (Romans 5:6; 2 Corinthians 12:7–10; Colossians 1:24). In other places, though, Paul either explicitly minimizes suffering in relation to future glory or equalizes it in light of the comfort received through Christ (Romans 8:18–23; Philippians 3:8–12; 2 Corinthians 1:5–10).[16] The Genesaic cosmogony leads one to suggest that none of the theological usefulness or postlapsarian necessity of pain or suffering would make sense unless pain had first been brought into the world through an error. Pain is fundamentally exterior to the purposivity of the Genesaic cosmogony, to the idea that the divine created a fundamentally good world.

It is only after the Fall that pain can be explained as a part of the divinely created world without denying divine benevolence, and this holds despite the fact that pain is simultaneously rendered as determinative for the meaning of being human. Genesis unfolds this paradoxical logic deftly: pain enters the world after mortals do, even though, as the etymology of *atsab* suggests, it is definitive for their material form. Still, mortals pay for this fault, the proof of which constitutes their very existence as mortals and the removal of which is impossible without the removal of their very existence (i.e., via their death). Pain marks the entrance into mortality and into the mortally deferred recovery of a prior painlessness—a painlessness that would, paradoxically, mark the existence, not of the mortal, but of the nonmortal.

Pain, then, reminds us both of what we are and of what we seek to be: immortal, divine, free of the weight of the telluric. Signaling the ontological divide between transgression and redemption, pain calls us to remember that what we are is the obverse of our desire and potential. For the religious imaginary taken by such an account, pain signals right from wrong in a far less abstract sense than one might think.

I began by arguing that on dominant theories, pain functions as a sign by which one knows that one has committed a wrong before the divine. But it is not just some abstract notion of the "divine" that is at stake here; it is the divine understood as a thetic order.[17] By "thetic," I mean that which is a principle, a *principium,* in the sense of being both an origin and a foundation. That which is a *theos,* to hear the Attic Greek root, is that which orders and founds, a beginning and a ground. Theticisms do not provide merely the scaffolding of a "world-view" but shape the meaningfulness of things; they structure the syntax and semantics of what Rorty (1989) calls our "final vocabularies."[18] Put simply, theticisms are frameworks that are determinant for the meaning of what we see, think, feel, judge, and reason. "That's just how it is." "There's a reason for everything." "I believe I will be saved." "This is the truth." A thetic order delivers ultimatums that help regulate the cacophony of human life.

Pain is one of the more, if not the most, epistemically obvious signals a given theticism can employ because of its de facto negativity. That is to say, aside from notable exceptions that I address in detail in chapter 2, pain is fundamentally experienced as that-which-is-to-be-avoided. Moreover, without alternative explanations, such as those that modern medicine would later provide, the religious–cosmological explanation of pain is sounded in the moral register out of which religion first speaks: debt (Graeber 2011).[19] I said earlier that pain has an etiology by definition, but, to be more precise, it has an economic etiology. Pain signifies a price to be paid. It will turn out that pain is integral, if not central, to the moral feedback loop of thetic orders, whether figured as God, Reason, Nature, the Good, or what have you.

Although this economic etiology explains how pain functions, it stops short of elucidating *what pain means,* what pain's replete sense is for a religious (Abrahamic) imaginary. That is to say, pain's meaning is not reducible to its cause (wrongdoing) or to its discrete demands (righting a wrong). Pain points backward to a wronging of and before God for which one must pay, a payment the completion of which is a result not of a fixed algorithm but of mediated judgment. Although it does not in and of itself necessitate content vis-à-vis its prescriptive obligation, pain orients one to the possibility of harmony with the *theos* in question. Pain is both proscriptive and prescriptive in a way that is *regulative.* It is, in that sense and whatever its precise parameters, a condition of the possibility of redemption and future promises, but always as indexed to one's lived experience.[20] The Abrahamic religious theory of pain can be summed up as follows: via an economy of debt, pain is theologically *regulative.* This is to say, pain orients and directs one as an individual with respect to the ultimate principles dictated by a given thetic order.

Neurobiological

In early Greek and Egyptian writings, pain is associated with object intrusion, whether of a material or immaterial sort.[21] Plato understands pain as an affection in the sense of an intrusion on the body or soul (Plato, *Phaedo,* 64d). The idea that pain is emotional-affective, however, goes back at least to Aristotle, for whom pain is a modality of touch and on a continuum with its (assumed to be) opposite affect: pleasure (Aristotle, *De Anima,* 3.2: 426b; 3.4: 666a). By the time of Galen, the idea of animal spirits moving through ventricles (nerves) took hold, and the emotional-affective aspects of pain were downplayed relative to stimulus–response patterns of the nervous system (Galen 1968, 5.9). This line of interpretation was followed by Avicenna in the Middle Ages and taken up again in the early modern period by da Vinci, Vesalius, Eustachius, and Descartes.[22] Throughout the nineteenth century and into the early twentieth century, the roots of Galen's model held. Biomedical arguments over pain largely centered on whether it was a question of specificity or intensity—whether pain constitutes a sense-modality of its own or whether it is instead a sufficiently intense stimulation of another sense-modality.

It is only in the last few decades, and especially since the advent of positron emission tomography (PET) and, later, functional magnetic resonance imaging (fMRI) technology, that the Aristotelian, emotional-affective view of pain has regained currency.[23] Pain is not its own sense-modality in the way that touch, sight, or hearing is. But it is also not simply a question of "intensity" of those sense-modalities. Pain is now understood as an event involving a complex, multimodal gestalt of sensory-affective components spanning multiple sense-modalities as well as an individual's organismic history.

The neurobiological theory of pain relies on an evolutionary account of the emergence of multiple sense-modalities over the course of the development of the human organism. Among other things, pain plays a crucial evolutionary role in two basic systems: (1) the avoidance system and (2) the restorative system (Wall et al. 2006,

3–34). The avoidance system is based on the quick-acting A-δ fibers that lead an organism to move itself away from the localized cause of pain; the restorative system, on the other hand, enlists the slower C nerve fibers to kick in afterward and to last long after the acute occurrence of pain.[24] These duller, less localized nerve signals limit the mobility of the damaged area such that repair is made possible. Pain thus serves two primary evolutionary roles: the prevention of initial harm through avoidance and the securing of repair through immobilization or mobility/activity reduction.

Both of these roles in turn serve the larger purpose of the preservation of bodily integrity. At the most general biological level, pain is a necessary condition of the ontogenetically adaptive and allostatic capabilities of an organism. In other words, pain is indispensable for the human to be able to respond to its own body and environment and maintain reciprocal harmony of and between each with the end goal of purposive action. Because its function is fundamentally adaptive, pain is positive in the sense of productively guiding action, except when it is absent (e.g., congenital analgesia) or when it becomes a syndrome and thereby maladaptive (complex regional pain syndrome [CRPS], allodynia, chronic pain of many sorts, etc.) (Wall et al. 2006, 232–33).

At this point, it may sound as though pain is merely a question of stimulus and response, but recent neuroscientific research shows such a framing to be far too simplistic. Kenneth Craig (1995) argues that the affective aspects of pain are actually more important biologically, but because the majority of testing related to the neurophysiological aspects of pain has historically been performed on nonverbal laboratory animals, it is no surprise that research in this area is lacking.[25] Although there are indeed determinable sensory-discriminative aspects to pain, the affective-cognitive aspects are central.[26] In other words, thoughts, feelings, and one's psycho-physiological history all affect the experience of pain, from its intensity to duration to even its initial occurrence. Pain is not like a light bulb. There is no simple on and off switch. It is less a current or flame, and more a force. Pain is not simple. Like gravity, we can measure it, feel it, alter it, study it, and even exploit it, but we still don't really know how it works.

In this light, thought experiments that focus on acute, noxious stimuli (e.g., holding one's finger over a candle) are bound to mislead inquiry concerning the meaning and character of pain as a whole.[27]

Focusing, say, on how the fear of a noxious stimuli can exacerbate the pain it elicits proves more promising. Some interpret the case of pain asymbolia (those for whom pain is experienced, but without unpleasantness, that is, people who feel pain without being in pain) to suggest that these two aspects are dissociable. Others disagree, but both camps maintain that both the sensory-discriminative and also affective-cognitive aspects are necessary for pain in fact to be painful.[28]

I refer to the current section as the neurobiological model of pain because it is in large part due to the technological advances of PET scans and fMRI that previously "subjective" questions of affect have become a topic in pain research.[29] This neuropsychological research has grounded first-person reporting of pain in third-person, technologically mediated analysis in novel and impactful ways. However, upon adding the affective-cognitive dimensions of pain into pain research through neuropsychology and neurobiology, the primary understanding of pain from evolutionary biology remains intact: pain, whatever its discrete cause and experiential characteristics, orients an organism to avoid potential or actual noxious stimuli and, secondarily, to allow for the healing of damage done by that cause.

On a neurobiological theory, *pain is adaptively regulative* via complex, intermodal sensory-discriminative and affective-cognitive interactions.

Humanist

One could address a number of texts to outline a "humanist model" of pain. Because of its immense effect on humanistic inquiry over the last four decades, I focus here on Elaine Scarry's (1985) *The Body in Pain*. Although Scarry stops short of didactic moralizing, she frames her discussion of pain through examples of torture and war. She expects this focus to have prima facie, though not necessarily universal, moral import:

> The deconstruction of creation is present in the structure of one event which is widely recognized as close to being an absolute of immorality (torture), and . . . the deconstruction of creation is again present in the structure of a second event regarded as morally problematic by everyone and as radically immoral by some (war). (22)

Scarry defines the act of torture as "extreme and prolonged physical [or psychological] pain" (59). The ultimate pain producers, torturers, are placed squarely and unquestionably in the realm of the immoral. For Scarry, being appalled by torture is "a basic moral reflex. . . . Torture is such an extreme event that it seems inappropriate to generalize from it to anything else or from anything else to it. Its immorality is so absolute and the pain it brings about so real that there is a reluctance to place it in conversation by the side of other subjects" (35, 60; cf. 143). That is to say, she focuses on torture because she takes it as the paradigmatic case in the public imaginary of both extreme pain and also morally blameworthy action. In its immoral obviousness, pain—in this case, the categorically undue pain of torture—functions both as a call for justice and as a foundation for ethical solidarity. That is to say, the existence of pain attunes us to ethical deliberation so as to join in projects of ameliorating pain wherever we can. What better phenomenon than one that is so intuitive, universal, and riveting for such an aim?

The Body in Pain seeks to reveal the unmaking of the world caused by torture and war, an unmaking caused by *causing pain.* Rejecting such unmaking of the world, Scarry's hope is that one works instead toward communitarian practices of making the world. This is a pervasive and persuasive humanist trope. For example, Paul Gilroy (2000, 17) writes, "the reconstruction of pain, disease, humiliation, grief, and care for those one loves can all contribute to an abstract sense of human similarity powerful enough to make solidarities based on cultural particularity appear suddenly trivial." Pain, as an archtypical human experience, is thought to carry special ethical powers for humanistic aims—humanists suppose that it makes people care and brings people together.

However, Scarry (1985) also argues that pain is an intensely private experience: no one can have my pain. "When one speaks about 'one's own physical pain' and about 'another person's physical pain,'" she writes, "one might almost appear to be speaking about two wholly distinct orders of events" (4).[30] Part of what makes torture so morally onerous is that it effects a "shattering of language" (172). There is a tension in Scarry's text between the subjective character of pain and the role language plays in expressing it. On one hand, pain is private, and articulations of it fail to convey the full character of one's experience. On the other hand, the communication about and meaning of pain are so powerful that it is taken as a moral bedrock for society writ large. Even when expressed solely through what Scarry defines as "prelinguistic" modes, such as cries, groans, and screams, pain still motivates action. As I argue in more detail later in this chapter, I disagree with the claim that language pales before pain. Pain only signifies in an explicitly linguistic context when arrested, not in excess. That is to say, the fully pained body, the body stricken with unbearable pain, *speaks* very loudly: it groans, cries, moans, yelps, and screams. So-called nonlinguistic expressions of pain should be considered at least as, if not more, articulate about disclosing the actual situation of a sufferer.

For Scarry, pain is both universal and singular, both comprehensible for all and forever indexed to one. She simultaneously leverages the subjective incommunicability of pain and its normative unquestionability. The fact that I feel the pain of others while not feeling the pain of the other seems to operate in an empyrean of analogical experience. Scarry never provides a sufficient explanation of how such a gap is possible, and distinctions between types of pain are effaced in the service of its normative gravity. This explanatory lacuna is, it seems, assumed to be forgivable in light of the profound confidence that the pain of others will be sufficient to motivate action toward a better, more just world. Scarry's humanist account presumes the epistemic obviousness of pain's undesirable nature as well as the inevitability of being motivationally oriented by the pain of another. Pain is the one simultaneously unique and universal human experience by which we can come to see each other as worthy of dignity and respect. On humanist theories, *pain is normatively regulative.* Pain orients and attunes us to how we ought to treat others. Pain is that phenomenon by which we learn the horror of harm and the demand for justice, equality, and respect.

Existential

As with humanist theories, there are a plethora of options from which to frame an existential theory of pain, but I focus here on Sartre because, among philosophers whose work falls under the banner of existentialism, he offers the most sustained analysis of pain. Importantly, he also offers an account that laudably takes pain to be phenomenologically distinct from suffering.

In a section titled "The Body" in *Being and Nothingness,* Sartre (1984, 332ff.) introduces his discussion of "physical" pain (his scare quotes) as a way to "understand the proprioceptive coenesthesia of consciousness." That is to say, he understands pain as a phenomenon that demonstrates the way in which consciousness is reflexively constituted by the total sum of sensations of one's bodily state. One of Sartre's central claims, which might seem strange at first blush, is that pain is not experienced as pain *of some thing* as much as it is experienced as *a mode of experience* as such. If I have pain in my eyes as I am reading, I do not sense pain in my eyes. Though I am of course able to localize the pain, the lived experience of that pain is not one of emanating from the area below my eyebrows and above my cheekbones. To see pain as such is the result of a nonphenomenological, third-person, diagnostic interpretation.

Rather, Sartre argues that I in fact experience "the-eyes-as-pain or vision-as-pain; [this pain] is not distinguished from my way of apprehending" the words on the page. This means, however, that pain *just is* my consciousness in that experience. Yes, "it is undeniable that pain contains information about itself; it is impossible to confuse pain in the eyes with pain in the finger or the stomach." "Nevertheless," Sartre continues, "pain is totally void of intentionality"—it is inaccurate to speak of the pain *of* seeing this or that; one instead experiences pain *in* seeing itself (436–37). In short, to say I have pain *in* my eyes misconstrues its lived experiential character. On the contrary, "pain is precisely in the eyes insofar as consciousness 'exists them'" (332). Pain is neither "in" my consciousness nor "about" something:

> It is simply a matter of the way in which consciousness exists its
> contingency . . . the pain is neither absent nor unconscious; it
> simply forms a part of that distanceless existence of positional
> consciousness for it-self. . . . [Pain] is not in space. But neither
> does it belong to objective time; it temporalizes itself, and it is
> in and through this temporalization that the time of the world
> can appear. (436, 400)

For Sartre, pain is ultimately a modality of experience, not a sensation within it. Pain is experienced not as about something but as the way in which a thing or set of things appears.

It is in this sense that Sartre's phenomenological account of pain reveals the constitution of human existence: beings "condemned to freedom" (623). Pain is a modality that reveals our fundamental and unalterable vulnerability to being, to all that is, was, and will be as we enjoy our temporary being-in-the-world. Traversing across every possible existential structure, pain reveals the condemnation of our freedom and, simultaneously, the freedom of that condemnation:

> What then is this pain? Simply the translucent matter of consciousness, its being-there. .... The pain exists beyond all attention and all knowledge since it slips into each act of attention and of knowledge since it is this very act in so far as the act is without being the foundation of its being. (438)

Sartre here further distinguishes between pain as it is lived and "pain-consciousness," pain as taken up by reflection. The latter is "a project toward a further consciousness which would be empty of all pain; that is, to a consciousness whose contexture, whose being-there would be not painful" (438). For Sartre, lived pain is not the same as this reflective consciousness of pain because lived pain does not have the convenience to distance itself from itself, a distance intentionality, being "conscious of" something, requires. I find this a crucial distinction with which to understand how some people—whether via group rituals or individual practice, whether BDSM, self-cutting, or extreme fitness events—experience pain without describing it as painful or who experience their pain as painful but nevertheless take pleasure in its painfulness. For Sartre, the widely disparate attitudes people take toward painful experiences are not a question of whether people experience pain (the condition of pain asymbolia being an obvious exception). It is instead a question of the complex, mutually determining relation between lived and reflective pain-consciousness.

Notably, this distinction in some ways mirrors the biological distinction between the avoidance and restoration systems. In the first case, one simply knows that something is/could be painful, and a cascade of prereflective responses sets about avoiding the presumed cause of the pain, ranging from motor signals leading one away from the cause's assumed location to yells that might solicit help from others in case one's attempts fail. Lived pain-consciousness does not involve understanding the cause of the pain, nor does it involve processes to heal from or otherwise protect oneself from its effects or possible return. Reflective pain-consciousness, in taking up the occurrence, context, etiology, and nature of the pain, does. Yet, both forms clearly feed into each other, and increasingly so over time. The child who, upon seeing how close its hand is to the flame, learns to withdraw has transformed reflective pain-consciousness into a modality of lived pain-consciousness. The child experiences the pain as imminent and thereby treats it as lived before it is in fact lived—they may even "feel pain" without any tissue damage. The play between lived and reflective is entangled when one "learns" to "receive" a pain signal from such a flame before there is any tissue damage, as anyone knows who has experienced pulling their hand away from a flame, assuming damage, only to find not a scratch.

Such a distinction notwithstanding, pain is understood existentially as proof of the obstinacy of the world and also our freedom—a price we pay, not to a divine, thetic order, but to existence itself. Pain reminds us of the fundamental ambiguity of our telluric condition; it regulatively attunes us to the nature of our existence; it guides and orients one's understanding of the contours of one's being-in-the-world. One might here wonder whether the "existentially regulative" and "normatively regulative" amount to the same thing. I think not. The existential experience of pain cannot proffer norms for living. While that experience might lead one to seek such norms, they do not follow, as if an inference, from it. Pain inaugurates, not consummates, an inquiry into the very conditions of experience. On existential theories, *pain is existentially regulative.*

Medical

While one aspect of the overall goal of medicine has always been the alleviation of pain, pain has a complex relation with the ambitions of medicine, and increasingly so since the nineteenth century (Bourke 2014, 131–58).[31] While medicine has historically been "bedside," with the rise of the clinic and, in particular, the emergence of the field of anesthesia in the mid-nineteenth century, palliation gave way to pathologization (Pernick 1985; Foucault 1994). As increasing technological advancements allowed health care practitioners to achieve unparalleled physiological accuracy across a broad range of diagnostic measures, the aim of the medical profession in the Global North shifted its primary focus from a Maimonidean to a Hippocratic mandate, or, in other words, from care to cure.[32]

This is not to say that, historically, medical practices ignored pathologization or, more broadly, diagnosis. I am only claiming that its primary focus shifted along with the unequaled diagnostic, life-altering, and life-sustaining capabilities brought about by recent technologies. It is the widespread trust in the ever-increasing technological ability to uncover physiologically based (of which, e.g., genomics is one domain) pathologies that has, in too many cases, exacerbated the suffering of those whose conditions do not have such a pathology.

The entangling of for-profit pharmacological and biotechnological ventures with medical practice has only further entrenched the emphasis on discrete material pathologies and, equally troubling, the multiplication of such pathologies (Gabriel and Goldberg 2014). Furthermore, the rise of anesthesiology as a domain of surgery-related medical practice in the mid-nineteenth century later found its non-surgical correlate with another new specialization in the late twentieth century: pain specialists and pain clinics. If you suffer from a condition that requires sustained pain management, your primary care physician will now send you off to such a specialist, for alas, it is not in their orbit of knowledge to care for such a person. In the United States, at least, that shift has been profoundly affected by the fact that chronic pain doctors currently operate in the wake of the early 1990s rise of policy-driven and legally buttressed pharmacovigilance, one incubatory ramification of the Nixon-era "war on drugs" that presidents from Reagan to Biden have to date largely maintained with damning confidence (Goldberg and Rich 2014).[33]

To complicate the matter even further, in the nineteenth century, pain without lesion—that is to say, pain without any physiological etiology—was considered anomalous (Goldberg 2012). It is now well documented that a number of quite common pain conditions occur without lesion. These include lower back, abdominal, and pelvic pain; tension and migraine headaches; fibromyalgia; and causalgiform disorders, such as CRPS. In other words, these conditions are not necessarily coextensive with chronic pain conditions *with* lesion or with a clear post-onset etiology, such as osteoarthritis, rheumatoid arthritis, diabetic neuropathy, or postherpetic neuralgia.

Despite these otherwise immense changes in medical theories of pain, the constancy of pain's meaning for medicine is remarkable. Diagnostically, pain is understood as a sign or symbol that leads to a physiological, causal explanation of that pain. Historically, this was typically thought to be due to tissue irritation, inflammation, or some other form of insult. Although pain researchers have increasingly recognized that this stimulus–response, materialist understanding of pain is false, clinical practice on the whole still often treats pain in such a manner.[34] Whether pain is a sign of an acute trauma or a nonacute condition anchored in a disease or syndrome, the semiosis of pain is taken as a knowledge-producing process that assists (or is assumed to assist) in leading a health care provider to the correct diagnosis, to the proper form of treatment, and, ideally, to cure. Pain provides medical practice with *gnosis,* with knowledge, and thereby orients both the ends and means of patient–provider relations. Despite its complexity as a phenomenon and as a variable component of medical aims, on medical theories, *pain is diagnostically regulative.*

The Regulative Role of Pain

In each of the five theories of pain I presented, it is striking that pain plays a regulative role (see Figure 1).[35] Theories are meaning-making devices. They allow phenomena to be understood such that they make sense within larger wholes and with respect to larger swaths of experience. While the scope of objects a given theory encompasses can be very large, theories typically operate within a particular *domain.* The religious–moral theory of pain, for example, operates within the domain of theology, which is why distinctively theological concepts, such as sin or providence, prove definitive for religious understandings of pain. The *function* of a theory refers to how explanations within a given domain put the phenomenon in question to use. For example, the humanist model operates within the domain of axiology, of morality, which is to say, of an account of values and norms. This means that pain is used to account for the evaluation of human life in that model; hence it has a specifically normative or norm-giving function. Finally, the *effect* of a theory is the primary consequence it has, not simply on an individual in the abstract, but on one's lived experience of the world. On all theories of pain, pain's effect is ultimately to orient one toward not-being-in-pain. One is oriented toward the goal

THEORY	DOMAIN	FUNCTION	EFFECT
Religious-Moral	Theology	Judicative	Allostatic Regulation
Neurobiological	Biology	Adaptive	Allostatic Regulation
Humanist	Morality	Evaluative	Allostatic Regulation
Existential	Ontology	Disclosive	Allostatic Regulation
Medical	Symptomatology	Diagnostic	Allostatic Regulation

Figure 1. Theories of pain.

of regaining homeostasis within the domain in question, specifically with respect to that domain's impact on one's sense of self and/or ability expectations.

For example, the neurobiological model interprets pain to orient one toward not-being-in-pain in such a way that one returns to a baseline of adaptive behavior. Another way of describing the allostatically regulative function of pain is that the force of pain, regardless of its specific content or lack thereof, is always in the shape of an imperative (see Klein 2015).[36] Without social factors that change its default meaning, pain is experienced first and foremost as to-be-avoided. To repeat, this can of course be overridden in a number of cases, such as various self-mutilation and bondage practices and the changes in second-order judgment such habituated practices effect. These are not counterexamples. On the contrary, they provide supporting evidence. Self-cutters, for example, describe cutting as a way to feel, as a way to regain affective control over themselves—inflicting pain provides, in the place of feeling nothing, an imperative, namely, to *not* avoid feeling.

With respect to all the models of pain we have discussed, the effect of pain is to allostatically regulate life: *pain is a command to reorient oneself.*[37] To be sure, the ends toward which one will reorient oneself in the face of pain will be diverse. Those ends will always be relative to the domain or domains in which and by which one interprets one's pain as well as the salient interpretative differences operative within that domain.[38] Still, in each domain that proffers a meaning for pain, pain functions as a command to reorient oneself. Pain orders one to regain a certain balance. It functions with the aim of reestablishing oneself and one's abilities relative to the domain in question and the function it serves. In each case, however, its semiosis is specifically conceived; it both commands and orients one relative to the domain under which it is interpreted. Indexed to a given theory and its respective domain and function, this reorientation might be with respect to one's relationship with God, one's organismic state, one's praxis toward human solidarity, one's reflexive attitude toward existence, or one's bodily and mental norms. Now that I have provided a provisional inquiry into dominant theories of pain, I turn in the next chapter to a phenomenology of pain.

2

A Phenomenology of Chronic Pain

> Far from being broken, the fantasy link between knowledge
> and pain is reinforced by a more complex means than the
> mere permeability of the imagination; the presence of dis-
> ease in the body . . . [is] challenged as to [its] objectivity by
> the reductive discourse of the doctor. . . . The figures of pain
> are . . . redistributed in the space in which bodies and eyes
> meet. What has changed is . . . the relation of situation and
> attitude to what is speaking and what is spoken about.
>
> —Michel Foucault, *The Birth of the Clinic*

While the previous chapter provided a survey of theories of pain and
argued for its regulative function, this chapter explores the limits of
such theories by demonstrating how constitutive and consuming, as
opposed to component, pain are fundamentally deregulative and disorienting. I first provide a detailed narrative of living with complex
regional pain syndrome based on my mother's experiences. This account, rooted in first-person experience, leads to an analysis of four
general structures that characterize the lived experience of chronic
pain as deregulative rather than regulative: forebodingness, beholdenness, bioreckoning, and disruption. Finally, I use these phenomenologically revealed, general structures of chronic pain to begin
deconstructing the ableist conflation of disability with pain, showing how that conflation fails to take into account the many forms and
meanings pain takes across the breadth of human experience.

January 1

10:00 A.M.

I opened my eyes this morning to a blur. Pain surged everywhere, but especially in my head. Mouth: dry. Hands: numb. Feet: not numb, just not there. As my eyes open, I worry I can't get out of bed. I don't know whether today will be "one of those days." I have an appointment in forty-eight hours with my pain doctor. At the last appointment, my pain meds were cut. The plan is to bring my dosage down at least 30 percent in four or so increments. There was no explanation for this except that the doctor said she was concerned the dosages were "too high." TOO HIGH? Too high relative to what? I know opioids are addictive. I know there is an opioid "epidemic." But these are statistics. I am not a statistic. I am a person. I am a chronic pain sufferer of more than twenty years. I am not an instance to which the fears of those facts relate. Prior to the cut, I was able to get out of bed at least a few days a week. What will I be like after the next cut? The fear of further pain and its debilitation closes in on me. I do not know what I will be able to do in an hour, much less tomorrow, and if I lack the surety of the sole medication that gives me a vestige of the ability to function, then what? The fear of tomorrow makes today's pain worse.

10:25 A.M.

Nausea sets in. If I vomit, my meds will exit with the bile. Jaw pain from TMJ will intensify, as will my neck pain, and that circuit will set my head in a vice. A vice clinched in a feedback loop of pain. No movement. No nothing. "Just focus on not vomiting," I tell myself between long breaths. Where is the Zofran? (Better than promethazine, the doctor said.) If I move, I'll . . .

I text my partner to bring it to me. I take the Zofran with a sip of water. I feel an immediate rush of nausea. "Hold it . . . hold it . . . hold it," I say to myself over and over again. I can do this. The nausea circles me like a vulture. Constant throbbing like a fog, clouding all my thoughts and memories and plans—this is the milieu in which I measure everything. *Experience* is a fancy term for *measurement*. Tacit and expressed, background and fore—pain can play both roles. I never know when spikes will occur; I never know when the light of the sun will become an enemy, when the voice of my partner and lover of thirty years will act as a chainsaw running through my head, or when the touch of my own children will set fire across my skin. I never know.

1:05 P.M.

I vomited. Five times. Dry heaving. Losing consciousness. Couldn't drink water the last few hours. Ambulance. Emergency room. My partner is trying to list out my medications. The nurse is "uncomfortable" administering my regular pain meds. My partner yells. The head nurse is contacted. We get a different nurse. This nurse treats us differently—I am now a "problem" patient. My partner is a family member who "interferes." They surely put something in my medical notes about the incident. My primary care doctor is unavailable, as is my pain doctor: it's a Saturday. I would have protested going to the ER: what can they do that I can't at home? All they can do is be late. All they can do is be actively obstinate about administering my legally prescribed medications. All they can do is treat me like an "addict."

January 3

I walk into my pain doctor's office. I feel ashamed. I feel she will judge me. Hasn't she always? Why was I in the ER, again, she'll ask. I'm a "chronic pain sufferer." I have diagnoses in my medical file that are "vague." My medical files probably say I "complain"—what if they use the word "malingering"!? I know I wield privileges due to being white—what if I didn't? What does the recording of those words do to a person, a person as they actually find themselves in a deeply unjust world? Try living in pain for twenty years. I am not a patient to my pain doctor; I'm a problem. I make her a lot of money. But, when all is said and done, she wants me to be gone. She wants me to stop complaining. I am a walking embodiment of the failures of medicine to heal and cure. She's given up figuring out what's wrong with me because I am a reminder of what she cannot do. Her specialty is pain management—management! How do you manage the unmanageable? How do you manage persistent chronic pain without a known etiology? I am unmanageable. I am. That is the message I hear between the lines, between the diagnoses, between the bated breaths of a medical machine choking on the smoke of its own failures.

January 13

This morning on the TV, someone was asked, "What are you looking forward to in life?" I didn't hear the answer. Maybe I blocked it out. I rarely experience my own future like that anymore. I experience others' futures, and I substitute theirs for mine. It's not that I can no longer imagine; it's that my present is too strong. My present is my history evaporating and my future lost to the pain I experience now. Except . . . except when I see my kids. Except . . . when I hear the words "I love you" from my partner or my children. Except . . . in those moments when another breaks me out of the circuit of pain. Daudet (2002, 9) said it best: "Very strange, the fear that pain inspires nowadays—or rather, this pain of mine. It's bearable, and yet I cannot bear it." Bearable, and yet I cannot bear it. That I am alive and that I even talk and walk does not mean what others take it to mean. They do not know what it is to live a life at once bearable and unbearable.

January 30

The pain specialist has a new PA. He didn't bother to read my case history. He walks in with the nerve to say "What brings you in today?" WHAT BRINGS ME IN? Is this some kind of sick joke? Where should I begin? Let the puppet show commence.

Of course, I can list my primary diagnoses without thinking—one never forgets those words "You have X." But what is this PA, who clearly didn't even read my file, able to understand of my history? Two decades of experiences and complications. Two decades of pain, the singular history of which cannot be conveyed in haste, if at all. Two decades of unknowns, misknowns, and someday-we-will-knows. He wants a summary and solution. He wants a patient he can fix. I am anything but.

Incident 1

The moss was wet as I hit my back on stone and wood. Twenty-eight years old. In a hurry. I asked the landlord to clean the stairs. I mentioned it five times. The pain was intense, focused on my lower back but also in my neck. It was not sharp or burning but dull and throbbing. It hurt to walk, sit upright, even to sleep if I moved in the wrong way. The pain often made it hard to focus. I had to take a number of days off. I took a while to go to the doctor because I didn't have insurance. My boss is mad enough to fire me.

Diagnosis: Herniated Disks (L4, C6)

Incident 2

I never felt the spider bite. Must have been distracted. Didn't I register its fangs somehow? Only after a sudden onset of fever, headache, and a strangely stiff neck did I notice that small bite mark, pocketed by a light red rash. Sickness comes quickly. I had no idea a spider could do such a thing.

Diagnosis: Viral Meningitis

Incident 3

My jaw had never hurt before. I was extremely active—always outdoors. That damn left side—so sore all the time. Was I grinding my teeth? That happens to many young professionals. It lasted for weeks and continued to get worse. I saw a dentist. "It's not grinding." Off to an oral surgeon. The MRI brought news I was not expecting.

Diagnosis: Temporomandibular Joint Disorder (TMJ)

Incident 4

No matter how much I sleep, I always feel tired. My muscles ache indiscriminately, but I don't have a fever. Perhaps related to the TMJ? An aftereffect of the viral meningitis or my back and neck injuries? I have headaches often. Sometimes mild, but other times they lock me in bed. It's hard to concentrate. I've been to two primary care physicians, a naturopath, and an allergist. No one can figure out what's going on. This has been going on for years. Finally, a new doctor connects the dots. It amounts to an admission of not understanding how the dots are in fact connected.

Diagnosis: Fibromyalgia

Incident 5

I've seen a chronic pain doctor for twenty years now. I've been diagnosed with and treated for herniated disks, viral meningitis, and TMJ. I have also been diagnosed with fibromyalgia and degenerative disk disease, though there is no "real" treatment for those. Among other things, I lately developed carpal tunnel and numbness and tingling in my extremities. I cannot lift a gallon of milk anymore; a half-gallon is at times a struggle. I have to concentrate to walk. I often cannot even get out of bed due to the pain. I feel isolated. Doctors seem tired of seeing me and seem to have lost hope of helping me. I finally saw a specialist at a Mayo Clinic. He thinks there is more to the story. This is an unusual diagnosis for someone like me, he says. Other doctors will disagree.

Diagnosis: Complex Regional Pain Syndrome (CRPS) Type 1

I do not "have" pain in the same way that I do not "have" a body. If I hold my finger over a flame, it is an entirely different experience from the pain through which I live. Smiling hurts. Movement hurts. Interacting with others hurts. Pain is a condition of my life. I do not experience pain events; I experience a world in pain. All my projects are unsteady under pain's fickle, immeasurable weight. The litany of diagnoses, the surfeit of medical events from doctor's appointments to ER trips, seem endless. I live the chronicity of my pain. How am I to explain living with, in the here and now, a chronic condition like pain? How does the life *lived* in pain match up with a medical establishment that only knows of its occurrence?

Having now offered a description of the lived experience of chronic pain, I turn to analyzing what *general structures* this description discloses. That is to say, I turn to exploring the essence of experiences like these. By doing so, I aim to demonstrate how the lived experience of chronic pain provides insights into the nature of pain of multiple sorts. By the end of exploring these general structures and what they reveal about the nature of pain, it will become clear how narrowly and unreflectively pain is conceived in the ableist conflation.

The Structure of Chronic Pain

Some people haphazardly, or perhaps ignorantly, use the term *phenomenology* to refer to descriptions of lived experience. Although there are significant, long-standing disagreements over the proper aims and methods of phenomenology, everyone agrees that description is, on its own, not phenomenology. Mere description is the stuff of literature, memoir, and the like. What distinguishes phenomenology is analysis that critically moves from descriptions of lived experience into claims about the general structure of *experience as such*. This might be experience as such with respect to all beings or all humans or, instead, with respect to generalizations concerning experiences of X, Y, or Z sort—those distinctions are already in the intraphenomenological weeds. What makes phenomenology distinct is the move toward claims at the level of existential structures.

Phenomenological accounts of pain, not unlike other sorts of accounts, confront a number of perplexing questions.[1] How does one understand pain's complex temporal nature? How is one's experience of pain affected by one's conceptualization of pain?[2] Can one analytically distinguish between pain characteristics and nonpain characteristics? Is pain a natural kind?[3] Given that any of the five (or more) sense-modalities can become painful if intense enough, is pain a distinct sensation or sense or is it instead a modality of other senses? What do we mean when we speak of being in pain? Is it the same as feeling pain? Is pain a distinct cognitive state? An affective state? An existential situation? Or all of the above? Is pain "private"?[4] If pain is a discrete phenomenon, whatever sort it may be, is "chronic pain" as well?[5] How is the experience of pain affected by factors of sociocultural, historical, racial/ethnic, sex/gender, and dis/abled difference? How, that is to say, do social conditions and concrete interactions affect pain experience, including empathetic responses?[6] How do the effects of increasing pathologization in our global, (neo) liberal, late capitalist world affect pain experience?[7]

Because pain is among the first concepts most people learn and because it is so regularly used in daily life across otherwise disparate cultural and historical contexts, it is easy to fall into the trap of thinking that pain is simple or obvious. I raise these questions, questions that cover a vast terrain of research and inquiry, to give a sense of just how complex the phenomenon of pain is. In what follows, my aim is to use the first-person description that opened this chapter to articulate the lived experience of chronic pain by focusing on the common features that create and give it shape. Better understanding its experiential structure will then provide a way to critique and analyze the theories of pain presented in the previous chapter.

Foreboding

One of the more salient features revealed by the narrative description of pain above is its role in coloring and co-constituting all of one's experience. Pain becomes the background condition against and through which experiences are measured and taken stock. Mariet Vrancken (1989, 438) writes, "Pre-scientifically, pain is that mode of being in which the body becomes the center of one's life-world." Living in pain, one does not awaken and think about one's agenda or long-term projects. One first assesses, or, more accurately, is forced to assess, one's pain. A central concept of phenomenology is "intentionality"—the idea that part of what distinguishes experience is the *about* or *for* structure of perception. When I go to the refrigerator to grab a drink, I do not experience each step or each brush of the air on my cheek or each position of my arm as I reach toward the fridge door. On the contrary, my experience is fundamentally oriented toward the object for which I aim: a glass of water. Consciousness is always consciousness-*of* some phenomenon, and this purposive structure shapes lived experience through and through.

Yet, the intentionality of purposive action itself becomes a problem in pain—a problem with respect to both the current moment and also one's ability to forge a future. It is not merely a question of distraction or purposive frustration. While living in chronic pain, foreboding becomes central: concern about the future as foreclosed and restricted becomes definitive of one's relationship to it. "As my eyes open, I worry that I will not be able to get out of bed." I use the term *foreboding* here because, unlike *anxiety,* which has no object, and *fear,* which has an object, *foreboding* operates ambiguously between these two poles, akin to but more expansive than the more simple concept of "worry" (Eccleston and Crombez 2007). Not only does one not know whether one should be concerned in the first place but one does not know precisely what one is concerned about.

Such pain is foreboding because it is not just the type of pain that might come that is at issue—for example, whether one's pain might get worse or change its qualities or effects—but the specific manner in which that future pain will affect one. This accounts for research suggesting that "the limitations imposed by pain often form the focus of people's coping efforts, rather than the pain per se" (Miles et al. 2005, 431). Put more simply, the fact that one knows neither what will come nor how it will come to affect one intensifies one's fear. This means that foreboding redoubles itself. Through the shift in concern from the potential quantity and quality of pain to the aporia of never knowing what's coming, foreboding feeds and amplifies the experience of pain. Foreboding also assists in accounting for the unique temporality of chronic pain: the dulling of the past and future and the circling back to the ambiguous present. "I rarely experience my future anymore."[8] It is not that one's imagination has diminished, however blurred one's cognitive alacrity may otherwise be. It is that the attentional and affective dimensions of one's orientation are forced into a box. To return to the preceding description, the inertia of twenty years of chronic pain, of multiple days bed-ridden, and of multiple clinical encounters where one's experiences and testimony are regularly disregarded or minimized—this inertia buttresses foreboding.

The description in the previous section also displays that pain exists at the overlap of dynamic sociocultural, politico-historical, and ethico-juridical systems, on one hand, and their singularization through the life of an individual, on the other. The meaning of pain always emerges at the intersection of the political and the personal. It is constituted by and occurs within "discursive systems of power," producing what Alyson Patsavas (2014) astutely calls "cripistemologies of pain." In light of one's history, could one overstate the effect of the doctor's or PA's perceived lack of concern—the "last stop" and final authority over one's institutionalized pain management? No. Such a factor cannot but further intensify. "Will the pain worsen?" opens onto "What effects will that worsening have?" which opens onto "I will have no recourse to relief." That the sheer reporting of one's pain in its full severity might further prove oneself to be unmanageable, to be beyond help in the eyes of one's last medical hope for assistance, is horrifying. This is not to mention the insult of the requirement to repeat such narrative convolutions at regular appointments—in clinics where one has long, often for many years, been a patient—to continue to receive what in some cases amounts to life-sustaining medication

(Newton et al. 2013).[9] Foreboding, as a phenomenological structure of the lived experience of pain, must be understood within social, political structures. The failure of pain science and the legislative and political nightmares of the "opioid crisis" cannot be separated from the way in which the structure of forebodingness will play out for a given individual. On the contrary, it is only by looking to the specific historical, sociopolitical structures in which a given individual lives that the meaning of this structure will become clear.

Beholdenness

For those living in chronic pain, the past, present, and future do not merely function differently. The very character of one's existence as a temporal being is different: one is forever waiting, forever on call. I refer to this general structure of chronic pain as *beholdenness*. To be beholden is not simply to be held by someone or something but also to be observed, as in being "under watch," and to be retained, as in a lawyer on retainer. One is monitored and on call, but by whom? This is not known. It could be one's doctor, the medical system as a whole, the legal system, one's employer, one's body—all are in principle "watching" and "waiting." At any point, pain may call for one's services, for being retained means that one is obligated to jump at such a call. One is never free from being retained; one is instead always in wait for the next moment one must respond.

Beholdenness is not the same as what Heidegger (2010) calls "thrownness." It is not the general condition of finding oneself already formed by and complicit in a world one did not create and in large part cannot alter. Beholdenness specifically names finding oneself at the same time (1) monitored, (2) on call, and (3) forced to respond when called upon with regard to one's bodymind. What occurs, for example, when nausea from a migraine strikes? One's body vehemently "calls in," and one must respond. Yet, even while actively responding to that nausea, one is still "on call" for pain, still monitored by and monitoring it, and forever compelled to respond yet again. These are not choices—they are forced upon one by one's relationship to pain itself.

With the beholdenness of pain one is never off the hook. The peace that might come from determinate localization or compartmentalization is put at bay. This is one frame to understand the claim "I do not 'have' pain in the same way that I do not 'have' a body."[10] How does one describe the relationality of pain to oneself if the language of "having" fails—if the "in" of "in pain" can find no locale, no borders? This paradox of bodiliness speaks to the porosity of the sense of self when conditioned by chronic pain. One feels not only out of control but actively under the control of another power—pain—as well as the many, conflicting practices surrounding its control. When one has been told that one's pain cannot be stopped or significantly alleviated, one must confront working to subdue an uncontrollable force that nevertheless controls one.

One is beholden by the pain shaping one's experience and, simultaneously, by the pain that breaks through, transforms, and realigns its relative stability as a background condition. This accounts for the paradoxical formulation: "unbearable, yet bearable." One can in point of fact handle it in the sense that one isn't dead or unconscious. One still goes on going on, however diminished. And yet, in many ways, one does not. It's overwhelming, too much, crushing: unbearable (cf. Crosby 2016). The teeter-totter of the paradoxical structure of the "bearable unbearable" produces fatigue, weariness, and burnout. Beholdenness captures this in its fundamental and tiring ambiguity: that which I am called upon to bear is itself indeterminate even in my very requirement to be on call to bear it (cf. Crombez et al. 1998; Vlaeyen and Crombez 1999). Beholdenness is characterized by capriciousness, ambiguity, and weariness—a product of the fundamental variability one experiences in the lived chronicity of pain.

Bioreckoning

Beholdenness is closely linked to another general feature of pain: bioreckoning. In chronic pain, one is constantly looking for a way to account for one's experiences—for reasons, causes, explanations, histories, and diagnoses. Whether through habitually localizing pain with respect to discrete sources or quantifying one's pain according to the McGill Pain Questionnaire, one becomes a diagnostician. But not just a diagnostician, for the story of how one got this way is never sufficiently explained by diagnosis. One is often asked to provide a full account of one's current state and the actions one takes or will be undertaking to mitigate the ongoing pain. One's "normal" action is preemptively altered based upon anticipation of future symptoms or limitations because one is always reacting to potential reasons for one's pain both now and tomorrow. Bioreckoning refers to the more general process of constantly accounting for and being able to give an account of one's bodily state—past, present, and future. Bioreckoning thus goes beyond medicalization, a well-established sociological concept that describes how medical frameworks shape understanding and perception, both personal and social. It also goes beyond Laura Mauldin's refinement of the concept, "ambivalent medicalization," which she describes as the way that "individuals are both empowered by and surrendering to the process of medicalization" (Mauldin 2016, 4). While ambivalent medicalization brings about a wavering relationship to various diagnostic states, bioreckoning brings about an injunction: one must monitor oneself. One cannot but monitor oneself when the stakes of such monitoring are assumed to impact one's flourishing not just day to day but even minute to minute.

The need for and use of bioreckoning is displayed well in Christine Miserandino's (2003) parable that goes under the moniker "Spoon Theory." This short story revolves around the metaphor of "spoons" as markers of physical and psychological energy. The "average" person might begin with, say, twenty spoons for a given day. A spoonie starts with less, and daily activities that don't require a spoon for others might for a spoonie. Shower—one spoon gone. Make breakfast—another. Schedule appointments and run an errand—two more. Also, spoons don't automatically transfer from one day to the next. What counts as "normal" activity is very different for a spoonie, and this is typically very hard for non-spoonies to understand. Someone might get up and appear totally "fine," and by the early afternoon, they are depleted. When one is out of spoons, one is out. Tellingly, Miserandino's parable is renowned among people who experience chronic pain and/or chronic illness. Such people and their larger communities use the term both to explain their experience and as an identity marker: "Oh, you're a spoonie too?" Tracking one's spoons requires constant bioreckoning.

The *bio-* in *bioreckoning* is meant to highlight the focus on biological cause and biological concerns, but, at the level of lived experience, this reckoning of course involves social and any other number of factors as well. There is a process of constant self-evaluation not just of one's energy levels but of all of one's feelings, movements, and even thoughts. Regulating all of one's activities in light of one's pain, detailing the events and diagnoses that led to it, remembering life before it—these are all part and parcel of the structure of bioreckoning.

Of the many practices that inform bioreckoning, diagnoses in particular take on a narrative life of their own, a subplot that can, in effect, subtend the real plot: the fully fleshed-out life. Bioreckoning can upend the stability of the story one tells about one's life as one seeks out or is given new etiologies and diagnoses—and thereby new histories and futures. This process is exacerbated by the fact that too many chronic pain patients must simultaneously prove their (invisible) pain to be real (to others) (Kugelmann 1999; Werner, Isaksen, and Malterud 2004). Thus the frustration: "What brings me in? Is this some kind of sick joke?"[11] Bioreckoning renders pain legitimate only insofar as it adheres to the hermeneutic strictures of what Foucault famously calls the anatomo-clinical gaze. As Eccleston, Williams, and Rogers (1997, 699, cf. 707–8) note, "when pain is no longer useful as a symptom, identity is challenged, weakened and at risk for both chronic pain patients and pain professionals." Often lack of diagnosis does not merely delegitimize symptoms; it delegitimizes persons. Bioreckoning involves constant biomonitoring and biovigilance especially and specifically insofar as medical legitimation is required to continue living on in chronic pain—for many people to function, their medical provider must regard them as having a "legitimate" condition.

Furthermore, the sociocultural dimensions of bioreckoning are not decided merely by the authority of medicine. They are also decided by the authority of symptoms as they are experienced—not "making sense" or not "adding up" is judged irrelevant by one's body. Experience does not serve reason by bending the knee. But that doesn't mean reason can't forever detain it. To live in pain is to be before a continual tribunal, the verdict of which can dissolve or solidify the cohesion of one's self. Bioreckoning contributes to the intensity of one's beholdenness and foreboding. Each co-constitutes each.

Disruption

Pain cannot be understood in terms of its mere occurrence. Instead, a *for*-structure is constitutive of the meaning of pain. Pain is always in a dynamic relationship pulled taut between past conditions that led to its emergence and a future state without it toward which it orients one. "What will today, what will tomorrow, be like?"—this is the ground floor of constitutive pain. Given my analysis of various theories of pain in chapter 1, it is now clear that pain's regulative function relies on its etiology. Without a cause, pain loses its regulative significance because it no longer has a basis, a reason, with respect to which it can *orient* one's action. This is the case whether that action is conceived at the level of the organism, as in the biological model, or at the level of the divine, as in the religious model, or at whatever level with respect to the other models, *mutatis mutandis.*

Chronic pain disrupts this regulative structure; it evicts one from being at home in one's own body. All orders that would otherwise direct one to reorient oneself are made worthless because in chronic pain, following those orders guarantees nothing. It is in this sense that chronic pain fundamentally disrupts experience. The very habits, rules, regularities, and other reliances by which and through which one understands and orients oneself are unknown—unknown and capricious.

Each of these four features, foreboding, beholdenness, bioreckoning, and disruption, alters the characteristics of the others. That is to say, they can exacerbate or mitigate each other. In light of these four features, one can better understand how chronic pain renders the forces that determine one's life constitutively disrupted. In this respect, chronic pain effects disorientation in one's ability to regulate one's activities and projects, even to the point of disrupting one's sense of self. Forever beholden, one experiences one's being in the mood of foreboding. One is condemned to bioreckoning the conditions of one's existence, forced by medical and social demands to account for why and how one is and will be. Disruption feeds back into foreboding and beholdenness and also places extremely high demands on one's ability to bioreckon. These demands are so high that one might give up, which is to say, lose hope that there is an account of the meaning of one's life in pain. Given these general structures of chronic pain, we can now turn back to an analysis and critique of the ableist conflation of disability with pain.

Of Pains and Sufferings

The ableist conflation involves multiple mistakes, and I am now in a position to better explain one of its central errors: its misunderstanding of the nature of pain, the nature of suffering, and the difference between them. Although many trade on the commonsense intuition that whatever pain is, it is defined by not being "enjoyable," a small amount of reflection proves this false. Exercise, partying to exhaustion, eating spicy food or past satiation: these are all instances where we inflict various forms of pain onto ourselves quite willingly and, in at least some sense, happily. Research about the variety of experiences that humans report as pleasurable, ranging from BDSM to self-cutting to flagellation, and whether undertaken under the auspices of religion, erotic communities, self-therapy, or what have you, also proves this false. Having said this, no one wants to suffer. People who purposely inflict pain, even extreme pain, on themselves do not report doing so in order to suffer: they do so in order "to feel" or to instead provide a different sort of "feeling" that can push against or negate "negative" feelings. As I understand research on these practices, their telos is aimed at a goal distinctly other than suffering *in and of itself* (Strong 1998; Stoller 1991).

Based on the phenomenology presented earlier, I contend that there are three distinct categories of pain. The first two categories involve two distinct sorts of experience, whereas the third is defined by just one.

COMPONENT PAIN	CONSTITUTIVE PAIN	CONSUMING PAIN
Feeling Pain | Being in Pain	Suffering | Constitutive Suffering	Extreme Suffering

Figure 2. Types of pain.

Component Pain

I define component pain as pain that enters into one's prereflective and reflective awareness but is not definitive for one's life projects. Component pain takes two primary forms: feeling pain and being in pain.

Feeling pain comprises unpleasant sensations that are of note, yet do not substantively enter into one's projects. What is meant when someone says "It hurt, but it wasn't that bad—I wasn't really in pain" or "I'm fine; it didn't hurt much"? I would argue that there is an implicit distinction at work between feeling pain and being in pain. At the level of lived experience, the primary difference is the extent to which pain affects one's projects.[12] I hit the tip of my elbow and wince. It may hurt for a second or two, but I go on with whatever I was doing. I stretch my leg out too far and feel a sharp tension in my hip. In both cases, a few hours later I probably won't remember that these events even happened. I certainly won't the next day. I am arguing that this is a case of feeling pain but not being in pain.[13] Unlike arguments concerning pain asymbolia, the distinction here is about, not cognitive/physiological capacity, but existential impact: to feel but not *to be in pain* means that pain doesn't meaningfully affect one. Feeling pain thus includes many liminal discomforts—phenomena to which we are often unsure about applying the word *pain*. We often use the qualifier *mild* to pick out this category. Feeling pain thus includes what Sheena Hyland calls "mild corporeal pain: ordinary, non-pathological bodily stresses and strains–experiences that are commonly referred to as 'aches and pains'" (cited in Käll 2013, 7–8).

Being in pain comprises unpleasant sensations that inform or orient one's short-term projects. Unlike feeling pain, being in pain indicates the fact that it is nontrivial existentially. Being in pain names a situation in which the emotional-affective and cognitive-projective factors of one's being are notably altered by one's pain. One does not simply feel pain after a tonsillectomy, nor does one simply feel pain during pregnancy or amputation (assuming anesthesia is not at play): one is *in* pain. When a person is sick enough to go to the doctor and is asked "How much pain are you in?" such a question is often ultimately less about the level of the sensation of pain and more about the extent to which the pain is inhibiting their action. Notwithstanding the logic of the McGill or Faces pain scales and their—I readily admit—necessity in certain triage situations, medicine is primarily interested in pain's functional effect on life activity because it is when pain responses impact life activity that pain most distinctly becomes a sign of something seriously amiss.

Constitutive Pain

Constitutive pain is pain that substantively and definitively enters into one's life projects. As with component pain, the distinguishing characteristic hinges on the way in which and quality by which pain shapes one's life and life projects. Constitutive pain takes two primary forms: suffering and constitutive suffering.

Suffering comprises unpleasant sensations that inform or orient one's long-term projects. One suffers when one's projects are substantively and prospectively shaped by the pain one is experiencing. That is to say, one suffers when a determinate component of one's future and sense of self is formed by being in pain. Note that this definition of suffering allows one to explain how, despite suffering, a person could become temporarily distracted or even experience happiness. Distraction functions to pull one out of one's suffering even if one maintains the same ultimate relationship to pain before, during, and after that distraction. If one understands distraction as this fleeting, temporary forgetting of suffering, it is not surprising that distraction can function both through innocuous examples (laughter, music, good company, etc.) and through noxious ones (e.g., self-cutting, substance abuse).

In the latter cases, the infliction of pain by cutting or other such means actually opens up the field of one's otherwise narrowed or foreclosed projects. This may seem paradoxical to those who have not experienced it, but to repeat from earlier, this is exactly what is reported by those who take such actions. Cutting allows one to give a physical form to one's pain, eliciting a response that exposes what one otherwise feels as intractable and incommunicable, including even to oneself. In doing so, self-cutting is experienced as the *diminishment* of the constitutive pain of suffering through an amplification of shorter-term component pain. Add to this that it is a well-researched fact that the expectation of pain can increase the actual experience of being in pain, and also, as I have defined things, of suffering. Understanding suffering in this way helps explain why foreboding can intensify the self-reporting of pain levels, even with respect to simplistic methods like the McGill pain scale, for foreboding names one way that pain affects not only one's sense and experience of self but one's sense of the future.

Constitutive suffering comprises constant unpleasant sensations that fundamentally orient one's long-term projects and one's sense of self. Constitutive suffering picks out cases in which suffering has become integral to one's everyday experience and sense of self. This may be due to its intensity combined with duration, the gravity of a given trauma, or the severity of impact from loss, among many other causes. Put otherwise, constitutive suffering is suffering that acts as a foundation of one's being-in-the-world. Such a definition explains the intuitive difference one would make between, say, the experience of recovery from open-heart surgery and the suffering of posttraumatic stress disorder or chronic pain that manifests most or all hours of the day. Depending on length, impact, and quality, heart surgery recovery is a case of being in pain or, perhaps, of suffering. The latter two examples, however, are cases of constitutive suffering. Even if, miraculously, one's chronic pain were to cease, it has become the default position. It marks the background against which a new, nonsuffering state would be compared.

Consuming Pain

Extreme suffering comprises constant or recurring unpleasant sensations so intense that one's experience primarily or solely consists of them. Take the migraine poetry of Jane Cave. She describes lying in her bed with a headache so strong it's as if she is "entombed in perpetual night" (Winscom 1795, 166–67). Claustrophobic darkness encroaches upon her, drowning out sense itself along with the last specks of light crawling through shuttered windows. "To languish on is worse than death," she exclaims, knowing that only the utter inertness of death could conquer the suffering that grips her. Why is she thus entombed? From where has this suffering derived its power? She knows full well: "its dire excess" dissolves her sight. This sheer excessivity of suffering is also noted by Emily Dickinson when she speaks of a "pain—so utter—It swallows substance up—" (Dickinson 1960). An excessivity of nothingness. To have a migraine headache every single day is, Cave suggests, extreme suffering.

In his essay "Useless Suffering," Levinas (1988) speaks of the suffering of suffering. He begins by noting that suffering indeed presents itself in the commonsense way we usually talk about pain: it is a fact, a datum of consciousness—it is a sensation. "Suffering is surely a given in consciousness, a certain 'psychological content,' like the lived experience of color, of sound, of contact, or like any sensation . . . but in this content itself, it is, in-spite-of-consciousness, unassumable. It is unassumable and 'unassumability'" (156). It is an experience that one goes through but cannot take up, cannot incorporate into how one understands the world. Many experiences refuse themselves to understanding, to consciousness. Love is one example. If I feel love for you, when I try to make this love clear to myself, when I try to analyze it, understand it, reason about or explain it, I will, on most accounts, necessarily fail. Love is an excess that goes beyond any articulation of it or any particular sensation or sets of sensations. Love can neither be taken on nor refused—I find myself in love. Extreme suffering "results from an excess, a 'too much' which is inscribed in a sensorial content," but quite unlike love, it is invariably experienced as negative in and of itself (156). Extreme suffering is when one finds oneself experiencing the suffering of suffering itself.

Torture comprises extremely unpleasant sensations inflicted by others that saturate one's experience and are intense enough to destabilize or destroy the conditions for the possibility of subjectivity. In torture, one is not simply in extreme suffering, for one knows that in torture, the goal, however constructed and executed, is thought to be achieved through suffering itself. Which is to say, the fact that one's suffering is intended to be insufferable is a powerful way, if not the most powerful way, to intensify that suffering—keeping in mind the role of foreboding discussed previously. Moreover, as Elaine Scarry has argued, torture's goal and in some cases effect is to destroy the very possibility to be. Torture seeks the total destruction of a person's world—both actual and possible. In torture, the very affectivity by which one exists as a human is turned against oneself into a weapon. More than any other phenomenon, torture destroys, and destroys completely, the conditions for a subject to exist.

What each of these distinctions is trying to get at should now be clear: the extent to which pain shapes one's world. At the level of ordinary language, there is no uncontroversial distinction between the concepts of "pain" and "suffering." By distinguishing different sorts of each in a manner that draws on the phenomenological aspects of and relationship between both terms, I hope to have done justice to the ways in which the terms are used and, also, to the ultimately different set of experiences that distinguish each.

Experience, Evaluation, and Pain

A careful dissection of various types of pain and suffering is not common in the history of philosophy. The overarching aim of this book is to argue that one reason for this is the ableist conflation of disability with pain and suffering. That which is assumed to be "negative" has been populated by a wildly large range of experiences, and it has been a dedicated commitment to ignorance of such phenomena by those engaged in otherwise careful inquiry that propped up treatise-length defenses of support for lives that, it turns out, simply reflect the station and character of the thinker lucky enough to produce them. For example, many thinkers—from most Stoics and Rationalists to most contemporary thinkers ranging from Beauvoir to Rorty to Levinas to Young—fail to analytically distinguish "pain" from "suffering," much less differing types of each.

Despite this state of affairs, pain has played and still today plays an enormous role in philosophical inquiry, especially with respect to ethical and sociopolitical philosophy. For example, while the role of pain in modern liberal theories is often de-emphasized in relation to equality or justice, liberal theorists, such as Judith Shklar (1989), have regarded pain to be the core minimal foundation of liberalism. We may disagree about the *summum bonum,* but not the *summum malum*: we all wish to avoid pain. But this is misguided. Some pain cannot be avoided; some pain should not be avoided; and some pain should be avoided at all costs. Our ethical and sociopolitical theories need to take such distinctions into account.

Aristotelian virtue ethics, Kantian deontology, Rousseauian social contractarianism, Millean utilitarianism, and care ethics—whether Kittayian, Heldian, or Trontian—all valorize the minimization of pain. However, no one, whether political theorist or ethicist, is in the business of keeping people from the possibility of component pain. Component pain is an integral part of human life; it is the condition of the possibility of any model of flourishing. The aim of moral and political accounts is to minimize constitutive and consuming pain. Those living with congenital pain insensitivity make this evident— without the ability to feel or be in pain, the toll on one's body can be enormous, and early death is, despite contemporary biotechnological advances, inevitable.

Although ethicists and theorists are certainly right in seeking the minimization of constitutive and consuming pain, this approach is not without complications. One ramification is that forms of life tied to or assumed to be tied to constitutive or consuming pain will not only be considered negative but be considered as potential targets.

Ethical and political theories are likely to aim to prevent or remove such forms of life. Lives of constitutive and consuming pain aren't just lives less worth or not worth living for ethical and political theories— they are lives the absence of which marks a truly just society. The profoundly difficult task, one that too many theories eschew, is to more carefully determine how this supposed category of lives is constructed.

The ableist conflation leads people to assume that many, if not most, disabilities involve constitutive or even consuming pain, which is not the case. Tellingly, the ableist conflation implicitly takes the distinction I have made between component and constitutive pain into account, for it is precisely in terms of the horizon of an entire life that a person living with disability is assumed to be suffering. The ableist conflation assumes, in other words, that the very conditions of the possibility of living with a disability are fundamentally constricted possibilities and that the pains one experiences are not mere components of a life. Combining the arguments in this chapter with even a shred of awareness of research in disability studies and philosophy of disability, one sees that this assumption is false. And it is to such research concerning disability that I now turn.

PART II
Disability

3

Theories of Disability

Our aversion to the very idea of being disabled forestalls our understanding the disabled from their perspective.

—Anita Silvers, "Reconciling Equality to Difference"

Ignoring some difficult features of people's experience of disability can't in the end advance the flourishing of people with disabilities.

—Erik Parens, "Choosing Flourishing"

Whereas the previous chapters attempted to dismantle the ableist conflation with respect to its understanding of pain and suffering, this chapter shifts to focus on how this pernicious habit of thought fails to understand disability. The ableist conflation renders "disability," a concept that refers to a profoundly complex set of phenomena, into an indefensibly narrow concept. I begin by laying out the complexity of disability before turning to why disability activists have been able to achieve success despite disability's complexity, namely, via a focus on shared experiences of ableist discrimination and oppression. After this bird's-eye-view introduction, I turn to discussing the three main theories of disability, personal, social, and postsocial, as well as the dominant models of each. Paralleling the analysis in chapter 1, I provide an analysis of the domain, function, and effect of these theories. In what follows, I focus on how the term *disability* is *used* to pick out various bodies, identities, and social groups. I do so by exploring disability's function across multiple domains of knowledge building and dissemination, ranging from religion to biomedicine to philosophy to political activism.

At the end of this chapter, I will be in a position to argue that the effect of individual theories of disability is to *exteriorize,* of social theories of disability to *politicize,* and of postsocial theories to *problematize.* I further argue that while the social theories of disability are regulative, giving one traction with respect to the project of living, both individual and also postsocial theories of disability fail in that respect. At the outset, it is important to note that the theories of disability I discuss herein are more diverse than theories of pain discussed in the first chapter, and they are more diverse in multiple respects. This is because disability has become not only a highly politicized issue but also a political *identity* from the mid-twentieth century onward. It has become so in ways that pain has not (yet) for people living in chronic pain or for people living with chronic illness.[1]

Tellingly, it is common for discussions of disability to begin by detailing and lamenting the difficulty of defining it. Nancy Eiesland (1994, 23–24) demonstrates this well:

> The differences among persons with disabilities are often so profound that few areas of commonality exist. For instance, deafness, paralysis, multiple sclerosis, and mental retardation [sic] may produce the same social problems of stigma, marginality, and discrimination, but they generate vastly different functional difficulties. Further, people with the same disability may differ significantly in the extent of their impairment. The level of impairment for a person with dyslexia may be dramatically dissimilar to that of a person with severe mental retardation [sic], though they can both be identified as having learning [or intellectual] disabilities. Finally, disabilities can be either static or progressive, congenital or acquired. The social experience of a person who becomes disabled as an adult may differ significantly from that of a person with a congenital disability. These dissimilarities make a broad definition of people with disabilities difficult, if not impossible.

More provocatively, Fiona Kumari Campbell argues that "disability" is a catachresis. "There is no literal referent for this concept," she writes. "As soon as we discursively interrogate 'disability,' its meaning loses fixity and generality, and ultimately collapses" (Campbell 2005, 127; also Campbell 2001, 43). A wide range of critical analysis demonstrates how the concept of disability is constituted by a dazzling panoply of intersections: history, technology, religion, law, medicine, economics, gender, sexuality, race, ethnicity, indigeneity, class, citizenship, politics, science, culture, policy, architecture, and so on (Nielsen 2012; Trent 2017). This breadth leads one to wonder whether the concept of disability is too incoherent, vague, or expansive to have analytic value. Should philosophers and theorists attending to corporeal variability, hearing that term as including both physical and intellectual disabilities, do away with the term? Are we all better off without it? I think not. Despite the difficulty of defining disability, this concept has important—perhaps even indispensable, given current conditions of realpolitik—social, political, and economic implications and has concrete meaning in people's lives. Furthermore, defining disability can be particularly helpful for identifying harmful ableist attitudes, practices, and norms, including in a manner that allows for real-world legal and political action against them.

From melanin levels to the tilt of a spine to the length of a femur to hemoglobin count to the pace and timber of pronunciation, ableist norms can range over anything and everything. The list is endless. As Lennard Davis (2013a, 271; see also Davis 2015), echoing Campbell, notes:

> it is hard if not impossible to make the case that the actual category of disability really has internal coherence. It includes, according to the Americans with Disabilities Act of 1990, conditions like obesity, attention deficit disorder, diabetes, back pain, carpal tunnel syndrome, severe facial scarring, chronic fatigue syndrome, skin conditions, and hundreds of other conditions. Further, the law specifies that if one is "regarded" as having these impairments, one is part of the protected class.

The Americans with Disabilities Act of 1990 (ADA) is one of the more important legally binding documents (relative to the function of a given contemporary nation-state) to be written concerning disability. Indeed, the ADA gave rights to what thereby became the United States' largest minority. One of the primary means by which disability activists achieved this milestone was by utilizing the social model of disability to reconceive of disability from a question of individual bodies to a question of an oppressed minority group. Impairment is a fact of human embodiment; disability is a result of stigma, discrimination, and oppression. Activists were able to achieve this legislative feat *despite* the heterogeneity of forms and meanings of disability listed earlier because what made that heterogeneity cohesive was a question of *shared discrimination* and *oppression.* Notably, they were able to achieve this legislative feat despite the fact that with various technological developments, the identity of this minority can shift and has in fact shifted at a pace and in a manner that, arguably, other social identities that share oppressions have not, or at least have not in the same ways.[2]

In short, disability rights have been won because it is not the natural but the social dimensions of disability that primarily define it for purposes of group identity, political solidarity, and the like (Barnes 2016).[3] I thus disagree with Campbell, and by extension Davis, that disability has "no literal referent." It does have a literal referent: experiences of discrimination and oppression the causes of which are rooted in ableism.[4] That a concept is "spoken in many ways," to invoke Aristotle's claim about being, does not relegate it to nonsense (*Metaphysics,* 1017a23). On the contrary, it might instead be an indication of the unique power that concept has for experience.

One of the more compelling and defensible definitions of disability, coined by Rosemarie Garland-Thomson, is *the experience of being non-normate.* The "normate" is the archetypal figure of able-bodiedness, that which informs what we mean when we speak of the "normal," "typical," "standard," or "able" body (cf. Reynolds 2019). That is to say, the "normate" is an ideal used to justify hierarchy and oppression on the basis of ability-status. Rosemarie Garland-Thompson defines the "normate" as the ideological figure carved out from the plethora of nonnormate bodily variabilities, variabilities which it need not consider and yet which constitute it by providing, through relief, its shape. The "normate" picks out

> the veiled subject position of the cultural self, the figure outlined by the array of deviant others whose marked bodies shore up the normate's boundaries. The term normate usefully designates the social figure through which people can represent themselves as definitive human beings. Normate, then, is the constructed identity of those who, by way of the bodily configurations and cultural

capital they assume, can step into a position of authority and wield the power it grants them. (Garland-Thomson 1997, 8)

Given the many ways there are to be nonnormate, there are many ways to be disabled. If disability is understood to mean "the experience of being nonnormate," then this includes the question of "regard" and the other's gaze noted with concern by Lennard Davis. Social factors always contribute to the creation and maintenance of the normate in any given sociohistorical context. Because "disability" is a function of ability expectations relative to any given domain, disability intersects with everything. That is to say, it intersects with all forms of identity and meaning making. Disability is constitutive of human life.

Even if one remains unconvinced and still finds the concept of "disability" so complex, broad, or vague as to be indefensible, this does not mean one cannot learn something by analyzing its deployment— across its meanings—in practice. In what follows, I focus on how the term *disability* is used to pick out bodies, identities, and social groups. I do so by exploring disability's function across multiple domains of knowledge building and dissemination, ranging from religion to biomedicine to philosophy to political activism, and mirroring, to the extent it makes sense, the analysis of pain in chapter 1. I organize this exploration in terms of three overarching theories of disability: personal, social, and postsocial.[5]

Personal Theories of Disability

To repeat from the explanation given at the beginning of chapter 1, I follow Thomas Nail (2016) in how I use the term *theory*. He writes, "The purpose of a theory or concept of [a phenomenon] is not to explain or predict every detail of empirical [phenomena of that sort]; a theory . . . aims to describe the conditions or sets of relations under which" those phenomena occur (11). To this I add that a theory aims to describe the set of relations or conditions under which a given phenomenon is experienced as meaningful.[6] My overarching goal is to understand, first, how theories of disability function to shape and orient lived experience and, second, how these theories taken as a whole shed light on the errors of the ableist conflation. I begin with the moral theory of disability, the first and most dominant *personal* theory of disability historically.

Moral

At the outset, it is important to flag a terminological issue. No language in antiquity (whether Hebrew, Greek, Coptic, Quechua, Sino-Tibetan, or what have you) contains what in English is today captured by the term *disability*. Some historians would extend this claim to medieval and early modern times across a wide range of languages at the time as well. In these epochs and the various cultures in question, one finds a number of distinct terms, including blindness, muteness, lameness, and paralysis, but no overarching concept of disability. In the same way that Foucault (1973, 387) claims that "man is an invention of recent date," disability historians argue that "disability" is an invention of even more recent date. Its emergence is thanks to, among other things, the recent development of myriad programs of population governance in the last few centuries that demanded populations be categorized relative to their relationship to contemporary forms of labor. Having said this, I will here follow the lead of disability historians in retaining the term *disability* despite the constant risk of anachronism (Rose 2003; Metzler 2013).

As I commented when discussing the religious model of pain in chapter 1, because I am working within the "Western" intellectual tradition, I here limit my treatment of what I am calling the "moral theory of disability" only with respect to Abrahamic traditions: Judaism, Christianity, and Islam. By looking to a number of textual examples, I argue that whether through sin or selection, disability ultimately marks an ontological and social exteriorization of the individual: one is judged outside how a person should be in both the natural (religious) order and also in one's specific religious community.

The Jewish Tanakh/Christian Old Testament at times seems to present no ambiguity concerning disability.[7] Take Exodus 4:11 as an example: "then the Lord said to him, 'Who has made man's mouth? Who makes him mute [מֶּלֶא], or deaf [שֵׁרַח], or seeing, or blind [עִוֵּר]? Is it not I, the Lord?'"[8] If God is creator, then are not all creations purposive? While implicit in the latter verse, the idea that people who are "mute," "deaf," or "blind" are nevertheless at a disadvantage is addressed explicitly in other passages. Consider Leviticus 19:14: "you shall not curse the deaf [שֵׁרַח] or put a stumbling block before the blind [עִוֵּר], but you shall fear your God: I am the Lord."[9] The purposiveness of all creation is affirmed at the same time that the social disadvantage of certain forms of creation is protected against. To mistreat those who are deaf or blind by virtue of their *difference* is to treat such people as if they were not God's purposeful creations. Yet, these texts do not argue that these are *mere* differences as much as they assume that they are differences that indeed make a difference to humans. It is not that being blind or deaf should be affirmed for the types of experience it brings about as much as it is that none of God's creations should be treated poorly. Indeed, the primary theological defense against the expected mistreatment of disability is an appeal to divine purposivity. God meant for certain people to be born "differently," and one should not treat them poorly insofar as such people are also God's creations.

And yet, when certain questions of priestly hierarchy and privilege come into play, disability can become a marker of exclusion *by God's own standards.* Leviticus 21:17–23 reads:

> No one of your offspring throughout their generations who has a
> blemish [מוּם] may approach to offer the food of his God. For no
> one who has a blemish shall draw near, a man blind or lame, or
> one who has a mutilated face or a limb too long, or one who has a
> broken foot or a broken hand, or a hunchback, or a dwarf, or a man
> with a blemish in his eyes or an itching disease or scabs or crushed
> testicles. No descendant of Aaron the priest who has a blemish
> shall come near to offer the Lord's offerings by fire; since he has
> a blemish, he shall not come near to offer the food of his God.
> He may eat the food of his God, of the most holy as well as of the
> holy. But he shall not come near the curtain or approach the altar,
> because he has a blemish, that he may not profane my sanctuaries;
> for I am the Lord; I sanctify them.[10]

Here disability allows one to partake in sustenance, in the maintenance of one's existence, but it categorically prevents one from privileged connections with the divine. The Hebraic treatment of disability displayed in this passage appears somewhat mild in comparison to an Attic Greek context, in which congenital physical disability could warrant infanticide or "exposure" *(ektithemi)* (Rose 2003; Golden 1981). While God or the gods decide the ultimate "fate" of the person born or living with a (or certain types of) disability, that life is acknowledged as outside either all or at least most parts of the moral universe of the actual human societies in question. That is to say, disability signifies ostracization and exclusion. On one hand, disability is understood as resulting in social exclusions such that the divine intervenes with maxims to care. On the other hand, the divine sets up its own limits as to the level of intimacy it wants with people with disabilities—and at least with respect to Leviticus, the divine certainly does not wish disabled people near the holy of holies.

In the Christian New Testament, things get further complicated. After the reference to the ancient commonplace that disability was due to sin, John 9:2–3 recounts that Jesus's "disciples asked him, 'Rabbi, who sinned, this man or his parents, that he was born blind?' Jesus answered, 'It was not that this man sinned, or his parents, but that the works of God might be displayed in him.'" After this comment, Jesus takes actions that lead to the blind man's healing. Here the display of God's "works" is presumably in the making able of the disabled man, even though Jesus clearly aims to decouple his sin or that of his family line from the presence of congenital disability (Mitchell and Snyder 2007). Jesus heals the man despite or regardless of the fact that no sin brought about his disability, playing with the long-standing link between disability and sin. Yet, at the same time, the act of making him "able" is, ultimately, still a sign of divine power—that is the real point.

This interpretation involves further layers, however, especially when one looks to the emphasis Jesus places on the "disenfranchised." Take as an example Luke 14:12–14: "He said also to the man who had invited him, 'When you give a dinner or a banquet, do not invite your friends or your brothers or your relatives or rich neighbors, lest they also invite you in return and you be repaid. But when you give a feast, invite the poor, the crippled, the lame, the blind [*kalei ptochous, anapeirous, xolous, tuphlous*].'"[11] The emphasis on such persons is a mainstay of the reported accounts of the historical Jesus. The "disabled" are included in the ambit of his concerns but are included *as social outsiders*, as the excluded.

While "the crippled, the lame, and the blind" are often referred to along with other groups, such as "the poor," financial workers (Luke 19:1–10), or sex workers (Luke 7:36–50), disabled people receive a unique form of treatment. Disability is more often than not taken up as a vehicle for displays of divine power. Tellingly, Jesus does not perform miraculous work on tax collectors or sex workers in the same manner as he does on those with disabilities. Disability alone is that form of creation Jesus *re*-creates. It is true that Jesus, unlike multiple moments in the texts of the Pentateuch, continues to split questions of purity from disability. Still, in the end, however, disability serves divine power through its repair, through becoming "abled."

Take Mark 2:1–12, where Jesus heals someone paralyzed to make a point about his authority to forgive sin:

> When he returned to Capernaum after some days, it was reported that he was at home. So many gathered around that there was no longer room for them, not even in front of the door; and he was speaking the word to them. Then some people came, bringing to him a paralyzed man [*paralutikos*], carried by four of them. And when they could not bring him to Jesus because of the crowd, they removed the roof above him; and after having dug through it, they let down the mat on which the paralytic lay. When Jesus saw their faith, he said to the paralytic, "Son, your sins are forgiven." Now some of the scribes were sitting there, questioning in their hearts, "Why does this fellow speak in this way? It is blasphemy! Who can forgive sins but God alone?" At once Jesus perceived in his spirit that they were discussing these questions among themselves; and he said to them, "Why do you raise such questions in your hearts? Which is easier, to say to the paralytic, 'Your sins are forgiven,' or to say, 'Stand up and take your mat and walk'? But so that you may know that the Son of Man has authority on earth to forgive sins"—he said to the paralytic—"I say to you, stand up, take your mat and go to your home." And he stood up, and immediately took the mat and went out before all of them; so that they were all amazed and glorified God, saying, "We have never seen anything like this!"

As with the passage from John 9, Jesus plays with the disability-as-sin trope. He mocks those for whom disability is understood as a price one pays for a wrong, as is the case for moral rationales of experiencing pain. His mockery of this idea is so intense that the physical-material transformation of the person with the disability is meant to be the punchline of such an idea's absurdity.[12]

In certain respects, the Qur'an treats disability similarly to the Jewish Tanakh and the Christian New Testament. Even if people with disabilities are affirmed as a part of creation, assumptions about their difference, including their "bad-difference," operate alongside divine purposivity:

> He frowned and turned his back when the blind man [عبس وتولى أن جاءه الأعمى] came towards him. How could you tell? He might have sought to purify himself. He might have been forewarned, and might have profited from Our warnings. But to the wealthy man you were all attention: although the fault would not be yours if he remained uncleansed. (80:1, translation from Dawood 1990)[13]

The Prophet Muhammad turns his back on a blind man, and he is called into question for this. How could the Prophet know that turning his back would be justified? The assumption, it seems, is that there could be a reason for which the Prophet's shunning of the blind man might be warranted. The text suggests that the Prophet could not know if this shunning was warranted in the case that the blind man might be saved, might be cleansed. The only reason not to shun the blind man is, it seems, if one saves him in not doing so.[14]

Despite these examples of religious shunning, belittling, moralizing, and leveraging the disabled for the purposes of divine displays of power, in some religions—and in certain contexts or with respect to certain cases even within the aforementioned religions—disability can mark one as chosen or elected. For example, Suzanne Bost notes:

> In his study of Mesoamerican corporeal ideology, Alfredo Lopez Austin claims that "physical defects were considered signs identifying men as individuals with supernatural powers," because people who were chosen by the gods were often marked in some visible way. It was believed by the Aztecs and the Maya—and, to a degree, by many of their descendants today—that illness was a sign of disequilibrium between man and the elements of the universe. (Lewiecki-Wilson and Cellio 2011, 174)

This is, on first blush, a very different conceptualization of the relationship between disability and the divine. It is by virtue of what is recognized as a difference that one is not viewed as selected for disfavor but instead selected for favor. What ties together the contradictory pairs of disability as a marker of disfavor (due to sin) versus a marker of favor (due to selection) is that disability serves to demarcate the extremes of religious singularization: the way in which one stands alone before the divine. On one extreme, disability marks transgression, a separation brought on by oneself or one's ancestors and one that takes a psychosomal toll on the transgressor and/or the descendants of the transgressor. On another extreme, disability marks selection by or even perfection as judged by the thetic order in question and one that takes a psychosomal toll on the selectee as a price for selection. The primary disanalogy is clear: in one case, it is the fault of either the individual or the group for whom the individual is now a representative—one's familial genealogy, one's past lives in reincarnational accounts, or one's actions in the current telluric life. In the other, it can be due to the capriciousness of the religious order, the parable of Job being a paradigmatic case. One might have done nothing blameworthy to deserve one's selection, but that does not therefore mean that one is not responsible to act upon or even be thankful for it. In either case, it is a price one pays. In either case, disability functions to singularize an individual as at the limit or exterior to the dominant thetic order via either capricious or retributive divine power. As stated earlier, whether through sin or selection, disability marks an ontological and social exteriorization of the individual: one is judged outside how one should be in both the natural (religious) order and one's specific religious community. Whether defended as a purposeful creation or transformed into a new creation, on moral theories, disability is an exteriorization from social and religious life. This exteriorization can be from the realm of the social in the sense of disregard, of being outside practices of care, or in the sense of selection, of being chosen as special by the divine as a display of power.

Medical

The medical model of disability is, arguably, the most prevalent theory of disability across the globe today, more so even than the moral model.[15] Disability activists first defined this model as a way to capture how disability is conceptualized within modern medicine and, insofar as most societies adopt the medical model, how disability is conceptualized by most people and institutions. On the medical model, disability is an individual tragedy due to genetic or environmental misfortune.[16] Accordingly, disability is understood on the medical model as a pathology in that term's etymological sense: it gives an account of suffering one is undergoing.

For example, in *Fundamentals of Nursing: Standards and Practice,* "disability" is mentioned nineteen times and each time is described in a way that conforms to the medical model (DeLaune and Ladner 2011). The social dimensions and meanings of disability are never mentioned, even when referencing the ADA (197)! In the majority of cases, "disability" is listed alongside illness or disease (e.g., 43, 62, 247, 312, 390, 490, 1305). Revealingly, "healing" is defined in the glossary as the "process of recovery from illness, accident, or disability" (1347).[17] In a 2006 textbook on medical terminology, *Medical Terminology: The Language of Health Care,* the meaning of "disability" is assumed to be so obvious that *it gets no definition at all.* The word is used four times, once in a definition of Alzheimer's ("disease of structural changes in the brain resulting in an irreversible deterioration that progresses from forgetfulness and disorientation to loss of all intellectual functions, total disability, and death") and three times in the context of explaining a form of "developmental disability" (Willis 2006, 388, 413–16). Whether one looks to basic or clinical science, it is hard not to conclude that disability's meaning in medicine is often assumed to be so obvious as to warrant no explanation.[18]

Then again, when put in the historical context of the rise of modern medicine, this uncritical understanding of disability seems inevitable.[19] Corporeal difference itself, a set of infinitely differentiated forms, became increasingly subject to pathologization as modern medical practice and corresponding biomedical technologies developed. From limb formation to learning patterns to functional movement to hemoglobin count to behavior, nearly all general forms and discrete formations of human being-in-the-world can be understood relative to a norm—and thus everything can become a question of the normal and the pathological/the abnormal. The statistically typical as defined by the medical gaze has become the hegemon of human corporeal forms. Any difference is potentially subject to pathologization because there is nothing the medical gaze cannot incorporate in its typology of human being. In-corporate: this can be interpreted literally, for the medical model situates disability and ability inside bodies.

Yet, saying that corporeal difference itself became subject to pathologization is still too broad. Semiotics underwrites the logic of medical diagnosis as a form of knowledge (re)production. Symptoms are understood as signs, as *semeion,* that refer to physical or psychological causes. Diagnosis cannot but rely on semiosis. It relies on the process whereby something functions as a sign or, in short, the action of signs.[20] That is to say, diagnostic pathology relies on the semiotic structure of symptomatology: the accounting for misfortunes in the service of correcting them. Misfortune is the hermeneutic key to medical and moral theories of disability, and to suffer a misfortune means that one bears a cost, whether moral, economic, bodily, and so on, in nature. In this sense, the moral and medical models share the core idea that disability is a price one pays for misfortune.

The influence of the medical model and its tragic figuration of disability is hard to overstate. For example, it is only insofar as disability is seen as fundamentally tragic that the logics of inspiration porn and pity porn, of the supercrip and Tiny Tim, can take hold (Harris 2014). For those unfamiliar with these tropes, I'll discuss each in turn. Inspiration porn is everywhere once you know how to look for it. Consider the many TV ads, posters, infomercials, and stories that involve a person with a disability doing some activity—often one that is completely "normal"—and it being described as a "tale of inspiration." A person with Down syndrome goes to prom. Someone with paraplegia becomes a successful litigator. A blind person becomes a professor. This framing only makes sense if one assumes that the person with a disability is fundamentally suffering or lacking to begin with. It then provides the presumed able-bodied viewer with an opportunity to feel good at seeing someone with presumed *misfortunes* experience or achieve something one wouldn't otherwise expect them to. It inspires the able-bodied viewer, who acts as if a parasite upon such experiences, to try harder, believe in the impossible, and never give up (cf. Kafer 2013, chapter 4).

Insofar as disability is understood as a sign of something unfortunate, then in overcoming it, one is praised, even revered. One specific figure inspiration porn produces is the "supercrip." Eli Clare (2015, 2) famously explains it this way:

> A boy without hands bats .486 on his Little League team. A blind man hikes the Appalachian Trail from end to end. An adolescent girl with Down syndrome learns to drive and has a boyfriend. A guy with one leg runs across Canada. The nondisabled world is saturated with these stories: stories about gimps who engage in

activities as grand as walking 2,500 miles or as mundane as learning to drive. They focus on disabled people "overcoming" our disabilities. They reinforce the superiority of the nondisabled body and mind. They turn individual disabled people, who are simply leading their lives, into symbols of inspiration. Supercrip stories never focus on the conditions that make it so difficult for people with Downs to have romantic partners, for blind people to have adventures. for disabled kids to play sports. I don't mean medical conditions. I mean material, social, legal conditions. I mean lack of access, lack of employment, lack of education, lack of personal attendant services. I mean stereotypes and attitudes. I mean oppression. The dominant story about disability should be about ableism, not the inspirational supercrip crap, the believe-it-or-not disability story.

Tropes like the "supercrip" fundamentally fail to appreciate how disability often has more to do with social obstacles than bodily obstacles. It is only through an uncritical acceptance of the ableist conflation that inspiration porn and pity porn get off the ground and "work" for their always-assumed-to-be-able-bodied audience.

The flip side of inspiration porn is pity porn. In failing to overcome disability, one is looked upon with compassion and mercy. One of the more egregious examples of this is Jerry Lewis's infamously degrading and damaging Muscular Dystrophy Association telethons (Longmore 2015). These telethons trotted out people with muscular dystrophy in a way that was fundamentally demeaning, treating them as subjects of pity whose existence was defined almost entirely by *needing help.* These telethons functioned as therapy for the able-bodied who need to experience others as worse off than them, who need to feel good by "helping" someone else, someone to whom they can feel superior.

In the ableist imaginary, the supercrip is praised while the crip is pitied, yet both provide inspiration to the able-bodied observer, who embalms the other's experience in the service of reinforcing their sense of self. The medical model of disability assumes that the misfortune of disability is located in an individual and experienced as tragic. It then goes one step further in redirecting the psychosocial effects of that misfortune into one and just one possible response: the hope for rehabilitation, repair, cure, palliation, or, in certain cases, early death.

In conclusion, whether prompting pity and promoting cure for the crip or provoking praise and peddling faux achievement for the supercrip, the medical theory of disability understands disability as a cosmic misfortune afflicting an individual. This misfortune is always assumed to have an underlying cause that could be discovered through symptomatology, whether via sophisticated diagnostic technologies or the careless gazes of hurried providers. On the medical model of disability, a person living with disability is expected to manage their experience of their embodiment as a problem to be solved. They are treated as outside the realm of the natural and the normal. Disability places one outside a wide range of norms, whether norms of "function," of "ability," or what have you. As with moral theories, on medical theories, *disability exteriorizes one from both natural and social life.*

Social Theories of Disability

Social theories of disability are based upon a core distinction: impairment versus disability. The classic Disability 101 example is that while one might be impaired through paraplegia and use a wheelchair to get around, what disables one while going from point A to B is the choice of architects and engineers to build stairs instead of ramps. Both with respect to its political and academic dimensions, the history of social theories of disability is complex, and a proper analysis would far outstrip the aims at hand (Shakespeare 2014a). Paralleling in some ways the enormous practical and theoretical effects feminist theory achieved by demonstrating that neither differences of gender nor sexuality is reducible to sexual differences and that inequalities resulting from these dimensions of human life are a product of mutable social norms and histories of oppression, disability activists made significant gains for people with disabilities by demonstrating that disability is not reducible to impairment and that disability inequality is by and large a product of mutable social norms and histories of ableism.[21]

Social

Social models of disability developed by activists have a complex global and multicultural history that spans different political, economic, and material conditions, making it difficult to summarize as a whole. Though there are overlapping and even conflicting lineages to the political and activist history of the social model of disability, one starting point was certainly the Union of the Physically Impaired against Segregation (UPIAS) in the United Kingdom, established in 1972 by Paul Hunt, among others (Albrecht 2006). UPIAS's version of the social model is often called the *strong* social model, which picks out its Marxist framework and almost ideological emphasis on the social conditions of disablement. These activists fought not for piecemeal improvements with respect to, say, accommodations but instead fought for a fundamentally different, more just organization to society based on an analysis of class conflicts brought about by capitalist economic organization. I can here broach neither that history nor the notable variations of the social model in other countries, including the way that the social model was deployed to conceive of disability as a "minority identity" in the United States. This variation followed quite directly on the heels of the civil rights movements and drew strength from multiple smaller movements and activism, including the Independent Living Movement started at the University of California, Berkeley through the work of Ed Roberts and others, also in the early 1970s (Nielsen 2012). Suffice to say, social models of disability take up the meaning of disability in its relation to social and political structures.

To the extent they can be separated, the history of the social model in academia is equally, if not more, labyrinthine than its activist history. Although already implicit in writings as early as Erving Goffman's 1963 *Stigma,* one of the first influential academic formulations of the "social model" of disability is Saad Nagi's 1965 paper "Some Conceptual Issues in Disability and Rehabilitation" (Goffman 1963; Sussman 1965, 100–113; Nagi 1970). Nagi's theory of disability distinguishes between pathology as "injury" at a cellular level; impairment as relating to decreases in system-level physiological processes; functional limitation as minimization of the person's abilities vis-à-vis completion of tasks; and disability as a long-term, *social role–based* inability correlated to a given functional limitation (Barnartt 2010). Perhaps because of its nuances, Nagi's model has had a continuing impact on clinical and public health fields (Verbrugge and Jette 1994; Snyder et al. 2008). Although Nagi clearly splits impairment from disability (and furthers adds the distinctions of active pathology and functional limitation), his focus on and elaboration of a "person's re-

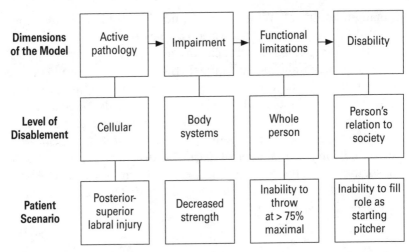

Dimensions of the Model	Active pathology	Impairment	Functional limitations	Disability
Level of Disablement	Cellular	Body systems	Whole person	Person's relation to society
Patient Scenario	Posterior-superior labral injury	Decreased strength	Inability to throw at > 75% maximal	Inability to fill role as starting pitcher

Figure 3. Nagi disablement theory, based on Nagi (1970) and Snyder et al. (2008, 431).

lation to society" was, it seems, not radical enough to make much of a splash in other domains, including for disability activism writ large.

Such technical and category-driven splits between impairment, functional limitation, disability, and disadvantage, among other terms, are today quite common in the social sciences, public health, and international law. For example, the International Classification of Impairments, Disabilities, and Handicaps, published by the World Health Organization in 1980, closely follows such an approach.[22] As Rannveig Traustadóttir (2009, 1) points out, however complex various downstream versions may be, the social model "has provided the knowledge base which has informed the international legal development aimed at full participation and human rights of disabled people." A survey of national and international classifications concerning disability would reveal numerous differences in definition, but the takeaway of such models is clear: the ultimate *effect* of impairment for a person's life is *socially mediated,* rather than being a mere fact of the person's body.

In summary, the social model of disability marks the most significant shift in understanding disability in history. Indeed, working to sever nurture from nature and necessity from contingency with respect to human abilities, the social model of disability has contributed to one of the more remarkable historical shifts in conceptualizing human embodiment. While there are notable and important intra-mural differences among the various types of social models, it is nevertheless the case that all social models fundamentally challenge the narrowness of the medical model. They move the location of the concept of disability from individual bodies in need of intervention to social practices and conditions in need of being designed and carried out more equitably. Bodily differences are not a fault but a part of life, and inequitable treatment is not a part but a fault of society. Put simply, on social models of disability, disability is a question of the sociocultural, historico-political environment in which a person lives. Disability becomes a question of the *polis*. On social models of disability, *disability is politicized.*

Biosocial

What could be called the "first wave" of criticism of social models gained momentum in the 1990s. For example, Susan Wendell (1996, 2001) argued in her landmark book *The Rejected Body* that the social model, especially the simplified version often deployed by activists, is ill suited to describe the experiences of people with chronic illness and chronic pain, especially with respect to their differential impact along lines of gender and, if one heeds work by scholars like Christopher M. Bell (2011) and Nirmala Erevelles (2011), also along lines of race, ethnicity, and nationality. Similar critiques homed in on how the social model undertheorizes or simply ignores disabilities that involve chronic pain, chronic illness, and conditions involving what I called in chapter 2 constitutive or consuming pain. To take another example, Tom Shakespeare (2014b) contends that the distinction between disability and impairment is ultimately untenable. He calls his own view a "critical-material" or "critical-realist" theory of disability. In short, he thinks that a defensible view of disability must involve insights from both medical and social models. As he puts it:

> Any researcher who does qualitative research with disabled people immediately discovers that in everyday life it is very hard to distinguish clearly between the impact of impairment, and the impact of social barriers. In practice, it is the interaction of individual bodies and social environments which produces disability. For example, steps only become an obstacle if someone has a mobility impair-

ment: each element is necessary but not sufficient for the individual to be disabled. If a person with multiple sclerosis is depressed, how easy is it to make a causal separation between the effect of the impairment itself; her reaction to having an impairment; her reaction to being oppressed and excluded on the basis of having an impairment; other, unrelated reasons for her to be depressed? In practice, social and individual aspects are almost inextricable in the complexity of the lived experience of disability. Moreover, feminists have now abandoned the sex/gender distinction, because it implies that sex is not a social concept. Judith Butler and others show that what we think of as sexual difference is always viewed through the lens of gender. Shelley Tremain has claimed similarly that the social model treats impairment as an unsocialized and universal concept, whereas, like sex, impairment is always already social.[23] (218–19)

The critical-realist model is surely an improvement in certain respects. Wendell and Shakespeare are right that there are conditions the suffering of which a just society could not fix. On the contrary, only specific biomedical technologies could fix them. And some simply cannot be fixed at all outside of unbelievable, science-fiction-like scenarios (take the case of anencephaly). When placed in the larger context of theories of disability, I find it more accurate to term theories like those of Wendell and Shakespeare *biosocial* because they push against conceptualizing individual bodies in contradistinction to the effects of social environments and instead argue that we must understand disability in all its messiness at their intersection.

Biosocial theories are of a kind with the claims of sociologists like Carol Thomas and Donna Reeve, who focus on both personal and social dimensions of impairment, including its often complicated psychological effects (Thomas 2004; Reeve 2014). Reeve frames her account as an investigation into "psycho-emotional disablism." Thomas and Reeve bring the biological, social, *and psychological* dimensions of impairment back into focus and demonstrate how impairments themselves, as it were, create effects, both personal and social, that can nevertheless prove resistant to social solutions for amelioration. A perfectly just and equitable society will not thereby solve the problems facing one with neuropathic pain, for example, as Shakespeare often points out, but it also might not "solve" certain forms of depression. Indeed, a perfectly just society cannot directly solve the destructive grind of one's temporomandibular joints for one with TMJ, the slow breakdown of one's body due to congenital pain asymbolia, or the suffering brought on by certain cases of schizophrenia, however much living in such a society would diminish the impact of "disability" in general as understood on the social model.

Biosocial models of disability offer a crucial corrective to the bifurcation of material embodiment and social life as put forward by less-than-nuanced proponents of the social model. On biosocial models of disability, disability is a question not just of the sociopolitical environment in which a person lives but also of how they experience their impairments and the extent to which various biomedical interventions—and the private and public research that supports them—can impact such experience. That is to say, on biosocial models of disability, *disability and impairment are politicized*. Despite the noted differences between social and biosocial models, I have argued that each should be conceived as social theories of disability that have a similar effect: they politicize experiences of disability.

Postsocial Theories of Disability

Given the reach of dominant critical projects ranging across the humanities and social sciences over the last half of the twentieth century, it is unsurprising to see their effect extend to disability theory. Social theories of disability have been subject to two primary critical appraisals. The first assails its linkage to and leverage of identity politics, arguing that disability is simply too heterogeneous to function as an identity. It is true that most hold one of the primary effects of social theories of disability to be the creation of a political identity. Although this has produced numerous positive effects, scholars like Lennard J. Davis argue that identity politics centered around disability are outdated and inept both theoretically and practically. They are especially so in light of increasing awareness of the need for intersectional concerns, whether with respect to the success of projects of social justice or to any given individual's self-understanding. On the contrary, the phenomenon of disability should lead us to *deconstruct* prevalent ideas about embodiment and disability, leading to what he terms a "new ethics of the body." Given their focus on the breakdown of core concepts or effects of social models of disability, I refer to frameworks like Davis's as *dispersive*.

The second primary critique assails the concept of impairment in a far deeper way than biosocial theories do, arguing that it is a historical construction that arose alongside shifts in governance just as the concept of "disability" did. For example, scholars like Shelly Tremain argue that a Foucauldian, genealogical analysis demonstrates that "impairment" does not refer to mere facts or states of affairs about individual bodies. On the contrary, "impairment" is a category arising out of governmental-juridical powers geared toward constituting the disabled subject. In short, on *genealogical* models of disability, both "impairment" and "disability" are constructs and techniques of governance that arose roughly around the eighteenth century. As they are the two most dominant types of postsocial theories of disability, I now turn to discussing the dispersive and genealogical models in more detail.

Dispersive

When I opened this chapter by pointing toward the complexity of disability, I foreshadowed one of the pillars of dispersive models of disability. These models are based largely on criticisms over the far-too-homogenous political construction and social deployment of the category of disability. Lennard Davis (2013a, 268–69) writes:

> We find ourselves in a morass in terms of identity politics and studies. There are various tactics one can take in the face of this conceptual dead end. One can object vehemently that X does indeed exist, that people have suffered for being X, and still do. Therefore, while there may be no basis in theory for being X, large numbers of people are nevertheless X and suffer even now for being so. Or one can claim that although no one has been able to prove the biological existence of X, they will be able to do so someday. In the gap between then and now, we should hold onto the idea of being X. Or one could say that despite the fact that there is no proof of the existence of X, one wants to hold to that identity because it is, after all, one's identity. Finally, we can say that we know X isn't really a biologically valid identity, but we should act strategically to keep the category so that we can pass laws to benefit groups who have

been discriminated against because of the pseudo-existence of this category. All these positions have merit, but are probably indefensible rationally.

If identities are products of social mediation—that is to say, if there is no such thing as identity categories without, at least in part, social constitution—then the social category of "disability" has no more absolute, fixed foundation than any other social phenomenon. Social kinds loop (Haslanger 2012). That is to say, historical contexts bring about structures that allow new *types* of persons to exist. Hacking uses the examples of the "hysteric" and the "idiot" as social kinds that were taken as accurately describing groups in the past—descriptions we today find not only inaccurate but morally deplorable (1999). Even with a more nuanced understanding of various social kinds, for Davis the hierarchies of disability within disability activism and studies should cause pause. And they should further cause one to wonder whether "disability identity" *should* in fact function as a social kind as it does today, namely, in a way highly tailored to the constraints of contemporary political reality.

For example, those with physical disabilities are typically at the top of the so-called disability food chain in terms of political optics, representation, and more. It is hard to imagine the ADA emerging on the heels of activism by people with eczema. Or those with fibromyalgia. Or . . . One could continue on with such counterfactual speculation for quite some time—the point is that any number of groups of people with disabilities appear ill suited relative to the calculi of disability politics under constraints imposed by, among other things, our late capital, settler colonial, neoliberal order. In short, social models of disability have created a political identity by carving prototypical forms of disability out of the cultural imaginary of the milieu of the twentieth century. A white, cishet, wheelchair-using man is an easier figure to leverage politically, so the assumption goes, than, for example, a Black, trans, queer women with invisible disabilities. Social models base their achievements in simplifications that actively ignore the fact that disability, as Davis argues, is so diffuse as to be conceptually incoherent. Is the social model effective as a strategy to create and sustain political solidarity? Yes. Is it based on a defensible ontological ground? No.

Davis (2013a, 271) brings this set of problematics to a head in the following way: "I think it would be a major error for disability scholars and advocates to define the category [of disability] in the by-now very problematic and depleted guise of one among many identities. . . . [Disability] must not ignore the instability of its self-definitions but acknowledge that their instability allows disability to transcend the problems of identity politics." In Davis's dispersive postsocial theory of disability, disability functions to disorient everyone for whom it is a possibility—which is to say, everyone. Disability is a hermeneutic of instability. It represents the flux and fluidity of being human, of the lived experience of human being-in-the-world in its many forms and figurations. Despite this flexibility, note that the "new ethics of the body" for which Davis calls nevertheless operates from a principle of sorts: corporeal variability. But because it is based on a fundamentally unstable category, because it is based on variability, such an ethics is without a normative foundation in any traditional sense. On dispersive models of disability, disability is an open question concerning the complex relationship between one's embodiment and the situation in which one finds oneself. That is to say, on dispersive models of disability, *disability is personally and socially problematized.*

Genealogical

Although Shelly Tremain is not alone in approaching questions of disability through a Foucauldian lens (Campbell 2001; Hughes and Paterson 1997; Hughes 1999), her groundbreaking edited volume *Foucault and the Government of Disability* acted as a flint spark for further genealogical approaches to the study of disability (Tremain 2005, 2015a). Tremain understands genealogy as a method that utilizes the analytic tools of textual archaeology in concert with the vast lexicon of Foucauldian critical concepts, such as biopower and the anatomo-clinical gaze (Tremain 2015b). What most clearly distinguishes genealogical models from other models of disability is their focus on historical conditions. For example, when one takes such conditions into account, the cogency of the core distinction between "disability" and "impairment" made by social models is thrown into disarray. As Tremain (2005, 10) puts it:

notice that if the foundational (i.e., necessary) premise of the social model—impairment—is combined with the preceding claims according to which modern governmental practices produce—that is, form and deform—the subjects whom they subsequently come to represent by putting in place the limits of their possible conduct, then it becomes more evident that subjects are produced who "have" impairments because this identity meets certain requirements of contemporary social and political arrangements. Indeed, it would seem that the identity of the subject of the social model ("people with impairments") is actually formed in large measure by the political arrangements that the model was designed to contest.

Tremain's overarching point is not merely that the concept of "impairment" is historically produced and contestable but that it was specifically produced by governmental and juridical practices to contain and interpellate particular populations, namely, those judged less valuable to the social and economic order and thus made fungible for enslavement, institutionalization, or other forms of state-sanctioned control. On Tremain's (2005, 11) account, "impairment" actually functions to "legitimize the governmental practices that generated it in the first place."[24] That is to say, the very logic of differentiation at stake in the distinction between disability and impairment operates relative to a standard whose ultimate arbiter is modes of governance, that is, power relations acting on and constituting subjects of a nation-state or other political order.

As Adorno put it (Richter and Adorno 2022, 19), to some famously, to others infamously, when discussing ongoing student protests against him, "I still believe that one should hold on to theory, precisely under the general coercion toward praxis in a functional and pragmatized world." In stark contrast to social theories of disability that welcome theoretical heuristics and shortcuts to achieve political and personal goals, heuristics that include what Spivak (2006) astutely calls "strategic essentialisms," postsocial theories seem to have little, if any, patience for such moves. On genealogical models of disability, disability is a question of the historical and political conditions through which one comes to understand and experience oneself as disabled as well as those through which others regard one. That is to say, on genealogical models of disability, *disability is historically problematized.*

There is much more to be said about all that a genealogical analysis of disability implies for understanding the ableist conflation. For the purposes at hand, I want to highlight the effect such an understanding has for the lived experience of disabled people. Although I find much merit in postsocial theories of disability, they are, in the end, existentially deregulative, the outcome I argued is true of personal theories of disability as well. That is to say, they neither help one gain or regain one's sense of self, nor assist in purposive action. To be fair, such concerns are often simply not part of many theoretical projects and certainly not part of these.

Recall that the ableist conflation undermines lived experiences of disability by conceptualizing disability in ways that flatten, hinder, or even eviscerate one's sense of self and purposivity. One of the ways it does so is by restricting available social concepts—hermeneutical resources—concerning disability, leaving public imaginaries to wallow in misguided personal, tragic theories of disability and in the ignorance of the actual varied lived experiences of disabled people. Although postsocial theories of disability are more defensible than personal theories, and are so on multiple counts, they also hinder or, at a minimum, are neutral with respect to the conduct of a life. I thus find that there is more work to be done sussing out the normative and theoretical implications of postsocial theories of disability as they bear on the lived experience of people with disabilities. This is not to say that these theories must be measured by their function or effect. It is only to say that such a limitation must be acknowledged and that such theories should be recognized as, at bottom, critical theoretical projects that leave much to be desired with respect to concrete projects of disability justice and broader social justice as well as with respect to contributing to the flourishing of actual, existing disabled people.

Theories of Disability

We have now discussed a number of prominent theories of disability, which I have here categorized as personal, social, and postsocial theories. As I did in chapter 1 concerning theories of pain, my aim is to provide an account of these theories as a whole. Is there, in fact, a defensible theory of theory of disabilities? I argue that there is, explain what it looks like, and clarify why it is important for judgments concerning disability theory.

"Almost by definition," Bill Hughes (2007, 673) writes, we "assume disability to be ontologically problematic." Multiple disability studies scholars and philosophers of disability have turned this (ableist) assumption on its head. As Titchkosky and Michalko (2012, 127) aptly put it, "that disability is conceptualized as a problem is what we take to be our problem in need of theorizing" (see also Scuro 2017).[25] I would argue that dominant theories of disability, when analyzed as a whole, shed light on how and why disability has become a problematic. Personal, social, and postsocial theories of disability converge in one crucial respect: they assume that disability regulates the conduct of a life, and they seek to leverage its regulation toward various ends. Following the schematic used to discuss theories of pain in chapter 1, I understand theories of disability as shown in Figure 4.

THEORY	DOMAIN	FUNCTION	EFFECT
Personal	Moral/Medical	Judicative	Exteriorize
Social	Political/Legal	Consciousness-Raising	Politicize
Postsocial	History/Hermeneutics	Heuristic	Problematize

Figure 4. Theories of disability.

I argued earlier that the effect of conceptualizations of disability are, in model-specific ways, to exteriorize in personal theories, politicize in social theories, and problematize in postsocial theories. To repeat the definitions given in chapter 2, theories are meaning-making devices. A *theory* allows phenomena to be understood such that they make sense within larger wholes and with respect to larger swaths of experience. While the scope of objects a given theory encompasses can be very large, theories typically operate within a particular *domain*. For example, personal theories of disability operate within two primary domains: moral/religious and medical. The *function* names how, within a given domain, the phenomenon in question is primarily utilized or deployed with respect to its effect on the sociopolitical order. For example, social theories of disability operate with respect to the domain of the political and legal, and their specific function is to alter the sociopolitical landscape for adjudication concerning specific experiences of disabled people insofar as they take themselves to be a protected (or should be protected) political/legal class. The ultimate function of social theories of disability is to raise consciousness about disability as a political/legal category and transform that consciousness raising into a specific effect: political action. The *effect* of each theory refers to the downstream intersubjective and cultural ramifications of taking that theory up as a dominant way to understand the phenomenon in question. For example, the effect of personal theories of disability is to exteriorize people with disabilities from the norms and often related activities of social and religious life. Even if one is brought back in—by divine selection, biomedical intervention, or the like—the default meaning of disability on personal theories is nevertheless one of understanding and/or actively placing a disabled person *outside*. To take another example, on social theories of disability, one can take up the meaning of disability in a manner that affords solidity and solidarity concerning one's political/legal identity and future as well as clarity over one's purposivity, which is to say, the effect of social theories of disability is to politicize experiences of disability. On postsocial theories of disability, on the other hand, one's lived experience is ultimately thrown into question. The primary effect of postsocial theories of disability is to problematize such experience, not to provide direct avenues for personal or political action, self-understanding, or social belonging more generally.

Note that in each case, the function of disability cannot be thought outside of both its normative and also its ontological rendering on a given theory. For example, the exteriorization in personal theories places disability both outside the limits of what a body is and also what a body should be.[26] Recall that the fact that those with "deformities" cannot enter the temple runs together description and prescription about embodiment. Being nonstandard and being excluded are two sides of the same Janus coin on such a theory. Another clear example of disability's ontonormativity, if you will, is demonstrated when one analyzes differing modern attitudes toward restorative, reconstructive, and even cosmetic surgery as opposed to, say, transabled surgery, surgery as a result of someone needing or desiring to "impair" themselves because they suffer their particular form of able-bodiedness (Reynolds 2016b). People of all ages with a host of "disabilities" are expected both to alter and also to desire to alter themselves "back" to an ideal state, even if, in the case of congenital disability, they have never been in that ideal/normal state. On the whole, surgical procedures considered to enhance an otherwise "normal" body are supported, even if the putative enhancement is primarily for aesthetic reasons and even if it runs counter to biological inevitabilities, such as aging. On the other hand, with respect to people diagnosed with body integrity identity disorder, more recently called body integrity dysphoria and many of whom identify as "transabled," the need to go blind, amputate one's arm, or become paraplegic has historically been seen by the vast majority of health care professionals and society at large as only conceivable as a psychological disorder. If one points out the formal similarity between these cases, the real stakes of these differing attitudes unveil themselves: with the case of disability, one is assumed to not enhance, not enable, not make more productive, and not fill-in-an-accepted-ableist-norm concerning one's life and body (Stevens 2011).

When I argued in chapter 2 that pain functions across its many theories as allostatic regulation, I indicated that one misunderstands pain's function if one thinks it simply directs one toward discrete norms, whether "reconcile yourself with God" or "take solidarity with other humans." On the contrary, models of pain are actively responsive to the agent each model aims to empower. However circuitously, every theory of pain aims to help one understand how one finds oneself, which is to say, aims to give one back to oneself.

When one turns to analyzing theories of disability, on the other hand, a more complicated picture emerges. Personal theories do not aim to give one back to oneself by returning one to a prior state; they assume that one can only become whole through change—change toward being "normal," "able-bodied," "standard." Social theories of disability, on the contrary, aim to give one back to oneself by valorizing disability identity in terms of its legal, cultural, and political power and by splitting social stigma from personal identity. Finally, postsocial theories are not at all geared toward giving one a way to understand how one should go about one's life; on the contrary, they are focused on historical conditions, genealogies of meaning, and the complexity of becoming and being a "subject," hearing that word with the complexity by which a figure like Foucault deploys it. While all theories of pain ultimately try to help one take up one's thrownness into the world, only social theories of disability actually work toward this aim. This crucial difference in theories of disability will become clearer when I turn to analyzing the concept of ability in chapter 5. Part of the issue with these theories of disability is that they are not phenomenological or, at minimum, not phenomenologically sophisticated. And, as I hope to have shown at this point, a phenomenological approach to disability has much to offer because it is better suited to investigating how people actually experience disability, including across the perhaps incommensurable breadth of the lived experiences captured by that term. Thus it is to a phenomenological description of disability that I now turn.

4

A Phenomenology of Multiple Sclerosis

> The telescoping of our lives into simplistic categorizations of good and bad, pain and pleasure, denies that the lives of people with disabilities, like all ordinary lives, are shot through with unexpected grace, overwhelming joy, and love returned. Life is simply a mixed blessing.
>
> —Nancy Eiesland, *The Disabled God*

> Developing a widespread, rich understanding of the phenomenal experience of disability from a social and political viewpoint, rather than a purely medicalized one, would go a long way toward establishing the conditions in which nondisabled bioethicists and health care providers could develop the moral perception and reasoning that would let them enter into constructive dialogue with the disability movement.
>
> —Joe Stramondo, "Why Bioethics Needs a Disability Moral Psychology"

In prison awaiting his execution, Socrates tells his friend Crito that "the most important thing is not life, but the good life [τὸ εὖ ζῆν]" (Plato, *Crito*, 48b). This claim, which has been celebrated in philosophy for millennia, rests on a prior, more problematic assumption: the good life is not possible in certain sorts of bodies. As this project began by noting, Socrates asks just a few moments beforehand in the dialogue, "Is life worth living with a body that is corrupted and in a bad condition?" "In no way," replies his friend Crito (47e). Socrates assumes that certain embodied conditions, those that are "corrupted" and in a "bad condition," can render life less worth living or not worth living at all. Yet, if one submits the idea of "the life worth living" to a more rigorous philosophical investigation by actually examining the lived experience of disabled people, this assumption appears indefensible. It fails to take into account the complex relationship between embodiment and well-being (Kafer 2013; Parens 2015; Kittay 2019).

"After learning of my diagnosis," Havi Carel (2013, 73) writes, "I had to overhaul all my plans, expectations, goals, projects and horizons. Most importantly, I had to rethink my idea of a good life." Although Carel is speaking specifically of lymphangioleiomyomatosis, a rare lung disease, her words ring true for anyone receiving a life-altering diagnosis, that is to say, a diagnosis whose ability transitions result in a fundamental modification of the majority of one's abilities and ability expectations. Carel's lived experience raises problems for Socrates's dictum, for it suggests that the state of one's body, even if the result of something ostensibly "bad" and "corrupting," can fundamentally change one's *idea of* a good life, of goodness, and even of life itself. Carel does not claim that this shift in her ideas occasioned by her body resulted in false or misguided beliefs, whether about the good life or what have you. On the contrary, she claims that this shift changed her epistemic framework as a whole. But how is this possible?

Simone de Beauvoir offers a key to help explain how and why embodiment plays such a powerful role, a key that can only be used after unlearning what we think a body is in the first place. Beauvoir (2011) writes that the body—understood as including, not separate from, the mind—is neither an object, nor a state, nor a condition but a *situation*; it is "our grasp on the world and the outline for our projects" (46). Our body is the *scene* of our life; it is integral to the narrative as well as all the action that plays out at any given moment. Pushing Beauvoir's claim a bit further, I understand "the body" as a synecdoche for a constitutively variable *field of relations and possibilities*—a field that constitutes, among other things, what we call our "abilities" and their corresponding ability expectations. That is to say, the body is a term used to capture *the primary way one finds oneself in the world as a purposive being.*

Let us return to Carel's account. She reports that upon experiencing such a profound shift in ability expectations, she had to overhaul and rethink all her plans, expectations, goals, projects, and even her idea of a good life. By virtue of a shift in the reflective relationship to her embodiment, she was forced to rethink the very structure by which and through which she is as a purposive being, as a being of possibilities always oriented toward future ends. In short, her body as *situation*, as the *scene* of her life, changed, and this transformed her understanding of her life as a whole. In the ableist imaginary, such changes are aberrations from the normal course of a life. If one pays any attention to research on aging (pick your time frame), that claim appears absurd, for the body as situation is not stable—insofar as it appears so, that is merely an illusion.[1]

Recall from the introduction of this book that a central component of the ableist conflation is the assumption that to be disabled is to lack or otherwise be deprived of a natural good. On such an assumption, to be disabled is to experience the loss/lack of possibilities that one would/should otherwise have. The ableist conflation stages the ever-shifting scene of embodiment through the dictates of a prejudiced script in which those who are disabled are simply worse off; the ableist conflation *forecloses upon* the lived experience of a wide range of bodily possibilities by predetermining their value and meaning; and the ableist conflation distorts the actual lived experience of humans as beings whose embodiment is situated in all manner of ways. It is for all these reasons that overturning the ableist conflation requires carefully attending to, not prejudging, the *lived experience* of disability. In other words, inquiry into disability requires the tools of phenomenology.

This chapter continues the task of dismantling the ableist conflation of disability with pain by turning to the lived experience of disability. I provide a phenomenology of disability via S. Kay Toombs's groundbreaking work, which focuses on the lived experience of degenerative multiple sclerosis (MS). My analysis of Toombs's phenomenology suggests that there are at least three general structures of the lived experience of disability: attentional (re)configuration, personal–social (re)configuration, and horizonal (re)configuration. Put simply, disability (re)shapes the salience and meaning of objects of attention at the level of the personal, social, and political. I conclude by discussing how this phenomenology bears on the theories of disability discussed in chapter 3. In short, I argue that social models best track the actual complexity of lived experiences of disability and also provide the most insight into these processes of (re)configuration.

A few caveats are in order. The first regards what it means to call what follows a phenomenology. I say that I am providing *a* phenomenology of disability and not *the* phenomenology of disability because I do not think there can be a phenomenology of disability as such. The extent to which this phenomenology can be generalized to multiple sorts of disabled experiences is left for further research and discussion. When I make claims about "general structures," then, I assume one will hear them in this provisional light. It seems to me that one of the upshots of work on "nonnormate" or disabled phenomenology is that more attention is warranted concerning regional structures relative to certain forms and modes of life and less to structures that rise to the level of human existence across the board (see Reynolds 2017b).

The second regards my choice of MS, which I take to be a particularly generative case through which to (1) understand multiple general structures at play for many sorts of disability experiences and through which to (2) examine the lived experience of disabled embodiment understood as a situation, as a scene. This is because MS involves an often unpredictable ebb and flow of variations of embodiment. Moreover, although many of these variations are explicitly *not* painful, as the ableist conflation would assume, others are. Thus MS refers to a disability the variable experiences of which are diverse enough to make it an unusually good candidate to inquire into general structures of multiple *kinds* of lived experiences of disability.

The third caveat concerns the relationship between a phenomenology of disability and the many theories and models discussed in the previous chapter. This chapter is not to be taken as defending the argument that the *best* model of disability will be phenomenological, which is to say, rooted in lived experience (or, to put a finer point on it, rooted in the insights that arise from research using methods in the phenomenological tradition). I do not make that claim here. I find phenomenology to be an indispensable and underutilized tool to examine the many phenomena of disability, yet I do not think there is any one model, method, or approach perfectly suited to understanding disability. It is simply too complex. On the contrary, it is only through a wholeheartedly pluralistic approach to disability that progress will be made both theoretically and practically.

A Phenomenology of Multiple Sclerosis

S. Kay Toombs was diagnosed with MS in 1973. As she describes her own research, she uses her lived experience to "reflect on issues relating to the experience of illness and disability, the phenomenology of the body, . . . the care of the chronically and terminally ill, the challenges of incurable illness, the meaning of vulnerability, and the relationship between health care professionals and patients" (Toombs 2012, 1). In one of Toombs's chief essays on the phenomenology of multiple sclerosis, "Sufficient unto the Day: A Life with Multiple Sclerosis," she begins with a page-long, small-print definition of the diagnosis of MS taken from a clinical neurology textbook (Toombs 1995b, 3).[2] By beginning this way, the first words of the essay are neither in her own voice nor rooted in her own experience. Instead, a medicalized, third-person perspective announces dryly, "Disseminated or multiple sclerosis is one of the commonest nervous diseases." The first piece of information Toombs and the reader discover about MS in this textbook is a question of statistical prevalence: it is "common." The authority of modern medicine, which is to say, the authority of the life sciences, including population-level statistics, gets the first word, and it says "common." Far from ceding authority to medicine, Toombs begins in this manner to expose that authority's limits, to expose how profoundly it covers over lived experience, including the *authority* of lived experience to determine the meaning of something like MS for an actual, existing, living person.

Toombs's own voice rings out decisively on the next page, "Every multiple sclerosis patient can remember the moment of diagnosis" (4). This moment notably echoes Havi Carel's account described earlier. Indeed, it is a common feature of narrative and phenomenological accounts of life-altering conditions that upon receiving the diagnosis, existential disequilibrium results. Toombs reports that "the future disappeared." She no longer felt "in control" of her life. One effect of receiving her MS diagnosis stood out above all others, though: "there was the overwhelming realization that, from that point on, I would live every day with uncertainty, never knowing (from one day to the next) what the extent of my physical capacities would be" (4).

This is not simply because degenerative MS involves shifting ability states—it is also because the precise *impact* of these shifts and these states is unknown in principle. Will there be curb cuts on the way to an appointment on a day Toombs cannot walk and uses a wheelchair for mobility? Will there be delivery services for healthy food on days she cannot make it out of the house or cook? Will her partner stay with her throughout all the ups and downs? Will what she experiences from day to day be consistent enough to make plans, whether short or long term?

> Over the past twenty-eight years (since the age of 30) my physical capacities have altered in a startling number of ways. At one time or another my illness has affected my ability to see, to feel, to move, to hear, to stand up, to sit up, to walk, to control my bowels and my bladder, and to maintain my balance. Some abilities, such as sensing the position of a limb, I have lost abruptly and then slowly regained. Some, such as clear vision in one or the other eye, I have lost and regained numerous times. Other physical capacities have disappeared and never returned. I can, for example, no longer walk because I am unable to lift my legs. This latter change has, however, been gradual. For a number of years, although the muscles in my legs gradually weakened, I was able to get around "on my own two feet" using first a cane, then crutches, and finally a walker for support. Several years ago I was forced to give up the walker and begin full-time use of a wheelchair for mobility. (Toombs 2001, 247)

This uncertainty did not simply throw her projects or goals into question; it rendered unstable the very conditions of the possibility of purposive action. Reception of a life-altering diagnosis like this—and, thereby, taking up its *meaning*—destabilizes not simply particular possibilities but the very ground of possibility: one's body understood as scene and situation. The body that once provided a foundation for her lived experience, including what "I can" do and what "is possible" more generally, was transformed into a variable "threat," or at least an unknown that could act to thwart, not promote, her projects.[3]

Part of this complexity has to do with the vagaries and euphemisms of language when it comes to carefully describing experiences of disability. As Alison Kafer (2013, 25) notes:

> "chronic" fatigue, "intermittent" symptoms, and "constant" pain are each ways of defining illness and disability in and through

time; they describe disability in terms of duration. "Frequency," "incidence," "occurrence," "relapse," "remission": these, too, are the time frames of symptoms, illness, and disease. "Prognosis" and "diagnosis" project futures of illness, disability and recovery. Or take terms such as "acquired," "congenital," and "developmental," each of which is used to demarcate the time or onset of impairment. "Developmental" does double duty, referring both to lifelong conditions, including those that develop or manifest in childhood and adolescence, but also implying a "delay" in development, a detour from the timelines of normative progress.

In addition to linguistic caprice, misinformation and catastrophizing also play a role. Toombs notes that in the early days of her diagnosis, she entertained many false ideas about what MS would mean for her. Some of these were due to the medical definition of that diagnosis. Indeed, there are a host of complex, dynamic expressions of MS. States of remission with respect to certain symptoms are common, yet they cannot be predicted with certainty, nor can the speed and specific character of the overall progression. Yet, sadly, Toombs's expectation of life with MS was framed in particular by a horrifying video from the MS Society, which effectively conveyed that she would have no choice but to watch her life disastrously fall apart. That is to say, they suggested that her future would not simply alter but disintegrate and compress in categorically and irremediably negative ways.

"The reality of my illness in the early days would have been other than it was if the initial 'message' had been portrayed differently" (Toombs 1995b, 6).[4] Under the guide of providing helpful information, this "informational" video misleadingly exacerbated the scope and type of disruptions MS would bring about:

> It is hard to express what that movie did to me, as it seared its way into my consciousness. I was still trying to understand what the diagnosis might mean for my life. . . . I yearned desperately for something—some evidence, some information about research, some positive example of a person living productively with MS—that would diminish the terror and give me a reason for hope. But, in large measure I lost my capacity for hope that night—not entirely, nor permanently, but for many months to come. . . . The only question that now re-

mained in my mind [after seeing the video] was how rapid my destruction would be. (Toombs 1995b, 5)

It is one thing to have global anxiety or concern due to a medical diagnosis of such gravity. It is another thing to have anxiety over the concrete, particular effects it will have on one's life. That is to say, it is one thing to feel general existential disequilibrium and another to think that one will specifically and inevitably become divorced, financially destitute, unable to partake in the life activities one finds meaningful and enjoyable, and so on—as that video from the MS Society suggested. The medical prognosis and the cultural imaginary about acquiring forms of disability like MS are stark enough, so why would a group designed as a support system for those with MS create an informational video that in fact inflamed its negative aspects?

If those running the MS Society still experienced themselves in terms of before versus after diagnosis; if prior to and throughout their diagnosis they assumed that using a wheelchair meant being wheelchair-*bound*; if the horizon of interpretation of their lived experience was, in short, shot through with ableism, then it is no wonder the video exacerbated rather than palliated. If those hypotheticals hold, then the only cure and only positive outcome is a return to the state before MS and the only relevant prognoses concerning MS are negative and world destroying relative to that before. That is to say, if ableism and the ableist conflation form one's hermeneutic field, disability is invariably a form of demise and deprivation. Under the aegis of the ableist conflation, one is forced to see only the worst, to see only degradation after a diagnosis like MS. Under that aegis, one can only see constitutive negatives, not possible positives. Under that aegis, one's horizon of interpretation is fixed to a point in the past that refuses to admit of possible change.

Both the diagnosis and the video present MS as merely a "compression" of possibilities and as a "gradual progression of disability" understood on a bad-difference view. Yet, neither of these presentations of "what MS is" makes even a rudimentary distinction between disability and impairment as the social theories discussed in chapter 3 would demand. Furthermore, both presentations assume that the referent for Toombs's *experience* of her body through the progression of MS will forever continue to be a well-defined, able-bodied, static "before." Some of Toombs's own analyses indeed operate along the lines of a dichotomy between life before the diagnosis of MS and life after, but this dyadic picture is ultimately misleading. It is not a question simply of "alteration," for MS was also creative. That is to say, Toombs's phenomenology suggests that MS caused Toombs to experience a *different world*. Even the lived experience of supposedly universal dimensions, such as space and time, changed:

> Loss of mobility (be it prolonged or temporary) transforms the character of surrounding space. . . . What was formerly regarded as "near" is now experienced as "far." . . . The answer to the question "is it too far?" no longer bears any relation to objective measurement of distance. It depends, rather on what is between "here" and "there." Are there obstacles that prevent the use of my scooter? Is the terrain suitable for a wheelchair? (It may also depend upon my level of fatigue.) (Toombs 1995b, 12)

The horizon of experience that would allow one to speak of a "before" or "after" itself shifts for Toombs, as do the very conditions under which she experiences any given "ability," including her relationship to space and time. Having now laid out the general contours of Toombs's account, I turn to examining the details of her phenomenology more closely. I argue that her account reveals the general structures of a disability like MS to involve attentional, personal–social, and horizonal reconfiguration.

Attentional Reconfiguration

Toombs's description continually highlights the import and variability of *salience*. That which is noticeable, or has the potential to be noticeable, can be of a qualitatively different kind for one with disability/impairment X than one without. Both that to which one attends and also the way in which one attends to multiple types of phenomena change based on one's embodiment, one's relationship to it, its interaction with a given environment, and others' relation to and regard of it. Not just the scope but the meaning of one's attention concerning bodily movement can be narrowed or widened. For example, one might shift from focusing on the possibilities of a particular part of one's body (e.g., "I can't move my leg") to the incorporation of this new restriction as a fact of the world (e.g., "Is there access for a wheelchair here?"). One now focuses on the possibilities of an entire field of experience. I call this feature of the general structure of the lived experience of MS *attentional reconfiguration*. Attentional reconfiguration can occur when, for example, the salience of an action, desire, or possibility shifts from one's body to the environment, in other words, when that to which one must explicitly attend to do X or Y becomes a question of the body's *relationship to* its environment: "I can't walk" becomes "Can I get there in my wheelchair?" "I want to cross the street" becomes "Are there curb cuts?" or "Is there an audible walk signal?" Wheelchair users, especially prior to legal interventions, were consciously left out of built environments (cf. Hamraie 2017).[5]

With respect to the changed character of physical space, it is important to recognize that those of us who negotiate space in a wheelchair live in a world that is in many respects designed for those who can stand upright. Until recently all of our architecture and every avenue of public access was designed for people with working legs. Hence, people with disabilities (and those who regularly accompany them) necessarily come to view the world through the medium of the limits and possibilities of their own bodies. One is always "sizing up" the environment to see whether it is accommodating for the changed body. For instance, I well remember that my first impression of the Lincoln Memorial was not one of awe at its architectural beauty but rather dismay at the number of steps to be climbed. This bodily perception is, of course, not limited to those with disabilities. . . . What is peculiar about this "seeing through the body" in the event of changed bodily function is that *it renders explicit one's being as a being-in-the-world. A problem with the body is a problem with the body/environment.* (Toombs 2001, 250, my italics; cf. Toombs 1995a, 12–13; Toombs 1995b 13–14)

In other words, when access, instead of impairment or accommodation, is the frame for one's interpretation of corporeal difference and variability, one begins more clearly to perceive the complex contours of both built and "natural" inequality and injustice. Both personal (e.g., impairments that result in nonambulation) and social (e.g., lack of elevators) factors can prove determinate for the purposivity of a life, but the causes, concerns, and complications each brings about are distinct, and distinct in politically decisive ways. We *can* make a world where the use of wheelchairs doesn't substantively limit one's life opportunities. Whether we do so is ultimately a question of political will. Why we currently do not is a reflection of the moral morass of all our social institutions that pretend to take the charge of justice and equity seriously.

If you have taken a Disability Studies 101 course, you'll know that the concept of access is revelatory for many people, not just those who identify as disabled. This is because so many are raised to believe in a naive theory of ability on which abilities inhere in and are discrete qualities or properties of a subject. Yet, even a cursory amount of reflection proves this picture flawed. "I can breathe" is no more descriptive of myself than it is of the environment that affords my breathing. A slight change to the proportions of oxygen and nitrogen in the air demonstrates this swiftly and decisively. A change to my social relations can also demonstrate this swiftly and decisively, as the phrase "I can't breathe" should immediately make clear today.[6] This is not to say that lung capacity is not a relevant factor in the conceptualization of the "ability to breathe"—it is instead to say that the conditions of the possibility of a given ability are never isolated solely in a subject. On the contrary, abilities are thoroughly relational. One must simultaneously look to the supports and structures in which "abilities" simultaneously *are* and *can become* abilities in the first place. And the hermeneutic strategies at one's disposal will in part determine how we explain those abilities, ability transitions, and ability expectations to ourselves and others. When Toombs, upon becoming a wheelchair user, cannot access location X because that location only has steps, a reconfiguration not just of space but of attention, salience, and sense has occurred. What it means to "be able to go to X" shifts from a narrow, ultimately illusory focus on merely oneself to a focus on access, to a focus on the interplay between oneself and one's environment. Attentional reconfiguration is in this sense a reconfiguration of horizon, of the frame or gestalt in which and by which one's world is experienced as meaningful.

To be sure, attentional reconfiguration can be disorienting. Especially with respect to noncongenital disability, Toombs's account suggests that the shift from previous ability expectations to new ones is difficult to work through. Part of this is because, in the case under discussion, attentional reconfiguration occurs in tandem with spatio-temporal transformation. That is to say, crip or nonnormate time and space are distinct from and transform normate time and space. For example, the supposed "objectivity" of space proves instead to be framed by the lived experience of "fit" (see Garland-Thomson 2011). Toombs (2001, 250) writes, "The dimensions of high and low also vary according to the position of one's body and the range of possible movements. From a wheelchair the top three shelves in the grocery store are too high to reach since they have been designed for shoppers who are standing up." The design and purposivity of things serves to inform one of one's place in the world quite literally (cf. Hendren 2020).

Of course, one can experience *I don't belong here* in nonbuilt environments as well. A hurricane strikes; one runs into predatory or territorially defensive organisms, and so on. In those cases, the salience of the *fluidity* of one's abilities will come to the fore quite explicitly. If one is ambulatory but, say, not able to run for whatever reason, that inability will become a primary determinate of one's survival (and one may well wish a fast wheelchair were at one's disposal). If one is allergic to the flora in a given area, and this temporarily makes one "unable" to run or maybe even to walk, that inability will instead become primary. If one is phenotypically "normal," yet the organism hunting one is faster, then that species-level difference in "ability" will become primary. Or perhaps other environmental factors come to the fore: the wind is too strong or the ground too sticky. In each case, personal, environmental, or species-level abilities (among other ultimately heuristic ways to carve up the phenomenon in question) will prove decisive as a result of their dynamic interaction in a given situation.

There is also attentional reconfiguration with respect to time. Toombs (2001, 258) writes:

> The transformation in being-in-the-world that occurs with disability incorporates not only a change in surrounding space and a disruption of corporeal identity, but also a change in temporal experiencing. Just as lived spatiality is characterized by an outward directedness, purposiveness and intention, so time is ordinarily experienced as a gearing towards the future. Normally we act in the present in light of anticipations of what is to come, more or less

specific goals relating to future possibilities. With bodily dysfunction this gearing into the future is disrupted in a number of ways. For instance, temporal experiencing changes in the sense that the sheer physical demands of impaired embodiment ground one in the present moment, requiring a disproportionate attention to the here and now. One is forced to concentrate on the present moment and the present activity rather than focusing on the next moment. Mundane tasks take much longer than they did prior to the change in abilities. For instance, when habitual movements are disrupted, the most ordinary activities such as getting out of bed, rising from a chair, getting in and out of the shower, knotting a tie, undoing a button, demand unusual exertion, intense concentration, and an untoward amount of time. (Think, for example, of the difference between the time and effort required to tie one's shoelaces using one, as opposed to both, hands—especially if one is right handed and only able to use the left hand to perform the task.) In this respect persons with disabilities find themselves "out of synch" with those whose physical capacities have not changed. This temporal disparity is not insignificant in terms of relations with others. "What's taking so long?" others ask impatiently.

Acquiring disability involves acquiring the need for *novel skills*. These might include doing old tasks in new ways, doing new tasks, or figuring out how to meet certain ends without engaging in certain tasks at all. This process means that one cannot initially take for granted how long things will take. At a deeper level, however, Toombs shows that the transformation is not just with respect to certain tasks or purposive action but with respect to one's everyday experience of time and space and one's existential relationship to how one finds oneself, past, present, and future. Toombs's phenomenology demonstrates how there will necessarily be an increased focus on the present, on the here and now, as these skills are being developed. Thinking far out in the future will be more difficult during such processes. As other parts of her writings make clear, this attentional reconfiguration can take another turn wherein, upon acquiring these skills and assuming stability with respect to one's condition, the time of certain tasks and the space of certain, especially daily sojourns become familiar again, and one can more easily look to the future.

Personal–Social Reconfiguration

We have seen already that disabilities like MS cause reconfigurations that defy simplistic comparisons, such as those based on a *before* versus *after* or *good* versus *bad*. Such simplistic comparisons, such binary ways of thinking, function only insofar as one operates with a naive concept of ability. MS also brings about a profound reconfiguration of one's sense of self and of others' regard. A shift occurs in the relative "unity" of the self as the injury, disease, impairment, or condition moves from "out there" ("my legs are not receiving signals concerning movement") to being constitutive of the self in at least some respect ("I am a wheelchair user"). Insofar as one's condition is variable—for example, if one is unsure of how much pain one will be in or if one's ability expectations will hold from day to day—all of one's projects are thrown into doubt. One's identity, especially insofar as it is tied to abilities thrown into question by one's condition, will become uncertain. This is an experience social models of disability are hard-pressed to appreciate fully.

These *personal–social reconfigurations* change the basic contours of one's lived experience as someone who is now regarded and judged by others as different, as nonnormate. "I can't go there" might now mean "That space is not designed for me." For example, one might discover, as Toombs writes, "a world that is in many respects designed for those who can stand upright." Attentional reconfiguration folds back not merely onto the relationship one has to oneself and to the world but also onto the world's relationship and regard *toward* oneself. Someone staring or even gawking at one can shift from an oddity easily brushed off to a regularity that impacts one's sense of self. The gaze of the other (whether doctor, family, stranger, or whoever) co-constitutes the way in which these shifts occur as well as their more specific effects.

Furthermore, whether the people around one figure these changes as a "struggle" or an "enemy" against which one must "fight" or whether they figure them as "opportunities for growth" is not an arbitrary designation (Toombs 1992, 1998). When a (temporarily) able-bodied person encounters a disabled person, their disability imaginary often runs wild, grasping incoherently at culturally culled metaphors and grossly misguided assumptions. Take as an example the following anecdote:

Whenever I am accompanied by an upright person, in my presence strangers invariably address themselves to my companion
and refer to me in the third person. "Can SHE transfer from her
wheelchair to a seat?" "Would SHE like to sit at this table?" "What
would SHE like us to do?" This almost always happens at airports.
The person at the security barrier looks directly at me, then turns
to my husband and says, "Can SHE walk at all?" We now have a
standard reply. My husband says, "No, but SHE can talk!" (When
I am unaccompanied people often act as if my inability to walk
has affected not only my intelligence but also my hearing. When
forced to address me directly they articulate their words in an
abnormally slow and unusually loud fashion—in the manner that
one might use to address a profoundly deaf person who was in the
process of learning to lip read.) (Toombs 1995a, 17; cf. Toombs
1995b, 16–17)

These types of situations, attested by numerous wheelchair users as
well as people with disabilities of other sorts, are problematic and re-
vealing. Ableism allows one to run from "You're disabled" to "You're
not like me" to "You probably can't do anything." This represents a
hyperinflation of the ableist conflation wherein disability is not simply a local harm but a global harm—a harm that affects one's overall
well-being and capacities. In this anecdote, and due solely to the fact
that one utilizes a chair for mobility, one is assumed to be able neither
to speak, nor to think, nor to fill-in-the-ableist-blank. Toombs's account suggests that part of the lived experience of becoming disabled
is to change one's understanding of oneself and others *in the light of
the ableism that structures so much of human life.* When one is forced
to reckon with an oppressive, widespread phenomenon like ableism,
and to do so in a way that now directly bears upon one's sense of self,
belonging, community, and the like, it is inevitable that personal and
social reconfigurations will follow. The sort of person one is and how
one understands oneself and one's place in the world *change.*[7]

Existential Reconfiguration

As I argued in chapter 3, the medical model of disability proves
wildly ill-suited to capture the complexity of experiences of disability. Toombs's analysis not only supports that claim but goes much

further.[8] There is an argument to be made that she largely deconstructs most theories of disability, for there are aspects of her phenomenology that could be used to support claims from each of the theories and respective models discussed, just as there are aspects that could be used to undermine claims from each. This marks a significant strength of a phenomenological approach to disability, for by digging deeply into the complexity of disability—in this case, MS—as it is actually experienced, the complexity of what it would mean to meaningfully define "disability" in general powerfully comes to the fore. Indeed, of all the takeaways on which one could focus in Toombs's work, the most important is the question of existence and transformation. Precisely insofar as one's person, social field, and lived horizon are reconfigured, novel transformations occur not just across various domains of one's life but with respect to one's life and its being *lived* as a whole. This is why I characterize the third general feature of MS borne out by Toombs's phenomenology as *existential reconfiguration*. Disability (re)shapes how one's life is *lived*.

On the whole, Toombs's account shows that while certain aspects of the world recede or compress, certain other aspects are at the same time opened, generated, and enriched. The quality of one's existing relationships may take on a new urgency, depth, or character—and they may also disappear as new ones arise precisely in light of one's ability changes. The understanding of space, both built and social, may be amplified or even transmogrified in light of new interests, new problematics, new activities, and new desires. Values change. Novel transformations emerge. The very texture and fabric of the experience of possibility can be made anew through the variability of the body and the relations it affords. More pedantically, the walking cane or some other assistive device, things which for many are but a helpful object from time to time when needed, might become beings through which and by which one lives. Such objects no longer exist as mere things and are no longer encountered as at hand. They take on new meanings. In short, alteration toward disability does not *entail* hedonic degradation.

Even small changes, like the shift from a heavy to a lightweight wheelchair, can have massive implications:

> Before I purchased a lightweight wheelchair, I was unable to wheel myself around because a standard model was too heavy for me to

operate. Consequently, I had to be pushed. I hated "being in" a wheelchair. It made me feel utterly dependent on others. It was a symbol of limitation. I used it as little as possible (even though that meant sometimes cutting back on social engagements). Then I obtained a lightweight wheelchair I could operate myself. I no longer needed to be pushed. "Using" rather than "being in" a wheelchair is an affirming, rather than a demeaning, experience. This phraseology is not just a matter of semantics. When I manipulate the chair myself, I am in control. I can go where I want to go "under my own steam." Thus, wheeling represents freedom rather than limitation. My wheelchair has become, in effect, my legs—an integral part of my body. (Toombs 2001, 259–60)

The ableist conflation gains traction by ignoring or denying the complexity and variability of disability experience. It can't comprehend the difference between "wheelchair-bound" and "wheelchair-free." It can only see a life constricted relative to dominant ability expectations, to ability norms cast in ableist molds, and to able-bodied priors that are treated as static constants. Using a wheelchair does not mean "not being able to walk." As Toombs makes clear, it in fact means *freedom to move*—assuming, of course, that it is in fact a good fit for the user. On the ableist conflation, there is nothing but constitutive suffering in disability writ large, but such a thought is laughably mistaken, especially in cases of congenital disability not concomitant with constitutive pain.

When an "able-bodied" person expresses pity to someone who, for example, was born without a phenotypical limb and says "You poor thing, it must be so hard without that!" the response is typically something like "Uh, no, I get along just fine" (hopefully followed by "please get away from me"). Whatever sufferings congenital disability can accurately be said to bring about, these are often due to, not degradation, but the structures and strictures of social spatialization and temporalization. An Autistic student might, for example, be disproportionately disciplined and cordoned off from other students. A wheelchair user might not be able to access certain areas because architects or other construction professionals have assumed that wheelchair users need not be considered or that they would rather take the chance of a lawsuit by means of the Americans with Disabilities Act. None of this is necessitated by the impairments in question.

Phenomenological accounts of disability make all of this especially clear. They place yet another nail in the coffin of the ableist conflation. Toombs (2001, 259) summarizes her phenomenology of MS and the insights it delivers as follows:

> In sum, then, phenomenology provides important insights into the lived body disruption that is intrinsic to the experience of loss of mobility. In particular, phenomenology discloses the ways in which this kind of bodily change necessarily alters the experience of surrounding space, disturbs the taken-for-granted awareness of (and interaction with) objects, disrupts corporeal identity, affects relations with others, and changes the experience of time.

The lived experience of noncongenital disability attests to a profoundly complex, multifactorial, and dynamic relationship between one's body and the world. It brings about attentional, personal–social, and existential reconfigurations, the valences of which are highly sensitive to the conduct and context of one's particular life and life projects. Toombs's account suggests that one way we should understand the many meanings of disability is via more fine-grained attention to how people actually *experience* it. On this view, being disabled is in many respects like any other significant facet of human identity: it shapes one's world. Whether one is shaped for good or bad and whether one is shaped a lot or a little depends on a host of factors. Some disabilities, such as pediatrically fatal conditions like juvenile Tay-Sachs, certain dissociative disorders, or those concomitant with severe and/or terminal chronic illness and chronic pain that constitutively undermine the stability, contours, and reach of one's life, can be world destroying. Others, like blindness, deafness, or many types of neurodiversity, can be world creating. Most disabilities, however, are somewhere in between—just like any other socially distinct form of life.

Ability Trouble

Different ways of being-in-the-world are not, by virtue of being different, worse ways of being. As Elizabeth Barnes (2016) has convincingly argued, most empirical evidence supports mere-difference views of disability, not bad-difference views. The cases in which disability turns out to be a bad-difference—and there certainly are such cases—are the exceptions, not the rule, if, that is, one wishes to make claims about "disability" as such. To focus more specifically on Toombs's scholarship, it is clear that impaired end states whose transition is profoundly difficult are not thereby intrinsically negative *by virtue of* the difficulty of their transition. A central implication of Toombs's phenomenology is that to understand the "disabled" body, one must return to the concept of the norm and, more specifically, to the role the concept of the normal body plays for judgment, desire, and action.

Eva Kittay (1999, 150), addressing her relationship with her daughter Sesha, who is physically and intellectually disabled as a result of Pura syndrome, speaks powerfully about this problematic: "that which we believed we valued, what we—I—thought was at the center of humanity, the capacity for thought, for reason, was not it, not it at all." Kittay realized that the capacity for reason, something she assumed was a normal and needed part of life, was not so, for, among other reasons, the caring bond between Kittay and her daughter Sesha was not predicated or constituted by Sesha's *capacities*. It was constituted instead by their *relationship* to one another. Through corporeal variability, through myriad forms of disability experience, and through the intimate intricacy of relations of care, the body reveals itself as situation, the whole of which marks the terrain of that ambiguous phenomenon we call "life." The moral and meaningful features of situations and of scenes are functions of *relation*—and so it is with embodiment. Assumptions about norms and normality, which infuse assumptions about the meaning of ability, more often than not mislead our attunement to the specificity of these relations, especially if shaped by narrow understandings of "disability."

Abilities are constitutively variable in meaning, value, and impact. That we attach enormous weight to some and not to others is often less a function of facts about bodies and more a function of the interaction between norms, values, and ability expectations. Comparing bodies is not like comparing this to that. Bodies are not mere objects, as so many recent thinkers from Husserl to Merleau-Ponty to Butler have demonstrated. If one must compare, it is instead like comparing bounded infinities. One can compare them, but only by bounding two in principle limitless and thus two in principle incomparable phenomena, which is to say, by treating them as if they were discrete wholes and not complex networks of interanimating relations. When the infinities to which we submit this subjunctive quantization are people, we risk the worst kinds of dehumanization (Smith 2011).

The ableist conflation performs precisely such a dehumanizing, normalizing move and, in doing so, reveals itself as the most pernicious kind of conceptual subterfuge. In feigning epistemic obviousness, it provides a refuge for ignorance and prejudice. As Lennard J. Davis (1995, 23) writes:

> we live in a world of norms. Each of us endeavors to be normal or else deliberately tries to avoid that state. We consider what the average person does, thinks, earns, or consumes. We rank our intelligence, our cholesterol level, our weight, height, sex drive, bodily dimensions along some conceptual line from subnormal to above average. We consume a minimum daily balance of vitamins and nutrients based on what an average human should consume. Our children are ranked in school and tested to determine where they fit into a normal curve of learning, of intelligence. Doctors measure and weigh them to see if they are above or below average on the height and weight curves. There is probably no area of contemporary life in which some idea of a norm, mean, or average has not been calculated.

It is here where the existentially transversal position of people with disabilities so clearly reveals the naive distinction between the able body and the disabled body in its absurdity. That one cannot access location X with a wheelchair or that one is treated poorly by educational systems due to being neurodiverse or that one cannot hold down a job due to persistent migraines is not merely a question of physiognomy or neurology or pathology or any number of other -*ologies* but is also and often more so about sociopolitical conditions and reigning ability expectations determinate of current social life and reigning sociopolitical order(s).

Having now examined phenomenological accounts of both pain and disability, one can see the many, importantly distinct differences between them. Even in the case of a noncongenital, degenerative disability like MS, one's experience is not defined by forms of constitutive or consuming pain. MS involves being in pain at times, to be sure, but intermittently so. Although MS brings about significant changes on many existential levels, they are mixed in their valence and depend significantly on context, uptake, and time. That is to say, how one experiences these changes and differences is highly contextualized with respect not only to one's sociocultural and individual context but also to the particularity of the difference in question (moving from walking to wheelchair use; dealing with fatigue; navigating new and differing social relations and forms of recognition, etc.). Chronic pain, on the other hand, does involve constitutive pain that is, on the whole, *negative regardless of such differences.* Thus a main takeaway of the overall analysis undertaken so far is that to speak of disabilities that involve constitutive pain is to speak of categorically distinct forms of disability. Given that most disabilities do not involve constitutive pain, *constitutive pain marks an exception to conceptualizing disability as a whole.* Furthermore, general structures of lived experiences of disability, even if a result of a transition from a comparatively "able-bodied" state, involve reconfigurations whose value and meaningfulness are highly variable and context dependent. In this light, the ableist conflation of disability with pain and suffering is misguided full stop, for it fundamentally mistakes the nature of *both* pain and disability.

I have now demonstrated how the ableist conflation's fundamental assumptions are wrong in their characterization of both pain and disability. Yet, those are not the only core concepts at play in the ableist conflation. At its foundation is an assumption about what "ability" itself is. It is to that topic that I now turn in the fifth and sixth chapters.

PART III

Ability

5

Theories of Ability

In vain we force the living into this or that one of our molds.
All the molds crack. They are too narrow, too rigid, and too
unyielding. Our reasoning, so sure of itself among things
inert, feels ill at ease on this new ground.

—Henri Bergson, *Creative Evolution*

Much of what befalls us remains to be interpreted.

—John Lysaker, "Being Equal to the Moment"

I began this project by asking how the concepts of ability and disability bear upon ethics, thought, and, in a word, life. Across the history of philosophy, conceptions of what we today call "disability" are shaped by the ableist conflation: the assumption that disability is a harmful lack and coincident with pain and suffering. From the triage unit to court bench, from common courtesy to principled thought, this conflation today ultimately functions as a mechanism of power to control, govern, and oppress nonnormate bodies, bodies marked as "disabled" in some way or another. In the first four chapters, I examined the two primary components of the ableist conflation: "pain/suffering" and "disability." On the basis of a coupling of theoretical-genealogical analysis with phenomenological investigation, I claimed that the ableist conflation is untenable. The ableist conflation misunderstands, mischaracterizes, and overgeneralizes the nature, history, and effects of pain and disability, as well as the relationship between them.

While I have offered explanations of various conceptions of pain and disability, digging into aspects of the lived experiences of and theories concerning each, I have not yet directly addressed why these two phenomena would have become so deeply linked in the so-called Western intellectual tradition in the first place. What installed this powerful, deceptively simple, and deeply fraught habit of thought into such a vast range of minds, practices, and traditions?

What is the *origin* of the ableist conflation? I am not referring to its historical origin but to its origin in the sense that term bears when thought as a *principium* or ἀρχή: as a ground or foundation for thought, as that by which an idea gains traction for one's reflection as a whole and the actions and practices that follow in its wake. In this chapter, I argue that the principle of the ableist conflation lies ultimately not in its understanding of pain or disability but in its conception of ability. That is to say, the problem of the ableist conflation is grounded in and originates from the implicit concept of *ability* operative across its various formulations and underwriting its central terms. On the ableist conflation, ability is understood as a function anchored in and wielded by an individual to control relevant outcomes within a possible future. On the ableist conflation, ability is understood as personal control over one's possibilities. Such possibilities become salient and vary in relevance relative to the manner in which they impact matters of concern. I term this the *theory of personal ability*. It is this theory that acts as the bedrock for the ableist conflation.

Unlike the treatments of theories of pain and disability discussed earlier, which ended in a critical, synthetic analysis of the various theories of the phenomenon in question, I take a different approach in this chapter. While the theories I discuss here will still be followed by a phenomenology in the following chapter, I do not provide a critical overview of dominant theories of ability; that task would require at least its own book-length study.[1] I instead analyze only the theory of personal ability, arguing that it is at the root of the ableist conflation. While this theory ties into a wide range of other theories of ability, I do not have space to make that case here. I instead aim to give an outline such that its general shape and impact can be better appreciated relative to the overall thesis of this book. In the following chapter, I turn to a phenomenology of ability that, it will turn out, contributes to the ongoing task—decades in the making by countless disability activists, artists, and scholars—of understanding ability in a genuinely, radically new way: *ability as access* or *ability as care*.

The Theory of Personal Ability

If one looks to the ableist imaginary at least as it operates in the United States today, an idealized body confronts one relentlessly in advertising, fashion, and a host of other vehicles through which consumerism ever engorges itself.[2] This perfectionist imaginary of how a body "should" be doesn't just saturate but also *organizes* society. For example, consider how foundational the binary between the perfect-healthy and defective-unhealthy is in discussions surrounding genetics and genomics. As Lennard J. Davis (2013a, 269) puts the matter:

> somewhere, in some empyrean there exists the platonic human genome. This genome is a book or text made up of letters sequenced in the right order without "mistakes." As such, it is in fact a sacred text. . . . Errors of transcription have ruined the primal perfection for the text. The problem is related to exegesis and amanuensis. Thus, people with genetic diseases have "birth defects" and are "defective."

The epistemological milieu of work in genomics treats the "human genome" as an originary perfection that should be duplicated *exactly,* such that every and all deviation is in at least some respect a "defect" from the sacred, perfect form (for a constructive counterpoint to this idea, see Shalk, 2018, 105ff.). As Davis points out, this desire for a perfect body as expressed in the framework of genomics is quite literally a desire for a perfect text. It resonates with a long history that echoes, to follow Jacques Derrida, an obsession with and result of what he, riffing off Heidegger, calls the metaphysics of presence (Derrida 1982). By the phrase "metaphysics of presence," he refers to systems of thought that operate upon a fundamental binary between presence and absence and that define the real and the true in terms of what is present. To return to the example at hand, the "true," "real," "natural" genome is the one that is perfect, that has no defects. That which is defective is not really, not truly, as it should be—not *really,* not *truly,* not *fully* human.

In this framework, one takes absences to mark that which is not really/fully there and which, thereby, has less meaning or, even, no meaning at all. The person born with two legs is really/truly/fully human in a way the person born without two legs is not. An absence relative to the imagined "perfect" form—a form that has "all" the things present thought to constitute a thing as what it truly is—renders one incomplete. *Ab*-normal. *De*-formed. *De*-ficit. *De*-viant. *Dis*-abled. Humans often, all too often, desire this idealized presence, which is to say, humans desire in ways that run counter to the variability of our actual existence. The idealized body, replete with *all the abilities* one "should" have, operates within this ontonormative metaphysics of presence; it presumes a binary between perfect and defective, between what things really are and should be and what they really are not and shouldn't be. In doing so, it denies the diverse variability of embodied existence by establishing that which is, in fact, not real, that which is an ideal, as *the* model for real, actually existing bodies and minds.

A driving force of ableism, in addition to the assumption of a standard body, is the assumption of the body's *perfectibility*. This can take the form of valuing the "standard" body as if it were itself a perfect body, implicit in the joy underwriting the locution "the baby is healthy!" The perlocutionary effect of such a phrase is to persuade that "everything is as it should be with this being," the painful opposite of which ends in surgeries, lawsuits, and traumas. Or the assumption of the body's perfectibility can take the form that the standard body is the only base from which a perfect body can exist, a view on which, for example, the Paralympic athlete, no matter their prowess and achievements, is, by definition, not a pinnacle of human athleticism. Ableism gains part of its affective and evaluative power through this *psycho-physio-perfectionism,* to which the capital-fueled medical establishment is—historically and still today on the whole—beholden. This bodymind perfectionism actively derides the sides of the proverbial and literal bell curve. Driven by lust after its fictional apex, a vast range of human activity lurches toward this reified and rarefied air in which the very conditions for its own maintenance are, woefully and ironically, wholly unsustainable.

In *The Autonomy Myth,* Martha Fineman (2004) argues that individual autonomy is today still one of the core myths underwriting the cultural-political landscape in the United States—and to be sure, at least some other places on the globe. She lists all the ways in which autonomy is definitive:

Autonomy is the term we use when describing the relationship between the individual and the state. . . . We think of an economically self-sufficient individual as autonomous in relation to society [more broadly] and its institutions. . . . The autonomy of the family . . . is expressed in the idea that it . . . is a "private" institution . . . [and] there is . . . the autonomy of individuals within the family, for which feminists have fought by exposing domestic violence and child abuse. (21)

Individual autonomy is a way of explaining what an individual should be able to do: it is a prescriptive framework for ability expectations that applies in principle to everyone. It is an idea and ideology that eschews dependence and interdependence for the allure of atomic independence. Yet, this is not merely a matter of political or societal imaginaries.

As Eva Kittay (1999, 45) notes in "Love's Labor," "a person who would do dependency work [Kittay's term for "caregiving"] . . . was viewed by Aristotle as the same person whose soul was defective in ways characteristic of a slave or a woman. Only the free male was thought morally capable of controlling the resources in the family economy and only he was granted the possibility of being a fully realized moral agent" (see also Friedman 1987). Certain types of dependent or caring relations were assumed to restrain—or indicate a definitive lack of—the abilities of the politico-philosophical subject. The language of "defect" and "defectiveness" is one of many ways to mark out this putative inability. Yet, to do so is to call "defective" what in many cases are biologically inevitable aspects of the course of a human life. This is not a minor but a fundamental and damning failure of thinking the meaning of being human.

On its own, the capable individual presupposed by the theory of personal ability is one whose abilities are possessions. This theory understands ability in terms of a thick concept of ontonormative perfectionism, reflecting both *posse* and *potis* in the stem of the Latin root for "possession": both "to be able" and "to have power" (*OED*).[3] On this view, abilities just are personal powers; what I can do tells me who I am because it is through the power relations I wield that I make myself known to myself and others. Ability is, in short, a sort of charm.[4]

The Charmed Pendulum of Ability

The person with exceptional abilities often receives praise because such abilities evoke awe. The very same abilities can, alternatively, evoke resentment and jealousy. Or, the perception of inability can elicit pity while—insofar as inability is equated with disability as interpreted through the ableist conflation—such inabilities simultaneously conjure fear. That pity and fear can be expressed in many ways, including hostility and anger. While the Jerry Lewis Muscular Dystrophy Association Labor Day Telethon continues to make significant money by evoking pity for people with visible physical disabilities, hate crimes against people with disabilities have in fact increased after the Americans with Disabilities Act (ADA) in the United States, the Disability Discrimination Act (DDA) in the United Kingdom, and related legislation (Sherry 2010; Longmore 2015). Furthermore, few disability-bias cases have been successfully prosecuted since the ADA.[5] While the self-professed Good Samaritan might give the disabled Vietnam vet a dollar, they might also vote against the expansion of Medicare or Medicaid and resent those "on disability." How is one to understand the asymmetry between these fundamental affective responses to varying types of abilities—praise or resentment due to awe and hostility or pity due to fear?

Taking inspiration from Gayle Rubin's (2012) influential "charmed circle of sexuality," Bethany Stevens (2011) crafted the charmed circle of ability (Figure 5). What Stevens's circle depicts so powerfully is the way in which norms fundamentally determine ability and the reverse. Depending on the strength of a given norm in a given situation and its affective-psychical tie to the person making a judgment concerning the practice in question, the overall existential impact will change accordingly. For example, what counts as "cognitive impairment" varies—and varies wildly—across historical epochs and various norms of intelligence. At various times, the concepts of the "moron," "retard," "idiot," and "feeble-minded" have all been medical terms of art. At other times, attitudes toward learning and cognitive differences were under the domain not of medicine but instead of society or the family or religion. Modes of identification, chosen or applied, codetermine not only how any given norm interacts but the very meaning of each of the terms at issue. For example, the line between "normate vision" and "visual impairment" is profoundly difficult to

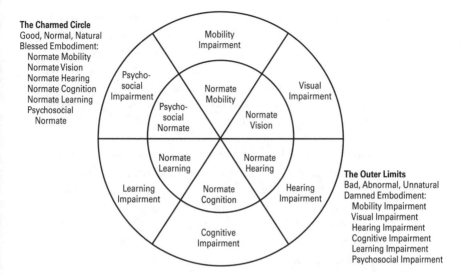

The Charmed Circle
Good, Normal, Natural
Blessed Embodiment:
    Normate Mobility
    Normate Vision
    Normate Hearing
    Normate Cognition
    Normate Learning
    Psychosocial
        Normate

Mobility
Impairment

Psycho-
social
Impairment

Normate
Mobility

Visual
Impairment

Psycho-
social
Normate

Normate
Vision

Normate
Learning

Normate
Hearing

Learning
Impairment

Normate
Cognition

Hearing
Impairment

Cognitive
Impairment

The Outer Limits
Bad, Abnormal, Unnatural
Damned Embodiment:
    Mobility Impairment
    Visual Impairment
    Hearing Impairment
    Cognitive Impairment
    Learning Impairment
    Psychosocial Impairment

Figure 5. The ability hierarchy: the charmed circle versus the outer limits. From Stevens (2011).

distinguish, as the global normalization of the prosthetic devices we refer to as "glasses" makes clear. That we even consider "blindness" to fundamentally demarcate a lack (as opposed to a different relationship to one sensory modality) is itself suspect on multiple fronts (Reynolds 2017b).

Alternatively, being bad at sports (whatever that precisely means) might be experienced as an inability due to the general privilege a given culture allocates to sports. Yet, to push Bethany Stevens's charmed circle of ability further to include Rubin's questions of sex, gender, and sexuality—and to include questions of racialization, ethnicity, and class as well—disability might be experienced as feminine by a male raised under patriarchal ideologies. Being good at sports might be experienced as masculine by a female raised under similar ideologies. Or it may fall along racialized ability expectations— such as, in the context of the United States, the racial stereotype of Black men being exceptionally good at sports, a skill often tied in the American racist imaginary to Black men who are economically impoverished and view it as the best economic way "up." Coming out as bi or gay or transgender or genderqueer might be experienced as, on one hand, taking certain control over one's identity or, on the other hand, an opening oneself up to potential pain, stigma, and danger, and thus a loss of control in a different aspect (or, if one pays attention to trans studies, likely a very complex combination of both). If you are economically well-off and can wield white privilege, such as Hugh Herr or Aimee Mullins, your experience of prosthetic use will be decidedly different from that of someone who has no access to prosthetics or even one who has access only to "standard," nonbespoke versions. These examples are all offered to demonstrate the extent to which how one experiences suffering or joy over one's perceived "abilities" or lack thereof relative to extant social roles will be affected by a wide range of culturally, socially, politically, and historically inflected ideals and norms. In each of these cases, one encounters a complex organism striving to live in a variable environment with a host of normative determinations that bound the parameters of its self-interpretation, self-determination, social recognition, and possibilities for political action. There are at least three central ways that the theory of personal ability makes one feel charmed: health, regard, and control.

Health

Today, when you woke up, what did your mind latch on to? Probably what you needed to accomplish: you focused on your projects for the day, starting with the necessities of modern life—coffee, brushing your teeth, a shower, and so on. But let's say you get a cold. Now you are forced to focus on your body: your nose runs, and you get tissues for it. You feel lethargic, and you lie down to rest. You may still focus on your projects and plans, but they will be altered or suspended in light of the illness. At the opposite end of such experiences, when one is "supremely" healthy—having, say, the remarkable energy of many children or the heart and lung capacity of professional athletes or specialized military personnel—this is often registered as being beyond "normal" health, a state one could justifiably call hyperhealth. Note that relative to a human life of even just twenty years, we all experience varying levels of this pendulum swing. However one defines it, *health is never simply maintained.*

For the purposes at hand, I will refer to "health" as that state in which we both are and also perceive ourselves to be in organismic homeostasis. It involves proprio- and interoceptive regulation, embodied and habituated ease of being-in-the-world, and a host of self relations that are always socially codetermined, as evidence for "health within illness" demonstrates so clearly (Lindsey 1996).[6] Although health is a multifactorial phenomenon, in a culture operating with the largely unquestioned assumption of "health" as a central goal of living well or, in a word, a culture saturated by healthism (Crawford 1980; Rose 1999; Roberts and Leonard 2016), it is an uphill battle to attend to the multifactorial nature of health, much less analyze and critique it. If an illness comes with persistent pain—say, a migraine headache or severe aches—one is forced to focus even more on one's body. Perhaps one can no longer open one's eyes in light or get out of bed. At that point, one likely isn't paying attention to one's projects any longer; they move all the way from attentional foreground to background to virtual disappearance.

But what should one conclude from the fact that one's projects are capable of receding to the point of evaporation—capable even if they are primary life projects around which one has shaped and oriented one's entire life? What type of being is the human in order for such a thing to be possible? Perhaps what we call health is a reverie of the theory of personal ability (Reynolds, 2022). Health is not a constant. Health is a negotiation. "Health" refers to a contesting set of values, an umbrella-idea to which we subject ourselves and take ourselves up as projects and yet about which we have no, or there are no, clear parameters.

It is helpful here to look at how we talk about such cases. We constantly speak in terms of the "I can" and "I cannot," in terms of ordinary language, first-person, active-verb equivalents of the (everyday, naive) concepts of ability and disability. "I cannot get out of bed; I am not able to." "I have given up on being a pilot; I can't do the job." "I can't do this anymore; this isn't for me." The "I can" and "I cannot" often form the primary language concerning such transitions or attitudes toward various possibilities, of such movements (heard in both a literal and also an existential sense) with respect to one's relationship to one's body as a touchstone of existence, as that through and by which we experience things as possible or not.

This language reveals an implicit understanding of health as tracking ability in the sense of the theory of personal ability, for note that in all of the concrete cases I've mentioned, we register our health in terms of "feeling good" or "feeling bad" along the lines of not simply pleasure and pain but the "I can" and the "I cannot." These are taken as two opposing poles of what could be called a neutral affective state. "Nonhealth" is not just about pathology and diagnosis, as we might think when we use those terms in medical contexts. On the personal theory of ability, nonhealth (or illness, if one prefers, for the purposes at hand) is not merely "not being healthy"—it is also about being in a negative affective state, which we often phrase and interpret as "being in pain." Note that the two poles are asymmetrical. "Neutral affect" is figured not as "not having pleasure" but as "not in pain." The negative component is more determinate than the positive for the conception of the central, neutral, anchoring term. This indicates that the meaning and possibilities of phenomena linked to the negative term will be taken to be more foreclosed than those linked to the positive. This is another reason why, as I've been arguing, the conflation of disability with "pain," "suffering," "illness," and even "death" is a normative guillotine. It doesn't simply shut down reflection; it actively evokes affective and intuitive responses rooted in fear and repulsion. The meaning of health and nonhealth delivers, on the theory of personal ability, a well-defined interpretation of the experience of abilities and the promise of ability expectations.

Regard

Teresa Brennan (2004, 119) writes, "When I judge the other, I simultaneously direct toward her that stream of negative affect that cuts off my feeling of kinship from her as a fellow living, suffering, joyful creature" (see also Guilmette 2016). If the logic of the ableist conflation is at work and someone falls ill or if someone is perceived to be disabled, one might pity them. One may, on the other hand, respond to them with hostility. The bullying of children with disabilities or other hate crimes against disabled people is one example of this (Sherry 2010). Attitudes that blame illness on wrongs done by one or one's family—including on moral models, sins—are a modification of such hostility or pity (specifically of a righteous sort).

On the contrary, one might praise and take inspiration from those with disabilities, if, that is, one falls prey to tropes of resilience and overcoming. I will use the term *regard* to refer to the many appraisals, judgments, and feelings of others that inform responses to the ability/disability state of another, including oneself. In each case, whether praise, pity, or enmity, one first exteriorizes the other: one perceives them to be in a state that one is not and, even if for that reason alone, as other than oneself. One takes distance. For example, what do "we" typically do when we are fearful? We seek to mitigate the control wielded over us by the fearful object or objects by increasing the distance between us. Running away is one option. Attack, the aim of which is subjugation—making distant by bringing under—is another. Fear, understood as a lack of control, effects a desire to counter the perceived power of the fearful object. Pity, however, can also act to reassert control over a fearful object. One way of doing so is by diminishing the import of the object. Pity lets people forget. Give an unhoused person a few bucks and go on with your day. Our judgments toward those who are thought to be experiencing conspicuous pleasure and pain are also dual. Those who are perceived to have extreme amounts of pleasure and power (think of the Great Gatsby, the Wolf of Wall Street, or Donald J. Trump) can end up praised, even revered. If one, however, interprets that pleasure through one's own comparative lack of pleasure, that awe can be instead transformed into resentment and envy. If moral considerations enter in, then these cases will likely be interpreted through frameworks of justice and injustice, and one's regard will be correspondingly altered.

With responses to those in pain, a similar pattern emerges. On one hand, one might pity a person in great pain. On the other hand, one might respond with hostility, whether that is expressed though ignoring their pain, delegitimizing it, or taking their pain as an affront to oneself. Appreciating the impact of the ableist conflation helps one understand the affective link between disability telethons and disability hate crimes. The range of regard running from praise to pity, esteem to enmity, is bounded by its relation to one's sense of control, one's adherence to the theory of personal ability, and how one conceives each in relation to one's larger sociopolitical context. Simply think about certain responses to the #BlackLivesMatter (BLM) movement. The #AllLivesMatter response is predicated upon understanding BLM as an incursion on the worth of non-Black lives; it interprets BLM as hostile and, with zero evidence actually suggesting so, places an "only" or "just" prior to its defining slogan. To interpret it as hostile, however, one must at minimum hold the pain and injustices to which BLM is a response as either insignificant, illegitimate, or irrelevant. There is no more effective moral intuition pump than pain, for expressions of pain demand a response, as chapter 1 in particular demonstrated. By discounting another's pain as illegitimate, as irrelevant due to its cause or due to the particularity of the object toward which it is oriented, one wields control to discount that pain and refuse a response.

Control

The two terms discussed so far—*health* and *regard*—are centrally determined by one's reflexive relation to oneself, for one's sense of self is altered when one perceives oneself to be outside of existential equilibrium. Yet, more precisely, in what ways does this shift in equilibrium occur? The always project-relative conspicuousness of abilities is often the primary frame through which the body is rendered conspicuous and thereby an object of judgment. If I have some trouble focusing, I may get a bit less work done than others. If I have significant trouble focusing, it may make me unable to do certain types of work entirely. It may also lead to diagnoses like attention-deficit hyperactivity disorder. But, more fundamentally, how do we imagine "being able to do something"? We imagine the things we want to do or come to have as under our control. Control is the key, the legend, to the meaning of ability on the personal theory.

When our abilities match up with our ability expectations and our experiential world, we sense ourselves at ease. We experience a satisfying accord with the world. "Control" is a shorthand way of naming this. When one takes into account sociocultural factors—for example, varying levels of emphasis on individuality and communality—the background against which control is understood will be rendered quite differently. For example, one may understand one's self-relation to control as relying in part or in whole on the grace of divinity or the help of others, including past generations, or, in the other direction, as due solely to one's own efforts: Horatio Alger–style bootstrapping and so on.

Though I have now discussed health, regard, and control, I have yet to sufficiently explain how they operate together—how they mutually shape and play off each other as fundamental comportments in which one finds oneself in the world under the sway of the theory of personal ability. The vectors of health, regard, and control inform such experience. Anti-aging products, the continually resurrected "nutritional supplement" industry, the many technologies or practices that putatively increase one's "abilities," whether in the form of psychotropics, genetic manipulation, or what have you, all of these demonstrate the way in which ability functions in relation to an active negotiation and mitigation of (perceived) pain, illness, lack of control, and "inability."

Existentialist philosophers like Heidegger, Beauvoir, Sartre, and Camus—as well as care ethicists like Gilligan, Noddings, Tronto, Kittay, and Held—would construe these relations as, ultimately, functions of our relationship to our fundamental (inter)dependency, a relationship that ever leads directly, of course, to death. Yet, reducing the various anxieties under discussion to the fear of death actually misses the forest for the trees. It is instead a question of the extent to which we perceive ourselves to be able to attend to the things about which we care. That is to say, the value of abilities is not ultimately a function of our relationship to death; it is a function of our relationship to the range and content of our concrete, lived, and often idiosyncratic concerns. Following Heidegger's (2010) assertion that the fundamental basis of Dasein, of human being-in-the-world, is care *(Sorge)*, the lived experience of homeostasis trumpeted by the personal theory of ability equilibrates according to relative control over one's concerns. In this light, the theory of ability as personal control, shaped in terms of health, regard, and control as discussed, is an attempt, a struggle, to believe that the world will always play to one's tune. To conceive of ability under the aegis of personal control is to conceive of a world under one's own control. This is a curiously prevalent and dangerously dominant way of thinking about the meaning of ability, of the "I can," and of any given human's relationship to the world.

The "I can" is invariably tied to the body. The way the theory of personal ability treats the relationship between one's body and one's experience as a whole, specifically through the features of health, regard, and control, is not the final say on the matter. On one hand, embodiment shapes the horizon of experience—it centrally and fundamentally determines what can and cannot be experienced, appear, and be disclosed to and for one as one finds oneself in the world. As Bryce Huebner (2016) incisively notes, "even if we begin from shared assumptions, embodied trajectories through socially structured space will impact what we think and what we see as a possibility." On the other, less ontological hand, the body has its own ways of being and ways of knowing that often do not (and perhaps in some cases cannot) rise to the level of conscious awareness, whether first or second order. It is in virtue of these quasi-proprietary beings, knowings, and doings of the body that one's embodiment can in and of itself sediment judgments, whether through its very comportment or its complex matrixes of response. It can do so often despite conscious efforts, as phenomena like implicit bias evidence well.

To the extent that bodyminds are both sites and agents of doings, beings, and knowings, the articulation of the abilities of an embodied being is simultaneously ontological and normative. Abilities are determined by possibilities ranging from the necessary (the ability to breathe oxygen) to the contingent (the ability to touch one's nose with one's tongue)[7] and from the forbidden (the ability for sexual stimulation in interaction with an especially vast range of objects) to the allowed (the ability to limit one's sexual activities with respect to the proper objects and in the proper ways). Abilities are determined by a range of ontonormative conditions variable with regard to mode (necessity/possibility) and value (positive/neutral/negative). Put more pointedly, abilities articulate how, why, and, in certain cases, whether a being *is* at all.

Given its import, one's conception of ability informs how one understands everything from "perception," "consciousness," "gender," "sex," "race," and "dis/ability" to even "being" itself. For example, if one thinks that the sexual category "male" is the only sexual category coextensive with the "ability" to "reason," as Aristotle did, one will think that women do not have that ability—and such an idea further assumes a binary split between both sex and also gender and corresponding "abilities," neither binary of which is in fact defensible. If I, like Peter Singer, think there is an ability category called "cognitive ability" that is necessary for moral worth, I will think that certain humans—which is to say, those born of other humans—have no moral worth. Such thinking removes those humans from existence in the moral universe entirely, and this is a prime example of my claim that in certain cases, abilities articulate whether a being is at all (Kittay and Carlson 2010).

There are numerous other cases where abilities are determinate in this way: if I define as existent only that which is reproducible under modern scientific constraints of experimentation, all manner of beings (and modes of being) are rendered nonexistent. It is, for scientific thinking, the ability to appear under such constraints that determines whether something is. Does this not mean that one's understanding of ability determines one's understanding of being? And the reverse? How is one to think this linkage?

To be sure, the preceding examples suggest at minimum that concepts of ability are mutually reciprocal in determining how one understands a wide range of categories by which we regularly judge humans: whether in terms of sex, gender, species, or other such concepts that demarcate central ways of being-in-the-world. But, more broadly, does this not mean that thinking ability is always an ontological undertaking? It is through "ability" or a cognate concept that any given phenomenon is bounded. Try to explain what something "is" without in any way referring to what it "can do." The possibilities and expectations that assumptions concerning "ability" pick out fundamentally determine the type, the specificity, and, in some cases, the singularity of a given being.

Thinking Ability

Return to a central conundrum of theory of personal ability—namely, that an ability can be a superpower in one context and a stigmatized form of embodiment in another context. This is hard to understand relative to the charmed pendulum and the features of health, regard, and control. If analyzed outside of that theory, however, it makes sense: *abilities articulate avenues of access.* For example, even if I am born with an entirely phenotypical corporeal structure—a structure that is considered "typical" or "normal" under the Linnaean classification of *Homo sapiens*—the oppressions I suffer may or may not have anything to do with the determinate structures of that category. They may have to do with acute occurrences (allergic flare-ups); they may have to do with the way I dress (fashion); they may have to do with the money I or my family or other connections leverage (class); they may have to do with the meaning of the perceived color of my skin (racialization); they may have to do with where I am from or where I am trying to go (ethnicity, nationality, indigeneity); or they may have to do with the makeup of my genitalia and my and my society's relationship to them and to those to whom I am attracted (sex, gender, sexuality). But the meaning of each of these phenomena is normatively inflected and ever relative to context, situation, and, in a word, history.[8]

This is why one and the same "ability" can be understood as offering one more access to the world (a positive-difference "superpower") or as taking it away (a bad-difference disability) or as neutral (a mere-difference disability). Insofar as "abilities" do not inhere in an individual but are relations of organism–environment interaction, to speak of an ability is to speak about access to meaning-making activities and the meaning-making contexts in which those activities are carried out—and are also desired to be carried out or not. To better understand what I mean by conceiving of ability in terms of access, I turn now to explore three examples of ability, aiming to do so in a way that does not treat them as charmed but instead treats them in terms of accessibility.

If all the oxygen on Earth were to disappear, every human and numerous other organisms would die. The ability to do anything for any given human would suddenly shift to an *inability* due to the lack of a structural support that is otherwise assumed to be constant. This, too, would mark a "change in one's abilities"—the change being that one's ability to primarily breathe oxygen would abruptly and fatally become an inability to continue living. Because there exists a seemingly intractable tendency to think of ability as located in an individual, the way in which environments fundamentally determine changes in "one's ability" is obfuscated, even though there are good reasons to think that they carry just as much power to alter one's so-called personal "abilities."[9]

Still, one could imagine the following response: "there were no changes in one's personal abilities when the oxygen went out of the room: the only thing that changed were conditions." If one assumes that the ability to breathe oxygen stops at an individual's respiratory system, one will think that the "ability to breath" is solely a question of an individual. Analogous to the error made in medico-individual models of disability, such an understanding of ability misses the forest for the trees (actually, it misses the forest for just one or two trees). To shed greater light on this mistake and to better appreciate what it means to make claims about "ability," consider the following heuristic distinction between individual, social, and human abilities.

Individual abilities are abilities that we take to reside in particular people. They are qualities, characteristics, or features, including dispositions. Person Y is better than person X at math. We might then say that person Y's personal ability to do math is greater than person X's. That ability is understood to be something like a predicate of the subject here named "person Y." We understand an ability such as this to be supported, above all else, by person Y's "intellectual ability." If so, salient environmental or technological factors—anything taken to be an "enhancing" or "conditional" support like early and exceptional education or the use of calculators—will be interpreted to modify, but not annul, such an understanding of ability.

Social abilities are abilities that we take to reside primarily in societal or political configurations. Many social abilities are necessary for modern life but not sufficient. This category of "ability" includes all those actions the performance of which cannot be explained except in explicit terms of interaction with a shared material environment. While whether I can walk is a question of individual ability, whether I can get on a train is a question of social ability. Person X's, Y's, and Z's ability to transport themselves in expected amounts of time in modern societies is made possible above all else thanks to taxation, the labor of those who build and maintain roads, a host of economic considerations related to the production of vehicles and other forms of transportation, road controls (stop signs, lights, guide paint), and other such things. Or, to take a different example, person X's, Y's, or Z's ability to interact in the vast majority of modern social exchanges is supported, above all else, in the continued creation, maintenance, and leverage of fiscal mediums (money) and various types of fiscal policy, ranging from inflation control and interest regulation to markets of numerous types across the world.

Human abilities are abilities without which no human could survive. In this sense, they can be considered necessary. One can continue living even if a machine breathes instead of one's lungs, but no human organism can survive without any oxygen whatsoever, at least given current technology and the evolutionary state of the human species at this point in time. The ability to physically incorporate oxygen is, in this sense, absolute. The same goes for the ability to drink water, to eat a minimally nutritious diet, to have location-specific shelter, and to have dependency workers provide for one in infancy, in times of certain forms of illness, and in many conditions pertaining to aging.

Consider, then, how these distinctions apply to the example of breathing. While breathing oxygen is indeed a human ability, both the individual and social ability to do so is highly mediated. If a construction worker is exposed to asbestos thanks to the negligence of management to run proper tests and that exposure, unbeknownst to the worker, leads to lung cancer, now the construction worker will have an "individual inability" to breathe well. Unlike the chess player, for whom we treat their skills, regardless of educational supports, as individual abilities, with the case of asbestos, we typically tell a history that excises personal responsibility for that individual and human (in)ability—we instead locate its "cause" at the level of the social.

But what about cases that involve widespread pollution? A government fails to pass clean air legislation and allows corporations or other actors to pollute with immunity, whether due to failures or absences of communication on the part of constituents, failures of whatever sort by their representatives, or, most likely, the power of money over representatives from actors who wish to so pollute. There is now a social inability to breathe well in a given area. Where do we situate the ability to breathe in such a scenario? We resist conceiving it as a question of individual ability or human ability. It is, it seems, a social inability and one for which we can chart a more or less direct cause. It is telling that we constantly grapple with the role of history when we undertake assigning values to the range of abilities salient for a given phenomenon.

Yet, as personal theories of disability discussed in chapter 3 demonstrate painfully well, when someone is born with or, in many cases, acquires a disability that causes them to, for example, breathe in nonphenotypical ways, our default is to think of that in terms of individual ability, not social ability. If someone is born with cystic fibrosis, we typically explain their ability to breathe as a question of individual ability. This will often be the case *even if* that person lives in an area with high levels of air pollution and even if their relationship to breathing is diminished because they cannot access the best clinical options for such a condition. My point here is as follows: concepts of ability, and narratives concerning them, result in large part from assumptions regarding cause, the relevant scope of determinate conditions, and assumptions regarding the relationship between cause and meaningfulness at the level of both lived experience and also the sociopolitical. It is thus not surprising that conservative arguments against welfare focus on acquired disabilities in the framework of personal negligence (at whatever stage of the life course, including blaming mothers) and then employ those examples to make sweeping arguments against welfare (or, for that matter, basic support for the conditions of existence) as a whole.

To see how this logic is expanded, take the example of a person who wishes to vote against a raise in taxes to pay for curb cuts—what is the ordinary justification? "Why should I have to pay for something I don't need?" "Why should I have to pay for something that not everyone needs?" The central implicit assumption in such a thought is that those who are not sufficiently like one at the level of "individual ability" do not require one's concern and, by extension, one's money or that culled from society at large. Although clearly underdefined, conceiving of ability as individual ability offers an easy and putatively commonsense way out: "Most people are ambulatory: I don't want to spend my money helping that small percentage of people who aren't." However, upon a little bit of reflection, it should be obvious that curb cuts help people of all sorts and in all sorts of situations. They will help nearly everyone avoid injury or death of themselves or others at multiple points over the course of a life: a distracted person with a baby stroller; a blind person who uses a cane; or nearly anyone glued to their phone. To summarize from earlier, the meaning of *ability* is ultimately a relational performance involving an individual and their socio-historico-environmental situation. At any given moment, this concert, hearing that term in its etymological sense, assumes massive levels of production and support.

What, precisely, can one do without a supporting environment? The bootstrappers—whatever their affiliation, libertarian, neoliberal, or what have you—have no answer to this question.

For example, when one says "she is good at chess," one may, depending on the circumstance, mean nothing more than that she can follow and anticipate serially predetermined, complex algorithms well. That one's abilities with respect to chess are only contingently trivial, however, is offset when one becomes a grandmaster or world champion—when the ability becomes exceptional not in relation to some but in relation to all others. For example, if you are Robert James "Bobby" Fischer, now your abilities might lead certain countries to go out of their way to help (or hurt) you. In the case of chess, a seemingly trivial ability expectation to which one would not think to tie substantial value becomes one to which immense value is tied, namely, once it becomes superlative in a given context. The point here is not to say that we shouldn't praise certain people; the point is to demonstrate the constitutive variability and context dependence of the value of those abilities.

One might counter with the following question: surely there are neutral or meaningless ability expectations, for example, the ability to count backward from a high number quickly and accurately? But what ability is that? The content of the ability in this example is misleading because its form is just one possibility brought about by the ability to manipulate the decimal notation of the Hindu–Arabic numeral system. That, to my knowledge, there are not situations in which that content (counting backward) is held as socially meaningful in no way disproves my point.[10] But to then claim that such content does not have value is not to say that the form of that ability is necessarily value neutral. There are any number of possible worlds (including this one) in which the ability to count backward might be highly valuable in certain contexts.

The claim I wish to highlight here is that an ability must count as an ability, must be deemed as such by one's societal context, to be an ability. In short, the normative component functions to judge which biological and ontological determinations prove relevant. If it doesn't count, that ability is what I'll call trifling. The more provocative conclusion to draw is that any iterable function of organism–environment interaction could either count as an "ability" or "disability" or instead be trifling. I am here using the term *function* in an extension of its mathematical sense: denoting a relation between an input or set of inputs that produces and is thereby directly related to an output or set of outputs given the calculative framework at play. Put more flexibly, the concept of ability extends to range over any iterable outcome produced by a determinate set of relations: abilities are repeatable mediations of interrelation.

Accordingly, the breadth of the range of such mediations is astounding. Moving one's forearm in the four cardinal directions; blinking a single eye in response to discrete patterns; photosynthesizing light; withstanding tons of pressure; speaking in quasi-patterns that are not recognizable as known languages—the examples could be multiplied ad infinitum. Which "abilities" did I just name? The ability (in part) to conduct an orchestra; the ability (for some) to communicate while experiencing locked-in syndrome; the ability to maintain sustenance for some plants; the ability to exist as a deep-sea organism or as anything worth naming in some celestial environments; the ability to "speak in tongues." Placed out of context, these "abilities" might seem valuable, trifling, or strange. But each names functions of organism–environment interactions that are or could be essential—and not only with respect to that organism's ability to survive or its identity but for what, how, why, and whether it is in the first place at all.

Let me return one last time to the example of Bobby Fischer by way of contrast. The form of the ability expectation in question ("to follow and anticipate serially predetermined, complex algorithms well") stops being irrelevant and inconspicuous when it takes on a very specific content ("the ability to play chess better than any human"). The value of this ability expectation is transformed due to the qualitative intensity of its specific content in a given sociocultural context. That Bobby Fischer is held to be better than any human at chess becomes a reason to single him out as an exemplary object of praise or blame. That chess is held by many as an esteemed and elite game across the "globe" is another reason. But such facts, to repeat what is, I hope, obvious at this point, are due to the contingency of the social values placed on playing chess at a particular historical point across a certain swath of the global human population relative to extant geopolitical power games.

By defining the ability to play chess as "the ability to follow and anticipate serially predetermined, complex algorithms well," do I not leave out a host of other factors? Does it not require an ability to physically manipulate objects, namely, the pieces on the table and the game clock or some device utilized to manipulate the latter objects? Does it not require an ability to assess the moves of the other player—typically, though not necessarily, through sight—and also to anticipate their moves though some theory of mind? The "ability to play chess" thus presupposes a host of bodily conditions, including those that afford focus, higher-order cognitive tasks, theory of mind, core corporeal manipulation of objects or commands to do so, and so on. Any given socially meaningful ability, whether at the level of form or content, will involve a complex of such "discrete" abilities.

The larger point here is that bionormative assumptions form determinate moments in the mediated process by which we identify and grant varying levels of value and meaning to a life based upon its perceived abilities in a given historical epoch.[11] For example, all human abilities require the presence of oxygen, which in turn requires the presence of an organ or organs by which to breathe, which in turn requires the presence of a planet with a biosphere highly similar to that of Earth, which in turn requires the presence of carbon, which in turn requires the conditions bringing about and maintaining the known universe, and so on.

Abilities are irrelevant as value-granting mechanisms not only when they are trifling but also when they are sufficiently strange. For example, the ability to be a contortionist, to manipulate one's body in ways that do not conform to phenotypical joint and ligament formation (whether due to hypermobility or dedicated training) is a unique form of ability that precipitates unique ability expectations. Relative to the politics of the Cold War, however, the person named the "best contortionist" in the world was afforded far less social value compared to the one named the eleventh world chess champion. The reasons for this difference are contingent.

There are certainly situations in which the set of abilities of the best contortionist would afford value, but the putative cultural "strangeness" of contortionism (historically tied, one should note, to the exhibitionism of freak shows and other such historical analogues) renders it of less value than playing chess, at least in the historical context discussed here (Garland-Thomson 1997). The very concept of the "strange" is fundamentally value-laden, and this supports my claim about the normativity of ability. To call an ability strange or trifling is to say that it does not enter into meaningful social relations as determined by extant values in a given context. The examples discussed herein suggest that where an ability form has substantive value, it is typically because that form is both assumed to apply to the "standard body" and corresponds to an activity or form of life held to have social value in a given context. The importance of the content and its valuation will thus vary accordingly with respect to that of its form. It will also vary with respect to the futures an ability is thought to afford, hence my insistent focus on ability expectations.

Returning to the example of breathing: in the vast majority of instances, the ability to breathe oxygen affords nothing meaningful in terms of social standing. It is often only when one requires assistance to breathe that we begin to give significant meaning to that ability. That meaning is sometimes considered so momentous that a life lived without technological assistance to breathe is often preemptively judged to be not worth living. The equilibrium of the charmed pendulum of ability is that in which living is experienced lithely, a life for which the consistency of control over one's concerns is at minimum stable. Today, in the United States at least, the most ably charmed is typically a white, heterosexual, cis, monogamous, able-bodied, employed, upper-middle-class, university-educated, low-debt, monotheistically religious, developed-nation-born, capitalism-supporting man. That this charmed figure is ultimately in control is, of course, an illusion, for that charming requires enormous supports and wields its power in many respects through structures of privilege.

Abilities are constitutively variable with respect to their form, content, and value. The meaning of any determinate ability must be thought through the relevant and complex relations, histories, and contingencies into and out of which it enters. Abilities are not reducible to the conditions of support requisite for a given ability; to understand any given ability at the level of its lived experience as well as larger social significance is supervenient on a host of conditions. But any given world and any given context will render a vast range of abilities—like touching one's tongue to one's nose or counting backward—mere triflings. On the other end of that spectrum, some abilities will be necessary to prohibit one's death, or its moral sanctioning. Or to reliably afford one's very entry into the world.

I have argued that the theory of personal ability turns out to be a question of the range and specificity of one's concernful dealings. It is these dealings that ultimately determine which abilities "count" as value conferring, neutral, or value detracting. If one can appreciate the complexity of ability and appreciate how misguided the theory of personal ability is, the question immediately arises, what would a more defensible and decidedly non-ableist account of ability look like? It is in the hope of responding to this question that the next chapter offers a phenomenology of ability.

6

A Phenomenology of Ability

> Not only the architecture, but the entire physical and social organization of life, assumes that we are either strong and healthy and able to do what the average able-bodied person can do, or that we are completely disabled, unable to participate in life.
>
> —Susan Wendell, "Unhealthy Disabled"

> All human beings need care, assistance, and a sustaining environment to live; disability disadvantage results from living in an unaccommodating environment; quality of life cannot be predicted in advance; disability can produce life advantages; what counts as disability changes over time and space; and the border between disabled and nondisabled shifts over a lifetime.
>
> —Rosemarie Garland-Thomson, "Human Biodiversity Conservation"

My aim in this chapter is to explore the general structures of ability understood in terms of accessibility, and I do so through a description of my family's communal practices of caring. It will turn out that *caring systems* are determinate for whether a given individual is ultimately "made able" (or not) in various respects. Thus what follows will, in the end, expand beyond phenomenological accounts of ability, care, and even caregiving to a phenomenology of caring systems.[1] I begin by laying out a *day in the life* of the lived experience of my family unit in caring for my brother Jason and for each other in our particular place and social context: Eugene, Oregon, in the 1990s and 2000s.[2]

"What aboutYou?"

8:30 a.m.

I wake up, and I am tired. A mandatory class awaits me in a little over an hour, the necessity of which flaunts the fact that I have delayed sleep phase disorder and share a thin, Sheetrock wall with my brother Jason, my best friend. Because of his particular mind and body, he requires twenty-four-hour care. A few years ago, after trying for years and years to get the state to help with his care, my family found a social worker who would not take no for an answer. She fought tooth and nail through labyrinthine bureaucratic red tape and succeeded. At first, Jason's dependency workers were day shift only. Only after 2010 did it become twenty-four hours. In our small house—part medical facility, part storage unit, and part "perpetual-home-repair" experiment—there was no place to put the donated, secondhand hospital bed except next to my room. For the majority of Jason's life, my family lived in that modest house on 34th Street. No, not the one of *Miracle on 34th Street* fame. Though that didn't stop my family and others from thinking of Jason's presence in our life—and any number of fortuitous events that happened under that roof—as miracles.

Given the particulars of my religious upbringing, miracles weren't terribly uncommon. But whichever indeed happened, happened in the thicket of an enormous amount of labor, luck, and long suffering. A good portion of that labor involved modifying our surroundings and practices—and creating new ones—to make things work. Built in the 1940s by my paternal grandfather, nearly everything was inaccessible, much less meeting Americans with Disabilities Act (ADA) standards. The doorways were narrow, stairs led to both entrances, electrical outlets were frustratingly sparse and finicky, and hot water was always in short supply. Mold, mildew, and dust allergies from below-code construction led to severe allergies for my mother and me. It was quite literally not made with a family like mine in mind.

Because of a pneumonia scare, Jason's health was thrown into question, and we got care that night, giving my mom a rare chance to sleep through the night—or at least to attempt to. I walk out of my room and say hi to Dolores. She is the dependency worker who had been with my family the longest and had in many senses become family—we trusted her to take care of Jason (or anyone else, had the situation arisen) just as we would and considered it obvious to invite her to all family events. Jason lit up whenever she entered the room. I would then say good morning to Jason. Unless he was receiving a lung treatment, I'd give him a kiss (or a few), hold his hand, hug him, and welcome the day through the joy that our being-together always conjured. After making my way to the kitchen, I'd assess the results of my father's earlier departure. Working in construction since he was a teenager (his father and father's father—the one who built the 34th Street house—worked in construction), Alan was accustomed to early mornings, ever pervaded by the smell of drip coffee and the frenzied rush to get out the door. He loved his job in many respects, but manual labor of that sort invariably takes a toll on one's body, a toll that exponentially increases with age. Upon being awake just a few seconds and in the course of about twenty feet, I was already in interpersonal communion with my brother, a like-family caregiver, and my father.

By that time, my mother's health issues had become more serious: TMJ, degenerative disk disorder, fibromyalgia, and more. Gail was Jason's primary caretaker, and she was adept at putting other people's needs before her own—even to her own detriment. She lived in chronic pain, and her body clock, due to both her health conditions and years of caring on both day shift *and* night shift, was malfunctioning beyond modern tools of repair. I would go into my parents' bedroom, knowing she had probably only fallen asleep a few hours beforehand, and kiss her gently goodbye. A light sleeper, she always responded. I protested that I shouldn't say goodbye each morning and wake her, but she insisted.

That day, two main events were on my horizon: (1) attending four classes, including taking an exam in Attic Greek and (2) playing a club soccer game. Studies suggest that in multichild families that include a child requiring intensive, twenty-four-hour care, the children who don't require care can often feel neglected in various ways. So, in addition to other ways of remedying this, my parents were careful to attend as many of my events as possible. Caregivers left around five, so that was impossible. Cue the role of my maternal grandparents. Both gave countless hours of their time to watch Jason (and learn his care routine in and out), and they were our ultimate backup, a backup without which we could not have ultimately functioned over the years. If one of the regular caregivers—Mom, Dad, employed workers, or I—could not watch Jason, then Papa Jack and Grandma Babe would step in. From the very beginning, we were always a five-person team, and once we had daily dependency workers, our core team was anywhere between seven and ten strong.

For the majority of Jason's life, he was healthy. Two issues threatened to thwart that general state: seizures and the average cold. Because Jason's immune system was weak on the whole, any run-of-the-mill sickness could turn quite quickly into something serious like pneumonia. We became *very good* at washing our hands regularly and making everyone else do so (on this front, we were quite prepared for certain pandemics). We also became vigilant about barring people who were actively sick from visiting Jason, an effort that was much harder than one might imagine ("it's just allergies" was a common refrain and, we learned, a scarily common lie).

Seizures were the most serious and threatening concern, especially because they could occur with very little warning. If Jason was in the middle of eating or even just swallowing saliva, the flotsam could get sucked into his lungs, which could lead quickly into bacterial growth and then pneumonia. Seizures were also serious because they would sometimes stop his breathing. This meant that my family was constantly ready for a potential near-death emergency. We had bags prepacked with necessities if he ended up needing to go to the intensive care unit (ICU), and we had a thoroughly tested relay system: if there was loud yelling of any sort in the house, everyone would immediately run to Jason.

Cell phones quickly became indispensable. I was one of the first kids in my school to have one, though that bluish black Nokia 5110 did not suffice to hide my poor, blue-collar status. Whenever I would get a text or call, I would check it. *Something could be wrong.* Whoever got contacted first was responsible for contacting every else. If I got the call, I'd immediately call my dad, Papa Jack, Grandma Babe, or, in certain cases, Jason's primary care physician. Our system had to be fast, efficient, and resilient. Though we bought that phone for communication about Jason, by the time of my freshman year in college, my cell phone had acted as a lifeline for calls at the edge of life and death about every single one of my intimate family members. During my teenage years and all throughout my twenties, whenever I heard the phone ringing, I immediately worried that someone I loved was in the hospital and dying. To this day, my blood pressure still spikes at the sound.

2:00 P.M.

One hour after my ancient Greek exam, my mom had an appointment with her chronic pain doctor. My dad took time off work to go with her. We had learned from past appointments that the MD would regularly discount my mom's testimony. For reasons I still can't completely understand, if the physician's assistant instead took the appointment, it was always far worse. Cocksure and seemingly lacking any training in empathy and health-promoting patient–provider communication, the PA at most appointments began with "So, what's bothering you today?" For a chronic pain sufferer, you might as well ask "Does the knife I just lodged into your skull hurt at all?" At the time, we hadn't seen the statistics concerning how sex and gender affect clinical treatment, especially with respect to questions of pain and pain management. But we had learned from experience. When we later read that research, we realized the extent to which being white had offset many of the troubles we would have experienced otherwise—a fact we should have known in the first place and the ignorance of which is our responsibility. If my dad was unable to take off work for my mom's appointments, I would skip class. Our family developed an intricate system and set of feedback loops to ensure we were always there for each other. We had routines, backups, and redundancies built in at every critical point. All of us, together, were always *on call*. Vigilance was necessity, not choice.

Care, Trauma, and History

Although this day-in-the-life account details multiple aspects of my family's history and that of each individual member, it does not capture a crucial aspect of the development of our caring system, namely, that it had been shaped by multiple traumas. For my family, the "what about you?" was always asked, and answers to it were always posed in light of the "what if you weren't here?" These traumas were productive in the sense that they fashioned how we would deal with future events. At the same time, these traumas were profoundly and irreparably destructive in the sense that they teetered on the edge of being *support undertows,* things that undermined or otherwise impaired our ability to care well.

For example, just a number of years earlier, during my first year of college (which I nearly dropped out of), almost all of my intimate family members nearly died. In September, just as I was beginning college, my father needed open-heart surgery after his cardiologist found his mitral valve to be dangerously faulty. Despite the success of the surgery, for the next three months, Alan was in and out of the ICU with every single "post-op complication" mentioned during the "this could happen" pre-op conversation. Just a week or two after the complications subsided, my mother was quickly scheduled for an emergency cervical neck surgery—a steel fusion between C4 and C7—in early February. After an fMRI, her neurologist was of the opinion that without this surgery, any fall could have paralyzed her from the neck down.

While Gail was still in a full neck brace recovering from a notoriously risky surgical procedure and while trying to communicate without hardly any use of her voice (her vocal cords were damaged during the surgery), she drove out to see her father, Jack. She called my grandfather every day, and something just sounded "off" that night. Papa Jack and my grandmother, Grandma Babe, had gotten a divorce after forty-eight years of marriage. As unusual as that was, they in fact became much closer and better friends after not living under the same roof and sharing the same bank account. But it meant they were each living alone, and "checking in" with each became increasingly crucial. Because my family was a "medical family," my mom brought a pulse oximeter with her, only to find out that Papa Jack was "satting" in the low eighties. In other words, his brain was getting so little oxygen that it was either on the road toward or already in the process of being damaged.

She immediately called 9-1-1. He was sent via ambulance to the ICU. Congestive pulmonary disease and emphysema from thirty years of chain-smoking did not assist his overall health state. Two nights after being admitted to the ICU, his regular lung treatment was entirely skipped. This omission of care threw him into a respiratory attack, which quickly led to full cardiac arrest. He coded—his heart stopped, and he technically died for a minute or two—but they were able to bring him back to life. A World War II vet, it was far from the first time he had escaped the jaws of death.

When Papa Jack was released from the hospital, we refused to let him live alone. Past stints in tertiary facilities sent him right back to the ICU due to infuriatingly negligent care. Shortly after he moved in to what used to be Jason's room, Jason came down with pneumonia. Because Jason's immune system was weak, pneumonia—serious for most—was deadly serious for him. He ended up in the ICU. Although he never coded, there was more than one day that he was touch-and-go. And we had learned long ago that every time Jason ended up in the hospital, it was dangerous. As I mentioned earlier, no nurse or doctor had ever worked with someone like Jason, which is to say, someone with muscle–eye–brain disease and the specific, unique style of being his life enjoyed. Without one of our family members present, clinicians were ill suited to know whether he was in distress, much less the extent or quality of it in comparison to his normal signs and patterns of his care.

These events led us to develop a strict rule: *never leave anyone alone in the ICU* and, to the extent possible, in secondary or tertiary care either. Our experiences as a family unit in these situations led us to confidently believe that good care in such settings would be impossible without an active, tenacious, and well-informed *advocate* for the person needing care being present in the room. Part of this belief was based on seeing how intensive care worked in the United States: twelve-hour shifts; too many patients per RNA, MD, and seemingly every other position; little time to read charts, much less properly annotate them—you name it. It was less an indictment of the caretaking abilities of the medical and administrative professionals in the ICU (though, with respect to certain uncaring individuals, it certainly was) and more an acknowledgment that the system of care in U.S. hospitals and medical systems is a failed system. And we were unwilling to let that system fail our loved ones and break the system of care we had ourselves worked so hard to build and maintain.

Structures of Systems of Care

Having now laid out a day-in-the-life description of my family's caring system, I turn to explore what it suggests about the more general structures of caring systems. I contend that the lived experience of care as thought from an interpersonal, systems perspective reveals at least three interrelated dimensions of attentional focus toward which the completion of care is carried out: the personal, social-interpersonal, and civic-political (Tronto 1993). I argue that these three dimensions reveal the fundamental orientation of caring systems to be *what about you?* Far from, but certainly involving, the "I can" and the "I think," it is the "what about you?" that defines the lived experience of caring systems. *What about you?* oriented and guided all of my family's actions. It was at the heart of all we did.

The following is a summary of these three primary dimensions and the particular practices of each:

- Personal
  - Provision of needs
  - Hacks
  - Backups
  - Individuality

- Social-interpersonal
  - Being on call
  - Virtue cultivation/maintenance
  - Knowledge gathering
  - Solidarity (ride or die)

- Civic-political
  - Income/wealth
  - Health care
  - Institutional support
  - Representation/activism

Personal

Jason required care for all of his basic material needs, from food to bathing to clothing. The daily and nightly routines of my family were fundamentally oriented around those needs. We not only developed rhythms of care but also became adept at reading Jason's body. This was a necessity because he was nonverbal, though in certain respects impressive at vocalizing in various ways and also deftly communicative through body language. If he was hungry prior to his normal lunchtime or needed to go to the bathroom outside of his normal schedule, we learned to know the signs. In addition to constant attentiveness to his well-being in real time, our attention to and the successful delivery of these basic material needs required a significant amount of time, labor, money, and knowledge. We had to figure out how to balance his nutritional requirements with foods that were easy for him to swallow and that he liked, which diapers were the most effective and least chaffing, the optimal temperature for bathing water, and much more. It was never simply a question of what he needed—it was always also a question of what he wanted and what would make him happy. And yet our environment—from the physical construction of our house to the temporal demands of modern daily life—was not conducive to this kind of care.

Because of this, we became adept at retrofitting and hacking. Even in environments more conducive to care, such modifications and corrections will be necessary due to the particularity of people and the complexity of situations of care. In my family's case, though, we had to figure out how to make things function in ways they were clearly never designed to. And not just with respect to the house on 34th Street but also with respect to the very forms of life most people assume as default in modern, wealthy societies: an eight-to-five job, "standard" health insurance, access to needed services for basic care, and a single income. Today, thanks to decades of policies benefiting the rich and systematically stripping away supports for the poor and lower middle class, most of these, but especially the last, are no longer the norm. They are simply no longer possible for the majority of Americans, not to mention most humans across the globe.

In addition to hacks, we developed redundancies and backups. The use of cell phones is a prime example of this—we needed fast and efficient communication systems to offset someone being unavailable or otherwise unable to help when needed. Good care doesn't fail when something goes wrong. It is layered and robust. If there was an important appointment or some other time-sensitive event, all of us knew about it, not just one of us. If a certain item was central to caring routines, we built up stores of it (even if that meant rationing certain items). To care well, the materials or "matter" of caring had to be distributed in breadth and depth.

Last, all of these foci of our caring system—provision of needs, hacks, and backups—were fundamentally shaped by individuality. We learned that Jason loved country music, bright colors, and ice cream. We learned that kisses and vocal affirmation were his primary love language. Caring for his basic material needs and developing hacks and backups were all in the service of caring not just for *anyone* but for Jason as an individual. His individuality was the north star of all our caring efforts.

Social-Interpersonal

It is clear from the foregoing description that an essential aspect of our caring system involved being on call 24/7. This was a demand that was both individual and also shared and interpersonal. Being on call functioned in terms of nodes within a network: when the system lit up for a need, everyone was activated and aware, even if everyone couldn't respond. Yet, being on call was not just a question of availability; it was also a question of comportment—of character, virtues, and habits. My family had to learn how to delicately balance understanding and graciousness (excusing crankiness, atypical outbursts or meltdowns, or any number of negative effects due to sheer exhaustion) along with holding people to the standards of the multiple caring virtues on which our caring system relied. As a whole, our intimately interconnected and responsive care system functioned as a method of *virtue cultivation*. It encouraged, maintained, and reinforced the types of virtues necessary to care for others and worked to shape each of us into a caring person, which is to say, it functioned to shape each into a type of person who embodied the requisite knowledge, practical wisdom, and complete set of virtues necessary to in fact *be* caring.

Being on call was also a question of knowledge. Any novel medical event—or relevant political event for that matter—meant that at least one of us, if not multiple members, would try to figure out what we needed to know to meaningfully inform and critique treatment plans and caregiving routines. We had to learn as much as possible because we knew that Jason's care inside of the American medical institutions of the Pacific Northwest state of Oregon was more often than not poorly tailored (or not tailored at all) to his body and mind. Most medical professionals had simply never worked with someone like Jason—setting aside those who, due to ableist prejudices, thought that they (and we) shouldn't have been caring for him in the first place. Our medical knowledge was a crucial tool to combat everything from understandable ignorance to outright prejudice.

To successfully be on call in this way and work toward becoming a caring person—along with all the knowledge and skills it demanded—required a fundamental value: solidarity. Although much ink has been spilled on the philosophical meaning and import of solidarity, it had a very simple and visceral meaning for my family: *ride or die.* No matter what happened and no matter the odds, we would never give up defending and being there for each other. Caring systems cannot care well without solidarity between all those involved.

Civic-Political

The personal and social/interpersonal structures of our caring system included a third, broader dimension: the civic and political. For much of my family's life, my father's gross income was just above the threshold deemed appropriate for certain types of support from the state. From the perspective of state and federal tax code, that a huge portion of his income went to basic supplies for Jason's care was irrelevant. My father, the youngest of a family of seven, was not given and did not inherit any wealth from his parents—beyond their house, there were no assets—and this meant that despite his intense labor, we always lived paycheck to paycheck, along with a constant dance with credit card debt.

The economic situation of my family, a situation centrally determined by governmental policies, not by effort of labor, was doomed from the start. The fact that my mother typically worked ninety-plus hours a week was irrelevant. She was a "homemaker." She was a home "caregiver." At least certain aspects of U.S. society give lip service to the rights and worth of those who require care, and yet most care labor goes unpaid. Especially for families with zero wealth and low income levels, this then creates a cycle of economic impoverishment. Our church community and numerous extended family members indeed helped us when we were in financial straits, but those types of interventions were (greatly appreciated) stopgaps, not solutions. And if we had lost health insurance, those stopgaps would all have failed, and we would have very quickly faced homelessness, which would have meant death for Jason and my mother and who knows what for my father and myself.

If my father had not had a full-time job with health benefits that extended to his dependents, Jason would have died before the age of one. The fact that health benefits were *essential* to the well-being of Jason and all our family members kept my father locked into a job with a verbally abusive boss for many years. Thankfully, he eventually found employment with a much better company and did so without the prospect of losing benefits or income in the transition. It should go without saying that the fact that the United States is one of the wealthier countries in the world by a number of metrics and yet more than half of Americans delay or do not get health care because they cannot afford it is a moral and political tragedy.[3] This is what happens when health care is guided by profit, not the care of human life.

Modern health care is one form of what could more generally be called *institutional support*. During fourth grade, my elementary school did a "spaghetti night" fundraiser in order for my family to garner the funds to buy a van with a wheelchair lift. Public transportation in Eugene, Oregon, was not a viable option for Jason, because of both the lack of infrastructure and the risks that it posed for his weak immune system. Think about that for a second: there were no state or federal mechanisms in place for my family to be able to have a suitable way to get Jason from point A to point B, even if points A and B were public spaces. Put bluntly, there were no institutional supports for his basic material needs, just as there are no institutional supports for the basic material needs of a significant portion of American families, regardless of their specific ability statuses. My family's story is a *typical* American story, though the failure of these supports is far graver and far more politically premediated with respect to American families of color, especially Black Americans.

Looking at the political debates raging in the 1990s and 2000s, the lack of political representation for lives like Jason's, families like mine, and caring systems like ours is staggering. This is not to diminish the spectacular achievements of disability rights activists in the last half of the twentieth century. But antidiscrimination laws are in many ways the thinnest of institutional supports, categorically failing to extend to cultural and political representation in broader ways (Russell 2019). Being able to sue for something is not the same as having basic supports to live one's life. It is not hyperbole to claim that the current U.S. political system is actively oriented against caring systems and the flourishing of the majority of people as opposed to the wealthy few.

With respect to trauma, I spoke earlier of *support undertows*. Although trauma certainly generates serious support undertows at personal and interpersonal levels, the most significant support undertow my family faced occurred primarily at the civic-political level. It is hard to overstate the impact of insufficient income and zero wealth due to familial legacies of blue-collar work, of employment-dependent and profit-driven health care, of nearly nonexistent institutional supports, and of paltry political representation. Each of these profoundly limited our ability to create, maintain, and improve our caring system.

To the contrary, each of these civic and political factors threatened to undermine and destroy our caring system. We were constantly aware that Jason's life could hang in the balance at the whim of a health insurance agency, political representative, state or federal judge, overworked health care provider, sudden personal financial emergency, or, for that matter, the loss of anyone on our team. The success or failure of our caring system—and the quality of the lived experience of each individual in it—fatefully turned on whether systems above and beyond our own cared for us as well.

An understanding of ability as access leads quite naturally to what Michael Sandel (2007) has called an "ethic of giftedness"—an ethic that understands that the majority of what and how we are is due to gifts of all that is around us and makes us up. I hope to have shown why the meaning of disability cannot be determined by reference to bodies or to environments but instead only in terms of the interaction and interanimation of each relative to caring systems. We build worlds that care or fail to care, and the moral weight of those decisions falls neither on fate nor circumstance but on us.

Conclusion

An Anti-Ableist Future

We must do more than simply extend the scope of morality.

—Margrit Shildrick, *Leaky Bodies and Boundaries*

Disability may well be "the fundamental aspect of human embodiment." *The* fundamental aspect? What a notion—that the universalizing experience of disability, states of dimensional dependence from our infancy through the end of life, might be the central fact of having a body, or rather *being* a body. It's an idea that could alter one's very sense of self, if we let it.

—Sara Hendren, *What Can a Body Do?*

As a bright-eyed eight-year-old in rainy Oregon, few things seemed cooler than Hollywood, California: the land of picture-perfect beaches, fast cars, and blockbuster movies. That summer, my film-industry uncle rode his Harley up I-5 through the towering Redwoods and into the land of Douglas firs to visit my family. Despite tales of A-list stars and the Sunset Boulevard life, the conversation around our dinner table that hot July night turned to the mundane: my uncle did not wear a helmet. In fact, he refused to. This alarmed my parents, eager to instill in me the idea that helmet-wearing was mandatory, no matter what I rode. In response, my uncle did not mince his words: "*I'd rather be dead than disabled.*"

Silence filled the room.

That fateful phrase hung on the air for what seemed like an eternity as Jason, my brother and best friend, sat next to him in his shiny new wheelchair, being fed by my father, Alan. My maternal grandparents, in the transitional thickets of age- and illness-related disabilities, sat on his other side. My mother, Gail, recently diagnosed with temporomandibular joint disorder (TMJ), fibromyalgia, and other conditions that would quickly lead her to become disabled, sat across the table as well.

I wasn't angry then, but I am now—not at my uncle but at that idea: *I'd rather be dead than disabled.* I soon came to know that many—far too many—hold it without compunction. I learned that the road to death for countless people with disabilities has been paved by that idea and by ones like it across millennia. Even those who might say it and immediately regret it, like my uncle, invoke an assumption about the worth of a life lived with disabilities that is as old as history itself. On his deathbed, Socrates asks, "Is life worth living with a body that is corrupted and in a bad condition?" "In no way," replies his friend Crito. The question of worthy life has always been a question of disability.

As my eyes panned slowly across the dinner table to gauge others' reactions, my mind's eye focused on a simple fact: the sheer existence of so many others seemed to prove my uncle wrong. My life, the lives of my brother, my grandparents, my mother, and the life of every disabled person I knew and know suggest the opposite. These lives suggest instead that being disabled is like any other significant facet of human identity: it shapes one's world. As I stated earlier, whether one is shaped for good or bad and whether one is shaped a lot or a little depends on a host of factors.

However far my arguments and the arguments of other disability scholars and activists across the globe go, we are decidedly far from a world in which disability is understood primarily as difference, not disadvantage; as shaping, not severing; and as complex and changing, not uniform and constant (Barnes 2016). We are far from this world despite more than a half-century of disability activism; despite decades of disability studies scholarship spanning the humanities and the social sciences; despite a rapidly growing field of philosophy of disability; despite laws protecting people with disabilities as a historically oppressed minority group; and despite increasing media representations and representatives that more accurately portray the rich complexity of disabled life. More loudly and more forcefully, *we need to talk about the worlds disability creates.* We need to talk about ability in terms of access and care and caring systems.

Such world creation will only become intelligible once we commit ourselves to questioning what it means to create worlds in the first place—what it means to build societies and communities that are caring, habitable, and sustaining of the worth of people with bodies and minds and abilities and disabilities of all sorts.[1] To this question, the lives of my brother and of my family suggest a simple and powerful answer—the meanings of *world creation, disability,* and *worthy life* are intertwined by a single thread: care.

It is not the "abilities" or "disabilities" of a person that ultimately create worlds worth living in. Care and caring systems create worlds worth living in. Caring systems create the webs of relations that make up the meaning and worth of any given ability or disability in the first place.

From Ableism to Caring Systems

People with disabilities, including people living in pain, have historically been given remarkably short shrift by philosophers, especially those working in ethics and moral theory. Numerous contemporary social-political philosophers—ranging from Nussbaum to Mills to Pateman to Kittay to Khader—have attempted to rectify the glaring insufficiency of historically dominant theories of justice for those who have been oppressed under their very auspices. Relational autonomists, such as Catriona Mackenzie and Natalie Stoljar (1999), have approached this issue through altering and expanding the notion of individual autonomy assumed by most canonical theories. These scholars, each in their own way, have carried out their critical work in the recognition that normative ethical theories have historically emphasized their principles and putatively rational grounding while deemphasizing their exemplars and sociomaterial grounding. That is to say, whether framed as a question of virtue (Aristotle), duty (Kant), social contract (Rousseau), or utility (Mill), such theories have focused more on the grounds or axioms that determine the worth of ethical action and less on the type of people for whom such action is intended to be relevant in the first place. This has led to serious gaps, whether one looks to assumptions that some people are "natural slaves"; that certain "races" render people without moral dignity; that certain "types" of people relative to eugenic constructions like "IQ" are outside the social contract; or that happiness is tied more or less directly to social utility, a thought that has historically been politically devastating and led to widespread torture and massive numbers of deaths of people with disabilities.

To take a few examples with respect to questions of disability more specifically, Martha Nussbaum and Amartya Sen have addressed this through the capabilities approach, a revision and expansion of Rawlsian political liberalism (Nussbaum 2000); Eva Kittay by offering a disability-centric theory of care ethics built off the work of Carol Gilligan and Nel Noddings (Kittay 1999); and Anita Silvers by revising social contract theory into trust-based contractualism, developing insights mined from Hume and Smith (Silvers and Francis 2005). For each of these scholars, the guiding question has been, how does one conceive of justice such that people with disabilities are not excluded? If Tobin Siebers is right that "all known theories of human rights, whether based on humanity, social contract theory, utilitarianism, or citizenship, exclude individuals from the rights-bearing community if they do not possess the specific abilities required for membership," then the meaning of disability is at the core, not the periphery, of conceptions of justice (Davis 2013a, 233; Siebers 2008, 178). Ability and disability are not mere factors in normative theories—conceptions of ability and disability constitute the very ground out of which normative theories are first built.

That the meaning of disability is at the core of conceptions of justice should lead one to wonder why disability has been featured so little in theories of justice across history. One explanation is that theories of justice have too often been constructed in and through abstractions. Unlike such theories, a fully naturalized and egalitarian account of justice, one that grounds its principles in the concrete experiences of the beings for whom its prescriptions are thought to bear, is beholden to the structures and singularities of experiences. If such a theory, if such an account of ethics more generally, wishes to ground its normative claims, it cannot do so primarily through an appeal to a second-order, quantitatively produced metric. That is to say, the evidence that it brings to bear must be thicker, must be grounded more concretely in the experiences of the lives to which it is beholden and for which it crafts its prescriptions. For example, although I do not deny that constructs like statistical normality play a role (and in at least some domains like epidemiology, should play a role) in praxis with respect to normative judgments, a more just route to ground such judgments is through a critical synthesis of empirical and reflective evidence and research about lives attested to be worth living and lives attested not to be. We can only get better at thinking about lives worth living if we do better in thinking about the complexity and variability of life and of worth—if we do better in thinking about *the life worth living.*

The answer to the question of the life worth living is already found in its genuine questioning, found in the suspicion that one will never have complete certainty of the answer, found in the conviction that we should cast our moral nets as widely as possible. The answer, then, is found in the hope of difference and change and the justices each evinces. Many lives and many ways of living them intertwine to lace the thick texture that defines value and worth. Lives lived with, in, through, and for disability are lives from which we might better glean the depth and richness of that texture. Even with disability education, the ableist conflation can impact the ability to think carefully about disability and related experiences. Until the ableist conflation is destroyed as a habit of thinking, it will always threaten a just, equitable future. An anti-ableist future is one in which we appreciate that the meanings of ability and disability are contested, variable, and relational. An anti-ableist future is one in which the voices of people with disabilities are raised, heeded, and made a touchstone for the past, present, and future. An anti-ableist world is one in which our thinking and action concerning disability become as complex as the phenomenon of disability itself.

The Future of Disability Politics

I have argued that the ontology of ability cannot be construed merely in terms of properties, characteristics, or dispositions of an individual. Abilities are always in constitutive and fundamental relation to structural, environmental, and intersubjective supports. This is not just a point about the formal definition of *ability.* One cannot attend to the meaning of ability, to how that phenomenon bears out at the level of lived experience, without looking to the constitutive supports and structures in which abilities are and historically can become abilities in the first place. In summary, abilities are relations. Some abilities are world creating; others are trifling. Some abilities form social identities; others form nothing at all. Some abilities appear only in tandem; others are singular. Depending on one's ends and the sort of ability in question, some abilities might best be conceived at the level of the human, others at the level of the social, others at the level of the personal; and others yet as a combination of these. When all is said and done, I have argued that to be able means to be supported to be able, to be *en*abled. Abilities articulate avenues and conditions of support. Ability is a question of access: it is a question not of how one is as an individual but of the interaction, interanimation, and interrelationship between oneself and everything around one.

Understood in this relational way, abilities cannot but constitute the ways in which I am, am taken to be, and can be. I am insofar as I am abled, which is always to say at the same time that I am insofar as I am disabled. It is in this light that the misguidedness and social damage of the ableist conflation and of ableism more generally are best seen. The ableist conflation links disability to pain—conceived as a necessary limitation—in a way that is predicated upon the theory of personal ability. Even if pain is limiting, that does not tell us about one's abilities insofar as abilities are the sorts of things that go beyond questions of the individual. In a world with lidocaine patches and opioids, some pain, even some chronic pain, is manageable. In a world without those, the story would be different. As admittedly simple as that observation is, it makes clear the failure of thinking ability in terms of the individual. In claiming that "I'd rather be dead than disabled," my uncle was wrong for lots of reasons. But chief among them was his weddedness to his world and his inability to see the world created by Jason's life within my family's caring system. Without Jason and my family, would I, too, have been so wed to my world? Would I, too, have thought, *I'd rather be dead than disabled*?

When I teach ethics or political philosophy, I begin by asking my students, what kind of world do you want to live in? I have yet to have a student respond, "I want to live in a world with people with disabilities." Yet, to imagine a perfect world as one without disability is to imagine a world without human bodies and minds, their impressive variability, and the worlds we create to care for them. We will always have people who are born in different and unexpected ways. We will always have people who through various events in life end up in bodies and minds that work in different and unexpected ways. This is both a fact and a good thing. Worlds worth living in are built by and through caring systems made for all sorts of people.

And yet, the world is built to care, not for everybody, but only for a few. It does not have to be this way, and despite the exponentially increasing effects of climate change, there is still time to change this fact. As Achille Mbembe (2017, 179) writes, "as long as the retreat from humanity is incomplete, there is still a possibility of restitution, reparation, and justice. These are the conditions for the collective resurgence of humanity. Thinking through what must come will of necessity be a thinking through of life, of the reserves of life, of what must escape sacrifice. It will of necessity be *a thinking in circulation, a thinking of crossings, a world-thinking.*" It is in such a spirit that I argue that *care creates worlds,* for we are who we are by virtue of those who have cared or failed to care for us, by virtue of the systems we—as a community, society, or body politic—have created or not created to care for us. The very conditions of our being and being well are predicated upon caring systems.

Rosemarie Garland-Thomson (2013, 336) writes, "the ability/ disability system produces subjects by differentiating and marking bodies. . . . As such, disability has four aspects: first, it is a system for interpreting and disciplining bodily variations; second, it is a relationship between bodies and their environments; third, it is a set of practices that produce both the able-bodied and the disabled; fourth, it is a way of describing the inherent instability of the embodied self." When my uncle made the choice not to wear a helmet, he simply didn't realize what he was doing. He wasn't thinking about the many, complex meanings of the ability/disability system. He wasn't thinking about his actions and words and the assumptions behind them. He wasn't thinking about variation, organism–environment interaction, sociopolitical practices, and the nature of the self. More concretely, he wasn't thinking about all the relations and interactions and caring systems that could make his life rich even if he went through significant ability transitions due to a motorcycle accident.

I always wear a helmet now. I, for one, would rather explore the worlds care creates than deny certain worlds worth on the basis of the only one I've known. I would rather work in community with others to make habitable worlds for all. That, perhaps, is a path on the way to caring better, a path I have learned from my brother and family and the beauty of our world. If, as Cornel West brilliantly discerned, justice is love in public, then care is world making for all.

So, let us discuss this, again, starting from the beginning.

Acknowledgments

There are so many interlocutors over the years to whom I owe immeasurable thanks for shaping and refining the thoughts and lines of inquiry presented herein. At the outset, I want to highlight my dissertation committee and readers: John T. Lysaker, Cynthia Willett, Andrew J. Mitchell, Rosemarie Garland-Thomson, and Eva Feder Kittay. From my time at the University of Oregon (UO), I especially thank Mark Johnson, Beata Stawarska, Daniel Falk, Scott Pratt, Ted Toadvine, Mark T. Unno, and Steven Shankman. The graduate teaching fellows at UO were fantastic, and I was honored to learn from Adam Arola, John Kaag, José Mendoza, and Sarah LaChance Adams. Joseph Fracchia in the Clark Honors College was the primary reason I fell in love with the humanities, and I am so thankful for his consummate teaching, research, and mentorship. I owe more than I likely realize to the passion and insights of my high school English teacher Sue Churnside and also to my history teacher Grant Conway. From questions of shoe fashion to high scholasticism, Rick Lee deserves appreciation. Many thanks to Lauren Guilmette, Becca Longtin, Kate Davies, David Peña-Guzmán, Simon Truwant, Gail Weiss, Lynne Huffer, Gregor Wolbring, Sander Gilman, Carmen Gomen, Jennifer Scuro, Amelia Wirts, Jennifer Gammage, Erik Parens, Elizabeth Dietz, Rachel Zacharias, Lilyana Levy, Susan Bredlau, George Yancy, Marta Jimenez, Louise Pratt, Jill Robbins, David Morris, Kelly Oliver, Michael Gill, Adam Newman, Robert Leib, Axelle Karera, and all those involved with the 2013 *Collegium Phaenomenologicum*. Thanks to two reviewers who gave fantastically helpful feedback on an earlier version of the manuscript, and thanks to Danielle M. Kasprzak and Leah Pennywark at the University of Minnesota Press for being so supportive of this project. Thanks as well for help and guidance from Anne Carter at the Press.
Foremost gratitude goes to the lives and loves that first taught

me both to question and value (dis)ability and the nature of experience and to question *what* matters: Jason, Gail, Alan, Papa Jack, and Grandma Babe. My family has been a support for me without which I would be unmoored, and they are the inspiration for all that I do. In many ways, my research is a way of thinking through and honoring the experiences of love, care, embodiment, and interrelations through which my family survived and, despite long odds, thrived.

My entry into philosophy was occasioned through a one-credit course in which I enrolled on little more than a whim. A certain "philosopher" (I knew not what that term meant) named John T. Lysaker taught the course. The materials intrigued me as had no others, and the following year, I took my first official philosophy course with John, one of many to come. I had no idea that this would be the beginning of a mentorship and friendship of which many dream but that few find. John has been the most supportive and, at the same time, most constructively critical guide. I teach with the hope that someday I will be to my students what he has been to me; I write with the hope that my pen will attain the lithe acuity and depth of his; and I practice philosophy with the hope that it will bear out the type of life he was the first to show me possible. I cannot express my gratitude for his presence in my life, except to say that without him, I would rue the life that would have transpired. John has made me not only a better philosopher but a better person, and for that, there is no adequate economy of gratitude.

Cynthia Willett displayed outstanding concern and offered inimitable advice. Her presence on my committee was marked by superlative levels of guidance and continual sparks of brilliance, and I feel truly lucky to have worked with and learned from her. Andrew Mitchell was invaluable on many fronts. His confidence in the origins and trajectory of this project both was invigorating and also helped me through hard times. I am grateful for being able to work with such a simultaneously caring and surgical, "ceiling-less" reader and thinker. Rosemarie Garland-Thomson believed in me from the outset, and she sustained my efforts more than she knows. I am thankful for all that she is, all that she does, and all the wisdom she has imparted to me—and all with her inimitable, characteristic grace that still carries me today. In more ways than one, I wouldn't be here without her. Eva Kittay has been an inspiration and existential touchstone for me in numerous ways. Her insights (in person and in her writings) have deeply informed what I do and how I think, and I feel as though I have been struck by philosophical lightning to be able to continue to learn from her, Sesha, and the entire Kittay family.

Lauren Guilmette is a model of the type of philosopher who not only changes minds but lives, and she performs such transformations with a level of care that serves as a genuine measure. As both a colleague and a friend, she is exemplary, and I thank her for all she has been, is, and will be. Katherine Davies has displayed unparalleled strength and friendship through thick and thin and has done so with her distinctive wisdom and insight. I am thankful for our continent-spanning friendship, and I greatly look forward to its future. Ryan Fics has especially enriched more recent projects in multiple ways, and I am thankful for all the provocations and guidance to which his singular mind and spirit has led me—and us, together. David M. Peña-Guzmán has been a steadfast, always electrifying interlocutor for many years, and I am forever appreciative of his seemingly endless acumen. I can't wait to keep writing and thinking together. Rebecca Longtin is a lone, bright star in existence's night sky, and I cannot thank her enough for all of her wisdom, kindness, energy, support, and ever-enlightening insights. Schnerp and I (and Finn) are very lucky.

The graduate community at Emory University, both inside and outside the Department of Philosophy, was welcoming and energizing, and it made for a wonderful graduate experience. Among the multiple conference communities from which I've learned much and benefited greatly, I want to single out the remarkable community of scholars and activists at the Society for Disability Studies and at PhiloSOPHIA as well as all those scholars and friends involved in the Emory Disability Studies Initiative (and many thanks to the Emory College and Laney Graduate School for supporting me as the inaugural Laney Graduate School Disability Studies Fellow). My gratitude goes out to the Andrew W. Mellon Foundation, in partnership with the Emory Laney Graduate School, for the 2016–17 dissertation completion fellowship that allowed me to finish this project while teaching that academic year at Dillard University in New Orleans, Louisiana. Thanks also to the Howard Hughes Medical Institute and the Emory College for support as an On Recent Discoveries by Emory Researchers (ORDER) Fellow from 2015 to 2016; it was an honor to teach and grow together with the other ORDER teacher-scholars,

Isabella Alexander, James Burkett, Sasha Klupchak, and Anne Winiarski. Many thanks as well for the leadership of David Lynn and Leslie Taylor.

To my close circle of friends (you know who you are), thank you for being there for me through thick and thin. Thank you for holding me together and lifting me up when I most needed it and most needed you. To Michael, especially, thank you for being a brother. Few ever find a companion like you, and not a day goes by that I am not grateful for all that you are and for every moment we spend together—past, present, and future. Our journey has only begun.

Thank you to my students at the University of Massachusetts Lowell, Dillard University, and Emory University: it was a privilege to learn with and from you. I also thank the editors of *Jahrbuch Litertur und Medizin,* Bettina von Jagow and Florian Steger, for allowing me to use some reworked materials from my essay "Feeding upon Death: Pain, Possibility, and Transformation in S. Kay Toombs and Kafka's 'The Vulture'" (vol. 6, 135–54) in chapter 2; Nicole Piemonte and *Review of Communication* for allowing me to use a couple sections from my essay "'I'd Rather Be Dead than Disabled'—The Ableist Conflation and the Meanings of Disability" (17 [3]: 149–63); and Ted Toadvine and *Chiasmi International: Trilingual Studies Concerning the Thought of Merleau-Ponty* for allowing me to use a very small amount of material from my essay "Merleau-Ponty, World-Creating Blindness, and the Phenomenology of Non-Normate Bodies" (19: 419–36).

The vast majority of this project was written between fall 2014 and spring 2016 (yes, seriously, that long ago). The book was to come out many years earlier, but, alas, fickle fate deemed it otherwise. Although I have made serious revisions (especially to the latter parts of the project) thanks to constructive feedback from many people, and although I have done my best to update things where feasible, a truly staggering number of books, articles, and chapters have been published since 2016 related to the many topics and literatures I engage, especially with respect to the rapidly expanding field of philosophy of disability. Given the long delays in publishing that can happen for any number of reasons, I hope readers will keep such timing in mind if they find themselves wondering why a more recent piece isn't engaged at this or that juncture and with respect to this or that argument. My next book will try to do justice to what has come out since that time and will, I can already say, update a number of claims I make in this project. I should also add that the acknowledgments for that forthcoming project will contain many, many new names of people, conference communities, and institutions who have been intellectually pivotal over more recent years. So if you are surprised to not see your name here (for example, my beloved Hastings Center and Georgetown colleagues), you will surely see it in future acknowledgments.

I want to thank from the bottom of my heart *all those* whose presence, insight, and work have informed and shaped this project and, through it, me. When all is said and done, though, this book is for Jason and Gail. I hope I did right by your lived experiences and your desire, need, and vision for a more just, less ableist world.

Notes

Introduction

1. Regarding the epigraph: reference to the Greek has been made in Aristotle (1926). I imagine hearing in tandem with this another of Aristotle's claims: "there is no demonstration of a principle of demonstration [*apodeixeos gar arche ouk apodeixis estin*]." *Metaphysics,* 1011a. Translation modified from Aristotle (1933).

2. I here use "canonical origins" without further qualification intentionally. If I were to specify "Western," I would risk giving in to racist, colonialist constructions of the West made to run from ancient Greece to nineteenth-century Germany. If I were to specify "West and East," I would then fall into further conundrums of multiple exclusions, canonical and otherwise. For example, where precisely is Islamic philosophy, given its ambit in many parts of Africa and other continents and its enormous historical role in the usual orbit of such a phrase? In sum, "canon" here functions as a placeholder for what many academic philosophers, for better or for worse, and too often without justification and in ignorance, *take to be* canonical texts in some "tradition" in history of philosophy.

3. In the spurious *Sense and Sensibilia,* it is also commented that "of persons destitute from either sense, the blind are more intelligent than the deaf and dumb" (437a15–17).

4. Take John Locke as another example from modern philosophy: "But if, through defects that may happen out of the ordinary course of nature, any one comes not to such a degree of reason, wherein he might be supposed capable of knowing the law, and so living within the rules of it, he is *never capable of being a free man,* he is never let loose to the disposure of his own will (because he knows no bounds to it, has not understanding, its proper guide) but is continued under the tuition and government of others, all the time his own understanding is incapable of that charge. And so *lunatics* and *ideots* are never set free from the government of their parents" (Locke 1988, 60).

5. See *OED,* s.v. "fool."

6. The question of what constitutes a "harm" in relation to given cases of disability is itself a major point of debate in philosophy of disability. Elizabeth Barnes (2016) provides a helpful overview. See also (Reynolds 2016b).

7. Take, e.g., the satirical post "This Woman Is Strong, Sexy, and Brave—Even If She Does Have Both Legs," Clickhole, http://www.clickhole.com/article/woman-strong-sexy-and-braveven-if-she-does-have-b-1219.

8. Arguments that tie "decency" to "disability" are subtle forms of this. Examples from recent government documents and news articles include Social Security Advisory Board (2009), David (2011), and White (2013). Such arguments are often couched in terms of *fiscal* sustainability, for example, take this quote from a *Fox News* segment: "Tanner said there must be a serious effort to put people back to work because the continued growth of these entitlement programs is unsustainable" (August 29, 2014). For example, it is because of the legacy of the ableist conflation that the *disability paradox* has become a research topic for social scientists: "Why do many people with serious and persistent disabilities report that they experience a good or excellent quality of life when to most external observers these individuals seem to live an undesirable daily existence?" (Albrecht and Devlieger 1999). This question is still alive today in scholarship spanning the social sciences and humanities (Hayward 2013). But this research program only makes sense if one assumes, as a matter of course, that disability is experienced as negative and of a kind with experiences of pain, suffering, and disadvantage. Unsurprisingly, the implications of the disability paradox are a pressing, ongoing issue for disability rights activism both locally and abroad (McMahan 2005).

9. Confusingly, not long after this statement, the authors directly engage the social model of disability and begin distinguishing between impairment and disability. They write, "Impairments often result in disabilities, but they need not. A disability is inherently relational: being disabled is being unable to do something. More specifically, to have a disability is to be unable to perform some significant range of tasks or functions that individuals in someone's reference group (e.g., adults) are ordinarily able to do, at least under favorable conditions, where the inability is not due to simple and easily corrigible ignorance or to a lack of the tools or means ordinarily available for performing such tasks or functions" (285–86; see also 319). Note that the definition is social only on the surface. It is framed as a question of *individual ability*. I'll return to this question in chapter 5.

10. Humanity+, "Transhumanist FAQ," http://humanityplus.org/philosophy/transhumanist-faq/. On the relation of trans- and posthumanism to disability and disability studies, see, e.g., Hall (2016), Kafer (2013), and DeShong (2012).

1. Theories of Pain

1. *OED*, s.v. "poena." "Avestan *kaenā* vengeance, reparation and, with a different ablaut grade, Old Church Slavonic *cěna*, Russian *cena*, and Lithuanian *kaina* all in [the] sense [of] 'price.'"

2. I say "presumption" and not "assumption" because assumptions are held whether or not one is confident about that which is assumed, whereas presump-

tions are held about things of which one is sure or takes oneself to be sure. For numerous glosses of the term *ableism,* see Campbell (2009). In a shorter piece, Campbell defines it as "a network of beliefs, processes, and practices that produce a particular kind of self and body (the corporeal standard) that is projected as the perfect, as the species-typical, and, therefore, as essential and fully human." Fiona Kumari Campbell, "Legislating Disability," in Tremain (2005, 127). Scholars and activists do not agree on the precise meaning of *ableism.* However, perfect consensus over that term is not necessary for the project at hand.

3. The hither side of the ableist conflation is the conflation of lives lived outside ableist norms with lives presumed to be able to *suffer nothing* and thus outside the purview of moral consideration due to moral status. E.g., Jeff McMahan (2002), following Singer's earlier arguments, takes such a stance with respect to the "congenitally severely mentally retarded," specifically in relation to their putative inability to engage in "prudential relations." A trenchant criticism of McMahan's views is presented by Kittay (2006).

4. Histories of pain are increasingly common, and although I cannot engage a comprehensive account of such histories due to the aims at hand, I would highlight the following sources: Bourke (2014), Moscoso (2012), Rey (1995), Wailoo (2014), Keele (1957).

5. The stakes of such a contestation are presented well by Said (1993, 318ff.). One might quickly object that if I were to consider certain Eastern religious traditions that treat pain and suffering as illusionary in various respects, my "religious model" would turn out quite differently. On the contrary, I would contend that the functional role of pain I here defend also captures what is at stake in deflationary models of pain. In short, pain still functions as a command to reorient oneself relative to a given order in deflationary models—it's just that the command in such a case is to *ignore* or sublimate that pain. I do not fully defend that argument here, so one will have to take this claim in that light. One might also respond that with sufficient bodily-mental practice, certain religious practitioners say they no longer feel or sense pain (such as in fire-walking practices). But if one takes that to be the case, it is not a counterexample, for my arguments do not aim to extend to examples where pain is neither sensed nor felt. See Armstrong (1970).

6. For a very short but helpful introduction to some of the issues Genesis 1–11, in particular, presents, see Rogerson (2004, esp. 18–26). Rogerson includes some discussion of the critical readings utilizing the documentary or Wellhausen hypothesis (DH/WH) that distinguishes between the Yahwist (J), Elohist (J), Deuteronimist (D), and priestly (P) sources. Although this hypothesis dates back to the eighteenth century, it was made foundational by Julius Wellhausen's 1876–77 *Die Composition des Hexateuch und der historischen Bücher des Alten Testaments.* For a recent analysis of the DH, see Baden (2012).

7. See Meeks and Bassler (1993). The Qur'anic account is nearly identical: "We said: 'Adam, dwell with your wife in Paradise and eat of its fruits to your hearts' content wherever you will. But never approach this tree or you shall both

become transgressors'" (2:34; see also 7:19). See also 20:120: "Thus did Adam disobey his Lord and stray from the right path." Due to this disobedience, the human is elsewhere described as contentious or as a disputer (خَصِيم) (36:77 and 2:204).

8. As a whole, the DH relies on the different usages of the name of God as one clue as to which documentary source is which. The names at issue are Elohim, YHWH, YHWH Eloheinu, and El Shaddai. I utilize the name "God" for simplicity.

9. With the exception of the clearly gendered punishment, I speak not of "man" but of humans with respect to the Genesaic account. As Robert Alter notes, the Hebrew term 'adam (אָדָם) does not indicate a male or man. With respect to Genesis 1:26, Alter (1996, 5) writes, "The term 'adam, afterward consistently with a definite article, which is used both here and in the second account of the origins of humankind, is a generic term for human beings, not a proper noun. It also does not automatically suggest maleness, especially not without the prefix ben, 'son of,' and so the traditional rendering 'man' is misleading, and an exclusively male 'adam would make nonsense of the last clause of verse 27." See also the translation by the Jewish Publication Society (1985).

10. Owing to the humanistic backdrop of my investigation, I do not here consider accounts that treat this separation from God as a sort of death or as even worse than death.

11. As the punning makes clear, 'adam as of 'adamah, "from the soil."

12. This formulation is, of course, heterodox insofar as I am not reading the prelapsarian relation of the human to itself and to creation as prelapsarian at all.

13. To be clear, I am here translating the pun from Hebrew into English without heeding the English etymology.

14. This line does not occur in any of the other gospels. See Aland (1982, 335).

15. See, e.g., 1 Peter 2:19–25: "For it is a credit to you if, being aware of God, you endure pain [λύπας πάσχων] while suffering unjustly. . . . If you endure when you do right and suffer for it, you have God's approval. For to this you have been called, because Christ also suffered [ἔπαθεν] for you. . . . When he was abused . . . he entrusted himself to the one who judges justly. He himself bore our sins in his body on the cross, so that, free from sins, we might live for righteousness; by his wounds you have been healed." As the notes to Luke 24:26–27 point out, the soteriology based upon Isa. 53 appears often (Luke 9:22, 9:43b–45, 12:50, 13:32–33, 17:25, 18:31–34; Acts 3:18, 17:3, 26:23). (Some scholars hold Acts to be written by the author of Luke.)

16. E. P. Sanders (1977, 23) speculates in his seminal work on Paul that a "history of attitudes towards suffering in Palestinian Judaism . . . would, I think, reveal that generally human suffering was considered to be divine punishment for transgression, except during the periods of religious persecution." Paul's views on suffering are in concert with prevalent views in Rabbinic theology of at least the Tannaitic period (105–6). On the overall role of suffering in Pauline soteriology, see esp. 466–74.

17. As ultimately a question of theticism, under different hegemonic regimes, "God" can easily become "nature" or "consciousness," etc. See Schürmann (2003).

18. When Aristotle argues in the *Metaphysics* that "there is no demonstration of a principle of demonstration," I would gloss this as the claim that that which is thetic, any given theticism, is founding and ultimately so. *Metaphysics,* 1011a. Translation modified from Aristotle (1933).

19. It is for this reason that although I have focused on the Abrahamic traditions almost solely through the Genesaic cosmogony, I am content to term my discussion as dealing with "religious theories" of pain, which is not to say that there are no exceptions but only that those exceptions would, it seems to me, be precisely that: exceptions. E.g., Graeber (2011, 56), when speaking of the transition from late second millennium Vedic poems to the Brahmanas, notes that the conclusion made by the Brahmans was quite simple: "human existence is a form of debt." Cf. also Ramey (2016).

20. Nietzsche (1966, 154) put it this way: "the discipline of suffering, great suffering—do you not know that only *this* discipline has created all the enhancements of man so far?" Or, to take another paradigmatic statement, "To see others suffer does one good, to make others suffer even more. . . . Without cruelty there is no festival" (Nietzsche 1967, 67).

21. See Keele (1957, 2). In what follows, I am drawing on both on Keele and on Gustafson's summary of Keele in "Categorizing Pain" (Aydede 2005).

22. Descartes's most famous claim about pain comes in *L'homme,* published fourteen years after his death.

23. See, e.g., Wall's (2000, 177) claim that "pain is not just a sensation but, like hunger and thirst, is an awareness of an action plan to be rid of it."

24. For a general explanation of this, see Wall (2000, 40–43). For a philosophically oriented explanation, see Grahek (2007, 141–66).

25. As Melzack and Wall (2003, 7) themselves put it, "the impact of the pain revolution is revealed by the contents of this handbook. The further we move from a stimulus-driven concept of pain, the better we recognize the validity of baffling pain syndromes that often have no obvious pathology to explain the presence of pain or its terrible intensity. They include neuropathic pains, backache, fibromyalgia, pelvic, urogenital, and other pains, which become increasingly comprehensible when we extend our diagnostic search to consider multiple causal mechanisms."

26. The language of this distinction goes back at least to Melzack (1973).

27. What's more, as Don Gustafson (in Aydede 2005, 237) nicely summarizes, "not even acute pain examples (a burn of the hand or blow to the thumb, etc.) cited by philosophers and others are conceived as simple sensations in current pain sciences."

28. As an example of an argument that they are dissociable, see Grahek (2007). For an example that they are not, see Klein (2007).

29. See, e.g., Price (2000).

30. Pain's private nature is a recurring theme in humanistic inquiry, especially

that which focuses directly on questions of illness or disease. See also Frank (1991, 29) and Woolf (1994).

31. This is not to sidestep long-standing debates over the internal morality of medicine, hence my phrasing "one aspect."

32. The central line of the Maimonidean oath reads, "May I never see in the patient anything but a fellow creature in pain" (Tan 2002). See also Meldrum (2003).

33. E.g., doctors whose focus is on making the lives of persons with chronic pain more manageable now face prohibitive conditions on opioid analgesic disbursement *regardless* of the particularities of the patient—actions that range from licensure to criminal prosecution. See Thernstrom (2010, 164–67). When overlaid with the fundamental materialism of the medical sciences (i.e., the assumption that phenomena under medical purview must have *physical* manifestations—specifically, manifestations that are *quantifiable* by current technological-diagnostic procedures), the question of pain's subjectivity, a given in the clinical literature on pain, is interpreted to mean that when no physiological etiology of pain can be found, a health care provider is not automatically out of bounds to question whether the patient is lying. For example, Rogers (2008) offers a *manual* on assessing whether a patient is lying, in this case, in the context of patients with mental illness.

34. E.g., see Gustafson's summary of research spanning from the mid-1970s up to the last decade by Wall, Melzack, Craig, Price, and Chapman in Aydede (2005, 234–38). Even explicit efforts to *improve* the undertreatment of pain fall into this trap. Regarding this project, another study has questioned whether its efforts, which employ numerical rating scales, provide any better outcome parameters than simply asking for binary (yes/no) responses (Meissner 2013).

35. As Mill (Mill and Bentham 2006, 282) writes, "what means are there of determining which is the acutest of two pains, or the intensest of two pleasurable sensations, except the general suffrage of those who are familiar with both? Neither pains nor pleasures are homogeneous, and pain is always heterogeneous with pleasure. What is there to decide whether a particular pleasure is worth purchasing at the cost of a particular pain, except the feelings and judgment of the experienced."

36. See Strong (1998) and Stoller (1991). Moreover, except in the ephemerality of a moment or in the abstractions of philosophers interested in the possibility of qualia, pain is never *just* a sign and never *just* a sensation. Phenomenologies of pain, as I argue subsequently, repudiate that possibility. My invocation of the term *imperative* is not meant to align wholesale my account of pain with imperativism in philosophy of mind. Because this literature is ultimately interested in pain only, or primarily, insofar as it is revelatory concerning questions of *consciousness,* the social, political, and historical (among other) aspects of pain are often lost. Moreover, when reference is made to the "phenomenology" of pain, it sometimes borders on a malapropism, merely referring to "what X experience is like" (literature, among other fields, is often far better at describing what X expe-

rience is like—phenomenology, distinctively, is a method aimed at uncovering general structures/features of experience and/or X sorts of experience). Tellingly, reference is rarely made to the phenomenological tradition, and concerns of phenomenological method are also too rarely addressed in the literature on pain in philosophy of mind. I thus find much of the "phenomenology of pain" occurring in philosophy of mind literature to be little more than investigations of experiences described under the constraints of *common sense*. In other words, I find too little *phenomenology* of pain. Defenders of imperativism about pain include Bain (2013), Hall (2008), Martínez (2011), and Klein (2007, 2011). The primary alternative position is representationalism, which, broadly, conceives the reporting of pain to represent some fact (or perceived fact) about the world. In other words, the phenomenal experience of pain is such by virtue of that experience's representational content. Defenders of various forms of representationalism regarding pain include Cutter and Tye (2011), Pitcher (1970), and Armstrong (1993).

37. As I argue at length in the next chapter, this regulation fails, and fails spectacularly when the pain in question is either constitutive or consuming.

38. E.g., with respect to medicine, cultural, historical, class-based, and genetic cohort–related groupings ("race," "sex," etc.) can significantly affect the interpretation of pain. One will, under a medical theory of pain, still ultimately seek its cause. There is a large literature on this topic, ranging from highly specific studies focused on a single triage unit to sweeping historical and cross-cultural analyses. E.g., see Sargent (1984), Staton et al. (2007), McNeill (2007), Kleinman (1986), and Bates and Rankin-Hill (1994).

2. A Phenomenology of Chronic Pain

1. In the phenomenological description provided, I draw on the experiences of my mother. But, in addition to that, I draw on insights from the following resources: Daudet (2002), Thernstrom (2010), Kestenbaum (1982), Kleinman (1988), Jamison (2014), Coakley and Shelemay (2007), and Lorde (1997). Provocatively, Ortega y Gasset remarked in 1950 that "no one has undertaken" a "strict phenomenology of pain" (141). Agustín Serrano de Haro, whose article I address in detail later, notes that Ortega must have been unaware of Buytendijk (1949). The assumption, to be clear, is that the phenomenologies of pain found among the earliest thinkers in the phenomenological tradition, such as Brentano, Stumpf, Stein, and Husserl, were not "strict" in Ortega's sense and not "more than an example" in my sense. Geniusas (2014) presents the problematic of these early phenomenological thinkers in relation to pain as addressing the question, "Is pain a sensation or emotion?"—but with an eye to determining the phenomenality of sensation versus emotion, not to that of pain itself. Recent candidates for a "strict phenomenology of pain" include Olivier (2007) and Grüny (2004).

2. See DeGood and Kiernan (1996), Bates and Rankin-Hill (1994), and Geisser, Robinson, and Riley (1999).

3. See Corns (2012).

4. Arguments in both philosophical and clinical literature often refer to Wittgenstein's arguments against private *language* in Wittgenstein (2003, §124). On this point, see Sullivan (1995).

5. Tellingly, there is research suggesting that time spent in a pain research facility itself intensifies pain experience. See Lamé et al. (2005).

6. Studies suggest that for some people, observing pain in another activates emotional and sensory brain regions associated with pain (in addition to their reporting of an actual noxious somatic experience). See Osborn and Derbyshire (2010), De Vignemont and Singer (2006), and Jackson, Rainville, and Decety (2006). Studies also suggest that the ability to form a cohesive narrative and have it *affirmed* by health care providers provides support (Evans, Shaw, and Sharp 2012).

7. To put a finer point on this question, what are the effects of the long history of what Foucault calls the "anatomo-clinical gaze" and the redistribution of space, time, and understanding brought about by the "reductive discourse of the doctor"? (Foucault 1994). If one effect of this gaze is the *necessity* of an identifiable cause, the fact that pain is often medically unexplainable *increases* as a problem. See Greco (2012), Salmon (2007), Nettleton (2006), and De Gucht and Maes (2006).

8. Relative age and perceived life expectancy are two notable factors that alter this temporality. See Richardson, Ong, and Sim (2006) and Améry (1994).

9. Studies suggest that this is notably worse for women (e.g., Werner and Malterud 2003). Class, locale, and race are also relevant factors (Day and Thorn 2010; Good 1992; Bendelow 1993; Tait and Chibnall 2014). Moreover, as Leslie Jamison (2014, 41) observes, "I've come to understand that the distinction made here between 'real' and 'unreal' doesn't just signify physical versus mental but also implies another binary: the difference between suffering produced by a force outside the self or within it. . . . These explanations place blame back on the patient and suggest not only that the harm inflicted is less legitimate but also that it's less deserving of compassion or aid."

10. Arguably the most famous investigation of the claim that I do "have" a body but also am embodied is Merleau-Ponty (2011, 1945). For a more recent book-length study, see Leder (1990).

11. That it is a PA (a person who is obviously not one's doctor) does not make a difference. That space, the medical office where one has met that doctor for twenty years, has a history. The newcomer who fails to take the time to learn that history trespasses and betrays the trust built there. Note also that the intersubjective position of the supplicant and patient is functionally similar, as the etymology of these terms makes clear. The supplicant is bent over *(sub-plicāre)* by virtue of their petitioning, their asking or begging *(petit-iō)*. The patient, who is as *patiēns* already under the weight of *(sub-ferre)* suffering undergoes further suffering by virtue of their entreaty, the drawing-up of negotiations *(en-trahĕre)* with the practitioner.

12. Congenital analgesia or pain asymbolia is a condition where people feel pain but aren't in pain. Put differently, they experience pain, but it isn't unpleasant. Neither bad nor good, for such people, pain is something more akin to feeling a breeze. I here treat this as an exception, and my use of the term "feeling pain" is broader than the use in literatures dealing with that condition. On my definition, feeling pain always involves unpleasantness.

13. This distinction may seem counterintuitive because we do sometimes use the term "in pain" with respect to such cases. "I was in a lot of pain when I hit my elbow a moment ago." I think, however, that the distinction I am making is better at explaining the phenomenologically distinct experiences of pain in question.

3. Theories of Disability

1. There are exceptions to this claim, especially surrounding certain types of chronic illness, for example, people living with AIDS/HIV. Furthermore, an argument could be made that the landscape is quickly shifting in a U.S. context for people in chronic pain who rely on opioids given the "opioid epidemic" (Goldberg 2014). As I address later, many texts that have been definitive for disability studies in the United Kingdom claim that disability-related political activism tends to emphasize structural oppression and neglect impairment (e.g., Shakespeare and Watson 2001). In the United States, with respect to the narrower category of chronic pain support and advocacy groups, the tendency is to emphasize impairment and neglect structural oppression (see, e.g., the American Pain Foundation, American Chronic Pain Association, International Association for the Study of Pain, and Pain Connection). I owe thanks to Florian Kiuppis and a working group on disability and chronic pain at the 2013 Society for Disability Studies for many fruitful discussions on this topic.

2. One cannot think "dis/ability" without technology, for one of the primary aims of modern technology is mastery over the body. When technology changes, so do the experiences and categorizations of disability. Disability requires that we address what Eduardo Mendieta (2012) calls *technosomaticity*: the way technology and bodies mutually shape each other.

3. To clarify, that these rights have been enumerated does not mean they have been sufficiently or fully enacted. The ADA is by no means a panacea, especially with respect to resources for enforcement and its inherent limitations as merely an antidiscrimination piece of legislation. The work of Marta Russell (2002, 2019) lays this out perhaps most clearly. My thanks to Elizabeth Dietz for pushing me to clarify this point.

4. One might here argue that this definition is circular, because "ableism" involves reference to "disability." I think that objection fails. On one hand, explanations of social phenomena are likely to involve some amount of circularity insofar as the historical conditions that create the very concepts in question are themselves historical creations. I take the work of Ian Hacking, among others, to make

this abundantly clear. If social kinds loop, then we should expect some circularity. Whether a definition of such sorts of phenomena involves some circularity should not decide the matter; on the contrary, the way in which the relationship between the social kind and the experiences to which it refers captures the determinate aspects of the phenomenon under consideration should decide the matter.

5. While various authors have provided overviews of theories of disability, these have been comparatively narrower in scope than what follows (see, e.g., Albrecht, Seelman, and Bury 2001; Wasserman et al. 2013). These overviews have also been primarily descriptive. My aim here is instead ultimately analytic in the hope of uncovering the larger conceptual structures undergirding and orienting these theories.

6. I agree with Sally Haslanger (2012) that social theories should not be merely descriptive but also ameliorative. That is to say, they should explain social phenomena such that adopting that explanation would make the world a better place. While I find this crucial, I take what I am doing in this chapter to not in fact be guided by ameliorative aims (that occurs instead in chapter 5 and, most specifically, chapter 6). On the contrary, I take myself, rightly or wrongly, as engaged in an attempt to analyze how theories of disability function.

7. A substantial literature within and on the periphery of disability studies argues for alternate understandings of disability within various theological frameworks, including those of liberation theology. Although I find such readings important and powerful in multiple respects, I do not address them in this book given the aims at hand.

8. Each of these terms is used in ancient Hebrew both literally and figuratively. Being without sight (עִוֵּר) is being without intelligence, as we also remark in modern English. As an aside, it is worth asking whether Moses is presented as having a speech "disorder" in the previous verse, when he says to God, "I am slow of speech and slow of tongue." His dysfluency is further contrasted with that of his brother Aaron a few verses later in 4:14. On the treatment of "speech disorders" and disability, see Eagle (2014) and St. Pierre (2015).

9. Or take Deuteronomy 7:18: "Cursed be anyone who misleads a blind [עִוֵּר] man on the road."

10. The meaning of blemish (מוּם) is understood as a stain, as a mark, that is either physical or moral (Strong 1996).

11. The word for "poor" is *ptochos,* literally "bent over," and is typically used to refer to one completely lacking resources. "Crippled" renders *anapeirous,* with -*ana* intensifying *peros,* which means "maimed" or "lame." This term can also be used figuratively (Aristotle speaks of those "*peperomenos pros areten,*" those incapacitated or unable to reach virtue). "Lame" translates *cholos,* which is literally "halted," dating back to Homeric usage, and "blind" translates *tuphlos,* literally "without sight," but it has both a literal and a figurative meaning, as with the Hebrew (Strong 1996).

12. To be clear, the act of "healing" is not straightforward here. This could

be read as a testament to the social model of disability: the "paralytic" is paralyzed by society, by the understanding that their paralysis is a product of their sin (or the sin of their family). When Jesus supports this person by disentangling the question of sin from their impairment, when Jesus makes their "disability" a question of societal norms and not intrinsic impairments, they are then able to walk. On such a reading, this narrative scene functions as a powerful metaphor of the way in which given social representations determine the *ability* of the people in that society, in that *polis*. To sufficiently address this, I would, at minimum, first have to broach the connection of *logos* with power *(kratos)* and being *(ontos)* in the Christian New Testament, specifically in the Gospel of John. Second, I would need to engage with liberationist interpretations of passages like this—readings that, whatever their merits, often run against the grain of historically dominant interpretations. Sadly, I cannot take on either such task here.

13. That disability would qualify as an exteriorizing category is also shown in verse 48:17, where, while speaking of fighting for the cause of Allah, the "blind, the lame, and the sick" are allowed to stay behind.

14. Bazna and Hatab (2005, 13) have argued that the Qur'an provides an understanding of disability that downplays individual impairments and instead valorizes "the degree with which" one seeks "the truth." They interpret the verse quoted earlier as communicating that "people with disabilities are to be treated with full regard to have the same subject-to-subject relations that are granted to the non-disabled."

15. As a reminder, for stylistic reasons, at times I speak of "models" and at other times of "theories," and the reader should take these terms to be synonymous.

16. There are some who distinguish the medical model from a rehabilitation model, which focuses more specifically (and in some senses carefully) on norms regarding function. Although this distinction is useful in certain contexts, I will here take the rehabilitation model as a variation of the medical model.

17. Similar patterns occur in Lewis et al. (2014).

18. Given the size of the literature of these areas, no sufficient literature review could be done to properly back up this claim. If one is skeptical, I suggest picking up a few such texts and testing out my hypothesis.

19. With the momentous shift from the humoral theory of Hippocrates and Galen to the germ theory of Louis Pasteur in the 1860s, symptomatology took a decisive turn inward. This led from explanatory schemas, such as nutritional disease (disease is produced not by microbes but by deficient nutrient) and autoimmune disease (disease is produced by the immune system attacking bodily tissue instead of infectious agents) to molecular genetic disease (disease is produced by the abnormal functioning of the patient's DNA) and Mendelian disease (disease is produced by the inheritance of a recessive mutated gene from both parents) (Thagard 1999, 20–36). Amid these revolutionary shifts in the understanding of the foundations of pathologies came the ability to explain not only

various diseases in terms of scientific etiology but any psychophysical difference, for "disease" is itself a category that relies on the distinction of "normal/abnormal" (Canguilhem 1978). To overly simplify things, as the ability to explain why people suffer (etiology) grew immensely, explanations for how people suffer (pathologies) grew.

20. See OED, s.v. "semiosis," "semiotic," and "sign"—whose oldest etymological roots trace back to the ancient Greek σῆμα, "sign" (see "seme"), and σημεῖον, "sign."

21. In the United States, the most obvious gain has been the landmark passage of the ADA in 1990, an act that created the largest legally protected minority identity in the country's history: people with disabilities. The social model is also at the backbone of large international human rights treaties, including the United Nations' 2006 Convention on the Rights of Persons with Disabilities.

22. Unlike the International Classification of Diseases, which focused on causes, the ICIDH focused on consequences of "disease" (World Health Organization 2001). Three of the largest differences between the ICIDH and Nagi's model are the joining of impairment and functional limitation, the definition of "disability" relative to abilities performed "in normal manner," and the restriction of "sociocultural factors" to the disadvantage that *either* impairment or disability brings about. The ICIDH is today referred to as the ICF, short for ICFDH: International Classification of Functioning, Disability, and Health.

23. I think this argument is too fast, but it would be a sidetrack to delve into why here. For a more detailed account of my concerns regarding this way of conceiving of impairment, see Reynolds (2021).

24. See note 23.

25. Careful readers will wonder why I don't bring up another side of the way in which disability is presented as a problem to be solved: what Scuro (2017) refers to as dismemberment and what Puar (2017) refers to as debility. These are ways of naming how unjust social structures and arrangements, in particular ableist ones, *make* people impaired and/or disabled in various ways. As the mea culpa in my introduction hopefully made clear (note that both of those books were published after the bulk of this project was done), this is one of the issues I hope to address in great detail in my next book, which is tentatively titled *The Meaning of Disability*.

26. Historical connections between the monstrous and various forms of disability are telling here (Eyler 2010; Metzler 2013). The *body that should be* is constantly formed through the powers that determine what a body is, just as *the bodies that are* are constantly formed through the powers that determine how bodies should be. Desire, always formed through perceived possibilities, seeks to act upon the body it takes to be present, but that body is determined above all else in terms of ability expectations. The "monstrous" offers the imaginary the hither side of ability expectations through the magnification of certain abilities along with the magnification of certain physical characteristics.

4. A Phenomenology of Multiple Sclerosis

1. This is related to claims I would make about how "health" can function as an illusion or, more precisely, a reverie. See Reynolds (2022).

2. Although research suggests that MS involves both genetic and epigenetic factors, the precise cause is still unknown. As medical historian Colin Talley (2008, xiii) explains in more detail, "multiple sclerosis (MS) is a disease of the brain and spinal cord that usually strikes adults between the ages of twenty and fifty and affects women more than men by a ratio of two to one. In the United States, estimates of the number of people with MS range from 266,000 to 400,000. Some argue that it may be even higher, but it is hard to know because of the difficulty in diagnosis, lack of access to health care for many, and unavailability of neurological expertise for some. The International Multiple Sclerosis Federation estimates that there are over 2.5 million cases of the disease worldwide. It has been established that there is a genetic predisposition for the disease. At some point there is an environmental assault which allows immune system cells to make it past the blood–brain barrier. The immune system then attacks cells in the central nervous system as if they were invading pathogens. . . . As the body tries to repair the damaged tissues, there is an overgrowth of glial or connective tissue between neurons. . . . Depending on where the damage occurs in the central nervous system, neural transmission and communication are disrupted, and various symptoms varying widely in form, pattern, and intensity are expressed. . . . The disease process is a continual one; it is only the symptoms that often remit and relapse over the course of many years and decades."

3. Nancy Eiesland (1994, 43) makes a comment along these lines when describing the experience Nancy Mairs had of MS: "She gained an awareness of her body that she had never had before" (see also Mairs 1996).

4. Reprinted as "Reflections on Bodily Change: The Lived Experience of Disability" in Toombs (2001).

5. It is perhaps worth noting that human organisms are left out "by design" with respect to well over 99 percent of the known universe.

6. One of the more worrisome gaps in Toombs's account concerns race (she talks a bit about sex and gender, and almost nothing about sexuality, all of which leaves one wishing for far more to be said). She does not name or reflect upon the ways that being white shapes her experiences of MS. Though it seems to me the tide is slowly turning, it sadly goes without saying that the intersection of ableism and racism (and especially anti-Black racism) is understudied in phenomenology, philosophy of disability, and disability studies. I address this in far greater detail, including engagement with the relatively small body of work that has in fact been done up to this point, in my forthcoming monograph.

7. I take it as obvious that these claims would need to be modified for congenital disability. I understand Toombs's account—or, rather, my analysis of her phenomenological account—not only to leave room for such modification but

to offer insights into what would help more clearly distinguish such lived experiences of disability.

8. An uncharitable reader might claim that the concept of "disability" does not receive the critical attention it should in Toombs's work. For example, in the article "Sufficient unto the Day," Toombs first deploys the word *disability* as a synonym for *dependency*. She writes that after her divorce, "for the first time I wondered if I would be able to manage on my own. The fear that I might become disabled intensified my anxiety about the future. I had always been very independent" (10). In the following paragraphs, she describes the progressive stages of her MS as a "gradual progression of disability" but then switches back to speaking of illness thereafter (10–11). It becomes clear that Toombs often employs the term *disability* under the auspices of a personal theory of disability, specifically the medical model, even though that use and understanding of the term are not in fact borne out by her own phenomenological investigation. Toombs presses over and over again how her self-perception of lacking a given ability is always in a dialectical relation with her socially and medically influenced pre- and postdiagnosis ability expectations. Tellingly, at no point in her phenomenology would it make sense to say "she is here speaking of disability." She describes the way ability transitions lead to sometimes minor, sometimes grave negotiations of personal ability expectations along with those of specific people, such as her first husband. She describes successes, such as getting her PhD, that would be judged as successes without qualification, successes that fly in the face of the "no future" to which the MS Society's prophesies condemned her. She describes stigmatization. She describes the specific effects of specific conditions in specific scenarios. She describes her expectations altering multiple times. Though I certainly think engagement with the field of disability studies would have enriched her analysis in many respects, a careful reading shows that Toombs's account is, when all is said and done, quite sophisticated in its treatment of the concept of disability, in many ways illuminating and providing more precision to the insights of social models.

5. Theories of Ability

1. That project is under way: *The Meaning of Disability* (the current, tentative title).

2. For the purposes at hand, I will gloss over a number of historical and philosophical issues related to the term *perfect*. Perfect relative to the discourses of health and medicine, the world of high fashion, Hollywood films, or what? Perfect relative to which historical time period or human culture? None of these are the same, and I consciously use the term here without qualification to allow for this range of ambiguity. I thus deploy it as a placeholder for whatever ideals of the body hold sway in a given situation or context. For a helpful discussion of the distinction between the ideal and the normal body, see Davis (1995).

3. This link is reflected in the Greek concept of *dunamis* as well. See Thesaurus Linguae Graecae, s.v. "δύναμις, εως."

4. As I argue later, even a simple distinction between individual, social, and human abilities demonstrates how the theory of personal ability is reductionist in ways that undermine the possibility of justice in even the thinnest of forms.

5. The trial over the death and torture of Eric Krochmaluk being an exception (Macfarquhar 1999).

6. As will, I hope, be obvious, I am avoiding storied debates over the meaning of health within the philosophy of medicine. My ends and concerns are different than those in that debate. Having said that, the best recent analysis, by my lights, is Kukla (2015).

7. Cf. Campbell and Stramondo (2017, 166), who discuss hitchhiker's thumb as an ability that doesn't (at least in this world—as far as anyone knows) have any value.

8. To more thoroughly analyze the concept of ability would require analyzing both ontological realities and also sociopolitical imaginaries, including what Ellen Samuels (2014) sagely calls *fantasies of (mis)identification.* See note 1 and the acknowledgments for the mea culpa concerning the limits of this and other chapters' investigations.

9. The effects of structural poverty are a powerful example of this. As the saying in social epidemiology goes, one's zip code is a better predictor of health than one's genome. As a further example, gluten allergies are typically represented as an individual "issue," whereas the near ubiquity of gluten in American food options is due in large part not to "how food is or should be made" but instead to cost-cutting practices ultimately rooted in profit-driven, capitalistic logics that have subsidized particular industries over others.

10. As Elizabeth Dietz noted to me, there are some examples: roadside sobriety tests, counting in the context of going under general anesthesia for a surgical procedure, and so on. But these are hyperspecific examples that, it seems to me, do not undercut the actual point being made here.

11. The 2001 U.S. Supreme Court case between Casey Martin and the PGA Tour, *PGA Tour, Inc. v. Martin,* further demonstrates the ambiguity of determining which abilities are "proper" or "essential" relative to a given domain, in this case whether or not walking during the last third of the qualifying tournament was an essential part of the ability to play golf (Cherney 2015; Parent 2002; Davis 1998).

6. A Phenomenology of Ability

1. A large body of humanistic and social scientific work could be marshaled to defend this thesis. Among other sources, see Reynolds (2016a), Piepzna-Samarasinha (2018), and Butler (2012).

2. A note on method: I here provide what could most accurately be called a *critical phenomenology* of ability (one that ends up showing that abilities are functions of caring relations and caring systems). In line with the growing number of proponents of critical phenomenology, I dub the following phenomenology

critical because of the way it deals with the social dimensions of lived experience across the levels of reduction, construction, and destruction (to invoke the three moments of the phenomenological method as Heidegger [(1927) 1982]) articulates them. This is the dimension that includes both and also operates between what Heidegger narrowly and problematically separated as the ontic and the ontological. This, I'd argue, is the dimension that Fanon insightfully termed the "sociogenic" and that Foucault analyzed in terms of the "historical a priori." On my understanding of critical phenomenology, it operates in a methodological space between traditional forms of phenomenology (whether transcendental, generative, hermeneutic, etc.) and critical theory. Because, along with the semantic, one must always heed pragmatic and rhetorical effects, the description that follows is in a narrative and stylized mode (cf. Paul Ricouer's work). My aim is, on one hand, to describe the lived experiences of the subjects in question under a version of the *epoche* and, on the other, to attend to the ways that one both cannot and should not "bracket" all of the relevant dimensions of the phenomenon under consideration. Indeed, the aspiration to suspend the natural attitude may in certain cases be precisely that which blocks one from more accurately seeing the phenomenon in question. Practically, this means that when I move to the (re)constructive moment and lay out the general structures revealed by the prior description under reduction, I include critical social analyses along with the more typical attention to general structures of first-person lived experience, and I heed the manner in which the latter are informed by histories of language, interpretation, and practice. Owing to space limitations, I only hint at the destructive or, if one reads Derrida, deconstructive stage, wherein I would engage in a critical analysis of the very concepts underwriting both the descriptive and the reconstructive stages.

3. See Carter (2018); see also National Center for Health Statistics (2017).

Conclusion

1. On this question, I have learned much from Kafer (2013) and Garland-Thomson (1997, 2015a).

Bibliography

Adorno, Theodor. 2007. *Negative Dialectics.* Translated by E. B. Ashton. New York: Continuum.

Adorno, Theodor. 2017. "A Conversation with Theodor W. Adorno (Spiegel, 1969)." https://cominsitu.wordpress.com/2015/09/01/a-conversation -with-theodor-w-adorno-spiegel-1969/.

Aeschylus. 2011. *The Complete Aeschylus.* 2 vols. Greek Tragedy in New Translations. Oxford: Oxford University Press.

Aland, Kurt. 1982. *Synopsis of the Four Gospels: Completely Revised on the Basis of the Greek Text of the Nestle-Aland 26th Edition and Greek New Testament 3rd Edition: The Text Is the Second Edition of the Revised Standard Version.* English ed. New York: United Bible Societies.

Albrecht, Gary L. 2006. *Encyclopedia of Disability.* 5 vols. Thousand Oaks, Calif.: Sage.

Albrecht, Gary L., and Patrick J. Devlieger. 1999. "The Disability Paradox: High Quality of Life Against All Odds." *Social Science and Medicine* 48 (8): 977–88. https://doi.org/10.1016/S0277-9536(98)00411-0.

Albrecht, Gary L., Katherine D. Seelman, and Michael Bury. 2001. *Handbook of Disability Studies.* Thousand Oaks, Calif.: Sage.

Alter, Robert. 1996. *Genesis.* New York: W. W. Norton.

Améry, Jean. 1994. *On Aging: Revolt and Resignation.* Bloomington: Indiana University Press.

Aristotle. 1926. *The Nicomachean Ethics.* Translated by H. Rackham. Loeb Classical Library. London: W. Heinemann/G. P. Putnam.

Aristotle. 1933. *The Metaphysics.* Translated by Hugh Tredennick and G. Cyril Armstrong. 2 vols. Loeb Classical Library Greek Authors. London: W. Heinemann/G. P. Putnam.

Aristotle. 1984. *The Complete Works of Aristotle: The Revised Oxford Translation.* Edited by Jonathan Barnes. 2 vols. Bollingen Series. Princeton, N.J.: Princeton University Press.

Aristotle. 1999. *Nicomachean Ethics.* Translated by Terence Irwin. 2nd ed. Indianapolis, Ind.: Hackett.

Armstrong, D. M. 1993. *A Materialist Theory of the Mind.* Rev. ed. International Library of Philosophy. London: Routledge.

Armstrong, Lucile. 1970. "Fire-Walking at San Pedro Manrique, Spain." *Folklore* 81 (3): 198–214. https://doi.org/10.2307/1259267.

Aydede, Murat. 2005. *Pain: New Essays on Its Nature and the Methodology of Its Study.* Cambridge, Mass.: MIT Press.

Baden, Joel S. 2012. *The Composition of the Pentateuch: Renewing the Documentary Hypothesis.* Anchor Yale Bible Reference Library. New Haven, Conn.: Yale University Press.

Bain, David. 2013. "Pains That Don't Hurt." *Australasian Journal of Philosophy* 92 (2): 305–20. https://doi.org/10.1080/00048402.2013.822399.

Barnartt, Sharon. 2010. *Disability as a Fluid State.* Research in Social Science and Disability 5. Bradford, U.K.: Emerald Group.

Barnes, Elizabeth. 2016. *The Minority Body.* New York: Oxford University Press.

Bates, Maryann S., and Lesley Rankin-Hill. 1994. "Control, Culture and Chronic Pain." *Social Science and Medicine* 39 (5): 629–45. https://doi.org/10.1016/0277-9536(94)90020-5.

Bauby, Jean-Dominique. 1997. *The Diving Bell and the Butterfly.* New York: Knopf.

Bazna, Maysaa S., and Tarek A. Hatab. 2005. "Disability in the Qur'an." *Journal of Religion, Disability, and Health* 9 (1): 5–27. https://doi.org/10.1300/J095v09n01_02.

Beauvoir, Simone de. 2011. *The Second Sex.* Translated by Constance Borde and Sheila Malovany-Chevallier. New York: Vintage Books.

Bendelow, Gillian. 1993. "Pain Perceptions, Emotions and Gender." *Sociology of Health and Illness* 15 (3): 273–94. https://doi.org/10.1111/1467-9566.ep10490526.

Bergson, Henri. 1944. *Creative Evolution.* Translated by Arthur Mitchell. New York: Modern Library.

Bourke, Joanna. 2014. *The Story of Pain: From Prayer to Painkillers.* New York: Oxford University Press.

Brennan, Teresa. 2004. *The Transmission of Affect.* Ithaca, N.Y.: Cornell University Press.

Buchanan, Allen E., Dan Brock, Norman Daniels, and Daniel Wilker. 2000. *From Chance to Choice: Genetics and Justice.* Cambridge: Cambridge University Press.

Butler, Samuel A. 2012. "A Fourth Subject Position of Care." *Hypatia* 27 (2): 390–406.

Buytendijk, F. J. J. 1949. *Über den Schmerz; aus dem Holländischen übersetzt.* Bern, Switzerland: H. Huber.

Campbell, Fiona Kumari. 2001. "Inciting Legal Fictions: 'Disability's' Date with Ontology and the Ableist Body of Law." *Griffith Law Review* 42: 42–62.

Campbell, Fiona Kumari. 2005. "Legislating Disability: Negative Ontologies and the Government of Legal Identities." In *Foucault and the Government of Disability,* edited by Shelley Tremain, 108–32. Ann Arbor: University of Michigan Press.

Campbell, Fiona Kumari. 2009. *Contours of Ableism: The Production of Disability and Abledness.* New York: Palgrave Macmillan.

Campbell, Steven M., and Joseph A. Stramondo. 2017. "The Complicated Relationship of Disability and Well-Being." *Kennedy Institute of Ethics Journal* 27 (2): 151–84.

Canguilhem, Georges. 1978. *On the Normal and the Pathological.* Studies in the History of Modern Science. Boston: D. Reidel.

Carel, Havi. 2013. *Illness.* Revised ed. London: Acumen.

Carel, Havi. 2016. *Phenomenology of Illness.* New York: Oxford University Press.

Carter, Shawn. 2018. "Over Half of Americans Delay or Don't Get Health Care Because They Can't Afford It—These 3 Treatments Get Put Off Most." *CNBS: Make It,* November 29. https://www.cnbc.com/2018/11/29/over -half-of-americans-delay-health-care-becasue-they-cant-afford-it.html.

Charon, Rita. 2006. *Narrative Medicine: Honoring the Stories of Illness.* Oxford: Oxford University Press.

Cherney, James L. 2015. "Sport, (Dis)Ability, and Public Controversy: Ableist Rhetoric and *Casey Martin v. PGA Tour, Inc.*" In *Case Studies in Sport Communication,* edited by James L. Cherney, Kurt Lindemann, Marie Hardin, Michael L. Butterworth, and Jeffrey W. Kassing, 81–104. Westport, Conn.: Praeger.

Clare, Eli. 2015 [1999]. *Exile and Pride: Disability, Queerness, and Liberation.* Durham, N.C.: Duke University Press.

Coakley, Sarah, and Kay Kaufman Shelemay. 2007. *Pain and Its Transformations: The Interface of Biology and Culture.* Cambridge, Mass.: Harvard University Press.

Corns, Jennifer. 2012. "Pain Is Not a Natural Kind." PhD diss., City University of New York.

Craig, Kenneth D. 1995. "From Nociception to Pain: The Role of Emotion." In *Pain and the Brain: From Nociception to Cognition,* Advances in Paid Research and Therapy 22, edited by B. Bromm and J. E. Desmedt, 303–17. Philadelphia: Lippincott-Raven.

Crawford, Robert. 1980. "Healthism and the Medicalization of Everyday Life." *International Journal of Health Services* 10 (3): 365–88. https://doi.org/ 10.2190/3H2H-3XJN-3KAY-G9NY.

Crombez, G., C. Eccleston, F. Baeyens, and P. Eelen. 1998. "When Somatic Information Threatens, Catastrophic Thinking Enhances Attentional Interference." *Pain* 75: 187–98.

Crosby, Christina. 2016. *A Body, Undone: Living on after Great Pain.* New York: New York University Press.

Cutter, B., and M. Tye. 2011. "Tracking Representationalism and the Painfulness of Pain." *Nous-Supplement: Philosophical Issues* 21 (1): 90–109. https:// doi.org/10.1111/j.1533-6077.2011.00199.x.

Daudet, Alphonse. 2002. *In the Land of Pain*. Translated by Julian Barnes. 1st American ed. New York: Knopf.

David, H. 2011. *The Unsustainable Rise of the Disability Rolls in the United States: Causes, Consequences, and Policy Options*. Washington, D.C.: National Bureau of Economic Research.

Davis, Lennard J. 1995. *Enforcing Normalcy: Disability, Deafness, and the Body*. London: Verso.

Davis, Lennard J. 2013a. *The Disability Studies Reader*. 4th ed. New York: Routledge.

Davis, Lennard J. 2013b. *The End of Normal: Identity in a Biocultural Era*. Ann Arbor: University of Michigan Press.

Davis, Lennard J. 2015. *Enabling Acts: The Hidden Story of How the Americans with Disabilities Act Gave the Largest US Minority Its Rights*. Boston: Beacon Press.

Davis, W. Kent. 1998. "Why Is the PGA Teed Off at Casey Martin? An Example of How the Americans with Disabilities Act (ADA) Has Changed Sports Law." *Marquette Sports Law Journal* 9 (1): 1–44.

Dawood, N. J., trans. 1990. *The Koran*. 5th rev. ed. Penguin Classics. London: Penguin Books.

Day, Melissa A., and Beverly E. Thorn. 2010. "The Relationship of Demographic and Psychosocial Variables to Pain-Related Outcomes in a Rural Chronic Pain Population." *PAIN* 151 (2): 467–74. https://doi.org/10.1016/j.pain.2010.08.015.

DeGood, Douglas E., and Brian Kiernan. 1996. "Perception of Fault in Patients with Chronic Pain." *Pain* 64 (1): 153–59. https://doi.org/10.1016/0304-3959(95)00090-9.

De Gucht, Véronique, and Stan Maes. 2006. "Explaining Medically Unexplained Symptoms: Toward a Multidimensional, Theory-Based Approach to Somatization." *Journal of Psychosomatic Research* 60 (4): 349–52. https://doi.org/10.1016/j.jpsychores.2006.01.021.

DeLaune, Sue C., and Patricia K. Ladner. 2011. *Fundamentals of Nursing: Standards and Practice*. Delmar: Cengage Learning.

Derrida, Jacques. 1982. *Margins of Philosophy*. Translated by Alan Bass. Chicago: University of Chicago Press.

DeShong, Scott. 2012. "On (Post)Human (Dis)Ability." *Subjectivity: International Journal of Critical Psychology* 5 (3): 265–75. https://doi.org/10.1057/sub.2012.15.

De Vignemont, Frederique, and Tania Singer. 2006. "The Empathic Brain: How, When and Why?" *Trends in Cognitive Sciences* 10 (10): 435–41.

Dickinson, Emily. 1960. *The Complete Poems of Emily Dickinson*. Edited by Thomas H. Johnson. Boston: Little, Brown, and Company.

Dohmen, Josh. 2016. "A Little of Her Language." *Res Philosophica* 93 (4).

Dostoevsky, Fyodor. 2002. *The Brothers Karamazov*. Trans. Richard Pevear and Larissa Volkhonsky. New York: Farrar, Straus, and Giroux.

Eagle, Christopher. 2014. *Literature, Speech Disorders, and Disability: Talking Normal*. Routledge Interdisciplinary Perspectives on Literature. New York: Routledge.

Eccleston, Christopher, and Geert Crombez. 2007. "Worry and Chronic Pain: A Misdirected Problem Solving Model." *PAIN* 132 (3): 233–36. https://doi.org/10.1016/j.pain.2007.09.014.

Eccleston, Chris, Amanda C. De C. Williams, and Wendy Stainton Rogers. 1997. "Patients' and Professionals' Understandings of the Causes of Chronic Pain: Blame, Responsibility and Identity Protection." *Social Science and Medicine* 45 (5): 699–709. https://doi.org/10.1016/S0277-9536(96) 00404-2.

Eiesland, Nancy L. 1994. *The Disabled God: Toward a Liberatory Theology of Disability*. Nashville, Tenn.: Abingdon Press.

Emanuel, Mike. 2014. "Census Figures Show More than One-Third of Americans Receiving Welfare Benefits." *Fox News*, August 29. http://www.foxnews.com/politics/2014/08/29/census-figures-show-more-than-one-third-americans-receiving-welfare-benefits/.

Erevelles, Nirmala. 2011. *Disability and Difference in Global Contexts: Enabling a Transformative Body Politic*. New York: Palgrave Macmillan.

Evans, Maggie, Ali Shaw, and Debbie Sharp. 2012. "Integrity in Patients' Stories: 'Meaning-Making' through Narrative in Supportive Cancer Care." *European Journal of Integrative Medicine* 4 (1): 11–18. https://doi.org/10.1016/j.eujim.2011.12.005.

Eyler, Joshua. 2010. *Disability in the Middle Ages: Reconsiderations and Reverberations*. Farnham, U.K.: Ashgate.

Fineman, Martha. 2004. *The Autonomy Myth: A Theory of Dependency*. New York: New Press.

Foucault, Michel. 1973. *The Order of Things: An Archaeology of the Human Sciences*. New York: Vintage Books.

Foucault, Michel. 1994. *The Birth of the Clinic: An Archaeology of Medical Perception*. New York: Vintage Books.

Frank, Arthur W. 1991. *At the Will of the Body: Reflections on Illness*. Boston: Houghton Mifflin.

Friedman, Marilyn. 1987. "Beyond Caring: The De-Moralization of Gender." *Canadian Journal of Philosophy* 17: 87–110.

Gabriel, Joseph M., and Daniel S. Goldberg. 2014. "Big Pharma and the Problem of Disease Inflation." *International Journal of Health Services* 44 (2): 307–22.

Galen. 1968. *On the Usefulness of the Parts of the Body. (Peri Chreias Morion.) (De Usu Partium.)*. Translated by Margaret Tallmadge May. Ithaca, N.Y.: Cornell University Press.

Garland-Thomson, Rosemarie. 1997. *Extraordinary Bodies: Figuring Physical Disability in American Culture and Literature*. New York: Columbia University Press.

Garland-Thomson, Rosemarie. 2011. "Misfits: A Feminist Materialist Disability Concept." *Hypatia* 26 (3): 591–609.

Garland-Thomson, Rosemarie. 2012. "The Case for Conserving Disability." *Journal of Bioethical Inquiry* 9 (3): 339–55. https://doi.org/10.1007/s11673-012-9380-0.

Garland-Thomson, Rosemarie. 2013. "Integrating Disability, Transforming Feminist Theory." In *The Disability Studies Reader,* 4th ed., edited by Lennard J. Davis, 333–53. New York: Routledge.

Garland-Thomson, Rosemarie. 2015a. "A Habitable World: Harriet McBryde Johnson's 'Case for My Life.'" *Hypatia* 30 (1): 300–306.

Garland-Thomson, Rosemarie. 2015b. "Human Biodiversity Conservation: A Consensual Ethical Principle." *American Journal of Bioethics* 15 (6): 13–15. https://doi.org/10.1080/15265161.2015.1028663.

Garland-Thomson, Rosemarie. 2017. "Disability Bioethics: From Theory to Practice." *Kennedy Institute of Ethics Journal* 27 (2): 323–39. https://doi.org/10.1353/ken.2017.0020.

Geisser, Michael E., Michael E. Robinson, and Joseph L. Riley III. 1999. "Pain Beliefs, Coping, and Adjustment to Chronic Pain: Let's Focus More on the Negative." *Pain Forum* 8 (4): 161–68. https://doi.org/10.1016/S1082-3174(99)70001-2.

Geniusas, Saulius. 2014. "The Origins of the Phenomenology of Pain: Brentano, Stumpf and Husserl." *Continental Philosophy Review* 47 (1): 1–17. https://doi.org/10.1007/s11007-014-9283-3.

Gibson, James J. 1979. *The Ecological Approach to Visual Perception.* Boston: Houghton Mifflin.

Gilroy, Paul. 2000. *Against Race: Imagining Political Culture beyond the Color Line.* Cambridge, Mass.: Belknap Press of Harvard University Press.

Goffman, Erving. 1963. *Stigma: Notes on the Management of Spoiled Identity.* Englewood Cliffs, N.J.: Prentice Hall.

Goldberg, Daniel S. 2012. "Pain without Lesion: Debate among American Neurologists, 1850–1900." *Interdisciplinary Studies in the Long Nineteenth Century,* no. 15.

Goldberg, Daniel S. 2014. *The Bioethics of Pain Management: Beyond Opioids.* Routledge Annals of Bioethics. New York: Routledge, Taylor and Francis Group.

Goldberg, Daniel S., and Ben Rich. 2014. "Pharmacovigilance and the Plight of Chronic Pain Patients: In Pursuit of a Realistic and Responsible Ethic of Care." *Indiana Health Law Review* 11 (1): 83–120.

Golden, Mark. 1981. "Demography and the Exposure of Girls at Athens." *Phoenix* 35 (4): 316.

Good, Mary-Jo DelVecchio. 1992. *Pain as Human Experience: An Anthropological Perspective.* Comparative Studies of Health Systems and Medical Care. Berkeley: University of California Press.

Graeber, David. 2011. *Debt: The First 5,000 Years.* Brooklyn, N.Y.: Melville House.

Grahek, Nikola. 2007. *Feeling Pain and Being in Pain*. Cambridge, Mass.: MIT Press.

Greco, Monica. 2012. "The Classification and Nomenclature of 'Medically Unexplained Symptoms': Conflict, Performativity and Critique." *Social Science and Medicine* 75 (12): 2362–69. https://doi.org/10.1016/j.socscimed.2012.09.010.

Grüny, Christian. 2004. *Zerstörte Erfahrung: Eine Phänomenologie des Schmerzes, Wittener kulturwissenschaftliche Studien*. Würzburg, Germany: Königshausen und Neumann.

Guenther, Lisa. 2013. *Solitary Confinement: Social Death and Its Afterlives*. Minneapolis: University of Minnesota Press.

Guilmette, Lauren. 2016. "Feminist Philosophies of Disability, Foucault, and the Ethics of Curiosity." *APA Newsletter on Philosophy and Medicine* 16 (1): 46–50.

Hacking, Ian. 1999. *The Social Construction of What?* Cambridge, Mass.: Harvard University Press.

Hall, Melinda. 2016. *The Bioethics of Enhancement: Transhumanism, Disability, and Biopolitics*. Lanham, Md.: Rowman and Littlefield.

Hall, Richard J. 2008. "If It Itches, Scratch!" *Australasian Journal of Philosophy* 86 (4): 525–35. https://doi.org/10.1080/00048400802346813.

Hamraie, Aimi. 2017. *Building Access: Universal Design and the Politics of Disability*. Minneapolis: University of Minnesota Press.

Harris, Scott Jordan. 2014. "Despicable Memes: How 'Miracle' Jokes and Inspiration Porn Demean Disabled People." *Slate*, August. https://slate.com/technology/2014/08/miracle-memes-and-inspiration-porn-internet-viral-images-demean-disabled-people.html.

Haslanger, Sally. 2012. *Resisting Reality: Social Construction and Social Critique*. Oxford: Oxford University Press.

Hayward, Hsien. 2013. "Posttraumatic Growth and Disability: On Happiness, Positivity, and Meaning." PhD diss., Harvard University. https://dash.harvard.edu/handle/1/11156671.

Heidegger, Martin. (1927) 1982. *The Basic Problems of Phenomenology*. Translated by Albert Hofstadter. Bloomington: Indiana University Press.

Heidegger, Martin. 2010. *Being and Time*. Translated by Joan Stambaugh. SUNY Series in Contemporary Continental Philosophy. Albany: State University of New York Press.

Held, Virginia. 2006. *The Ethics of Care: Personal, Political, and Global*. Oxford: Oxford University Press.

Hendren, Sara. 2020. *What Can a Body Do?: How We Meet the Built World*. New York: Riverhead Books.

Henry, Michel. 1975. *Philosophy and Phenomenology of the Body*. The Hague: Nijhoff.

Holmes, Oliver Wendell, and U.S. Supreme Court. 1927. "U.S. Reports: *Buck v. Bell*, 274 U.S. 200." https://www.loc.gov/item/usrep274200/.

Huebner, Bryce. 2016. Review of *Cognitive Pluralism,* by Steven Horst. *Notre Dame Philosophical Reviews,* September.

Hughes, Bill, and Kevin Paterson. 1997. "The Social Model of Disability and the Disappearing Body: Towards a Sociology of Impairment," *Disability & Society* 12 (3): 325–40. doi: 10.1080/09687599727209.

Hughes, Bill. 1999. "The Constitution of Impairment: Modernity and the Aesthetic of Oppression." *Disability and Society* 14 (2): 155–72. https://doi .org/10.1080/09687599926244.

Hughes, Bill. 2007. "Being Disabled: Towards a Critical Social Ontology for Disability Studies." *Disability and Society* 22 (7): 673–84. https://doi.org/ 10.1080/09687590701659527.

Hull, John. 1997. *On Sight and Insight: A Journey into the World of Blindness.* London: Oneworld.

Husserl, Edmund. 1983. *Ideas Pertaining to a Pure Phenomenology and To a Phenomenological Philosophy: First Book: General Introduction to a Pure Phenomenology.* Translated by F. Kersten. *Collected Works,* vol. 2. The Hague; Boston: M. Nijhoff; Kluwer Boston.

Husserl, Edmund. 1989. *Ideas Pertaining to a Pure Phenomenology and To a Phenomenological Philosophy: Second Book: Studies in the Phenomenology of Constitution.* Translated by Richard Rojcewicz and Andre Schuwer. *Collected Works,* vol. 3. The Hague; Boston: M. Nijhoff.

Jackson, Philip L., Pierre Rainville, and Jean Decety. 2006. "To What Extent Do We Share the Pain of Others? Insight from the Neural Bases of Pain Empathy." *Pain* 125 (1): 5–9.

James, William. 1967. *The Writings of William James: A Comprehensive Edition.* Edited by John J. McDermott. New York: Random House.

Jamison, Leslie. 2014. *The Empathy Exams: Essays.* Minneapolis, Minn.: Graywolf Press.

Jewish Publication Society. 1985. *Tanakh: A New Translation of the Holy Scriptures According to the Traditional Hebrew Text.* 1st ed. Philadelphia: Jewish Publication Society.

Johnson, Mark. 1993. *Moral Imagination: Implications of Cognitive Science for Ethics.* Chicago: University of Chicago Press.

Jones, Therese, Delese Wear, Lester D. Friedman, and Kathleen Pachucki. 2014. *Health Humanities Reader.* New Brunswick, N.J.: Rutgers University Press.

Kafer, Alison. 2013. *Feminist, Queer, Crip.* Bloomington: Indiana University Press.

Kahane, Guy, and Julian Savulescu. 2012. "The Concept of Harm and the Significance of Normality." *Journal of Applied Philosophy* 29 (4): 318–32. https://doi.org/10.1111/j.1468-5930.2012.00574.x.

Käll, Lisa Folkmarson. 2013. *Dimensions of Pain: Humanities and Social Science Perspectives.* Routledge Studies in the Sociology of Health and Illness. Abingdon, U.K.: Routledge.

Kant, Immanuel. 2012. *Lectures on Anthropology.* Cambridge Edition of the Works of Immanuel Kant in Translation. Cambridge: Cambridge University Press.

Keele, Kenneth D. 1957. *Anatomies of Pain.* Springfield, Ill.: Charles C. Thomas.

Kestenbaum, Victor. 1982. *The Humanity of the Ill: Phenomenological Perspectives.* 1st ed. Knoxville: University of Tennessee Press.

Khader, Serene. 2011. *Adaptive Preferences and Women's Empowerment.* Studies in Feminist Philosophy. Oxford: Oxford University Press.

Kittay, Eva Feder. 1999. *Love's Labor: Essays on Women, Equality, and Dependency.* New York: Routledge.

Kittay, Eva Feder. 2006. "At the Margins of Moral Personhood." *Ethics* 116 (1): 100–131. https://doi.org/10.1007/s11673-008-9102-9.

Kittay, Eva Feder, and Licia Carlson. 2010. *Cognitive Disability and Its Challenge to Moral Philosophy.* Metaphilosophy Series in Philosophy. West Sussex, Mass.: Wiley-Blackwell.

Kittay, Eva Feder. 2019. *Learning from My Daughter: The Value and Care of Disabled Minds.* Oxford: Oxford University Press.

Kleege, Georgina. 1999. *Sight Unseen.* New Haven, Conn.: Yale University Press.

Klein, Colin. 2007. "An Imperative Theory of Pain." *Journal of Philosophy* 104 (10): 517–32. https://doi.org/10.2307/20620051.

Klein, Colin. 2011. "Imperatives, Phantom Pains, and Hallucination by Presupposition." *Philosophical Psychology* 25 (6): 917–28. https://doi.org/10.1080/09515089.2011.625121.

Klein, Colin. 2015. *What the Body Commands: The Imperative Theory of Pain.* Cambridge, Mass.: MIT Press.

Kleinman, Arthur. 1986. *Social Origins of Distress and Disease: Depression, Neurasthenia, and Pain in Modern China.* New Haven, Conn.: Yale Univeristy Press.

Kleinman, Arthur. 1988. *The Illness Narratives: Suffering, Healing, and the Human Condition.* New York: Basic Books.

Kugelmann, Robert. 1999. "Complaining about Chronic Pain." *Social Science and Medicine* 49 (12): 1663–76. https://doi.org/10.1016/S0277-9536(99)00240-3.

Kukla, Quill [Rebecca]. 2015. "Medicalization, 'Normal Function,' and the Definition of Health." In *The Routledge Companion to Bioethics,* edited by Jonathan Arras, Elizabeth Fenton, and Quill [Rebecca] Kukla, 515–30. New York: Routledge.

Lamé, Inge E., Madelon L. Peters, Johan W. S. Vlaeyen, Maarten van Kleef, and Jacob Patijn. 2005. "Quality of Life in Chronic Pain Is More Associated with Beliefs about Pain, than with Pain Intensity." *European Journal of Pain* 9 (1): 15–24. https://doi.org/10.1016/j.ejpain.2004.02.006.

Leder, Drew. 1990. *The Absent Body.* Chicago: University of Chicago Press.

Leder, Drew. 2016. *The Distressed Body: Rethinking Illness, Imprisonment, and Healing.* Chicago: University of Chicago Press.

Levinas, Emmanuel. 1981. *Otherwise than Being or beyond Essence.* Translated by Alphonso Lingis. Martinus Nijhoff Philosophy Texts. Boston: M. Nijhoff.

Levinas, Emmanuel. 1988. "Useless Suffering." In *The Provocation of Levinas: Rethinking the Other,* edited by Robert Bernasconi and David Wood, 156–67. London: Routledge.

Lewiecki-Wilson, Cynthia, and Jen Cellio. 2011. *Disability and Mothering: Liminal Spaces of Embodied Knowledge.* 1st ed. Critical Perspectives on Disability. Syracuse, N.Y.: Syracuse University Press.

Lewis, Sharon Mantik, Shannon Ruff Dirksen, Margaret M. Heitkemper, Linda Bucher, and Mariann Harding. 2014. *Medical-Surgical Nursing: Assessment and Management of Clinical Problems.* 9th ed. St. Louis, Mo.: Elsevier/Mosby.

Lindsey, Elizabeth. 1996. "Health within Illness: Experiences of Chronically Ill/Disabled People." *Journal of Advanced Nursing* 24 (3): 465–72. https://doi.org/10.1046/j.1365-2648.1996.02135.x.

Locke, John. 1988. *Two Treatises of Government.* Translated by Peter Laslett. Cambridge Texts in the History of Political Thought. Cambridge: Cambridge University Press.

Longmore, Paul K. 2015. *Telethons: Spectacle, Disability, and the Business of Charity.* Oxford: Oxford University Press.

Lorde, Audre. 1997. *The Cancer Journals.* Special ed. San Francisco: Aunt Lute Books.

Lysaker, John. 2014. "Being Equal to the Moment: Form as Historical Praxis." *Philosophy and Literature* 38 (2): 395–415.

Mairs, Nancy. 1996. *Waist-High in the World: A Life among the Nondisabled.* Boston: Beacon Press.

Macfarquhar, Neil. 1999. "8 Are Charged in Tormenting of Learning-Disabled Man." *New York Times,* February 17. http://www.nytimes.com/1999/02/17/nyregion/8-are-charged-in-tormenting-of-learning-disabled-man.html.

Mackenzie, Catriona, and Natalie Stoljar. 1999. *Relational Autonomy: Feminist Perspectives on Automony, Agency, and the Social Self.* New York: Oxford University Press.

Martínez, Manolo. 2011. "Imperative Content and the Painfulness of Pain." *Phenomenology and the Cognitive Sciences* 10 (1): 67–90. https://doi.org/10.1007/s11097-010-9172-0.

Mauldin, Laura. 2016. *Made to Hear: Cochlear Implants and Raising Deaf Children.* Minneapolis: University of Minnesota Press.

Mbembe, Achille. 2017. *Critique of Black Reason.* Durham, N.C.: Duke University Press.

McKim, A. Elizabeth. 2005. "Making Poetry of Pain: The Headache Poems of Jane Cave Winscom." *Literature and Medicine* 24 (1): 93–108.

McMahan, Jeff. 2002. *The Ethics of Killing: Problems at the Margins of Life.* Oxford Ethics Series. New York: Oxford University Press.

McMahan, Jeff. 2005. "Causing Disabled People to Exist and Causing People to Be Disabled." *Ethics* 116 (1): 77–99.

McNeill, Jeanette. 2007. "Unequal Quality of Cancer Pain Management: Disparity in Perceived Control and Proposed Solutions." *Oncology Nursing Forum* 34 (6): 1121–28.

McRuer, Robert. 2006. *Crip Theory: Cultural Signs of Queerness and Disability.* New York: New York University Press.

Meeks, Wayne A., and Jouette M. Bassler. 1993. *The Harpercollins Study Bible: New Revised Standard Version with the Apocryphal/Deuterocanonical Books.* 1st ed. New York: HarperCollins.

Meissner, W., S. Mescha, J. Rothaug, S. Zwacka, A. Goettermann, K. Ulrich, and A. Schleppers. 2008. "Quality Improvement in Postoperative Pain Management: Results from the QUIPS Project." *Deutsches Ärzteblatt International* 105 (50): 865–70. https://doi.org/10.3238/arztebl.2008.0865.

Meldrum, M. L. 2003. "A Capsule History of Pain Management." *JAMA* 290 (18): 2470–75. https://doi.org/10.1001/jama.290.18.2470.

Melzack, Ronald. 1973. *The Puzzle of Pain.* Penguin Modern Psychology: Motivation and Emotion. Harmondsworth, U.K.: Penguin Books.

Melzack, R., and P. D. Wall. 2003. *Handbook of Pain Management: A Clinical Companion to Wall and Melzack's Textbook of Pain.* China: Churchill Livingstone.

Mendieta, Eduardo. 2012. Review of *Heidegger among the Sculptors,* by Andrew Mitchell. *Society and Space,* July 1. https://www.societyandspace.org/articles/heidegger-among-the-sculptors-by-andrew-mitchell.

Merleau-Ponty, Maurice. 1945. *Phénoménologie de la perception.* Paris: Gallimard.

Merleau-Ponty, Maurice. 2011. *Phenomenology of Perception.* Translated by Donald A. Landes. Oxon, U.K.: Routledge.

Metzler, Irina. 2013. *A Social History of Disability in the Middle Ages: Cultural Considerations of Physical Impairment.* Routledge Studies in Cultural History. New York: Routledge, Taylor and Francis Group.

Michalko, Rod. 1999. *The Two-in-One: Walking with Smokie, Walking with Blindness.* Animals, Culture, and Society. Philadelphia: Temple University Press.

Midgley, Mary. 1983. "Duties Concerning Islands: Of Rights and Obligations." *Encounter* 60 (2): 36–42.

Miles, A., H. V. Curran, S. Pearce, and L. Allan. 2005. "Managing Constraint: The Experience of People with Chronic Pain." *Social Science and Medicine* 61 (2): 431–41. https://doi.org/10.1016/j.socscimed.2004.11.065.

Mill, John Stuart. 2006. *The Collected Works of John Stuart Mill.* Vol. X. Indianapolis, Ind.: Liberty Fund.

Mill, John Stuart, and Jeremy Bentham. 1987. *Utilitarianism and Other Essays.* Penguin Classics. New York: Penguin Books.

Mills, Charles. 1994. "Non-Cartesian 'Sums': Philosophy and the African-American Experience." *Teaching Philosophy* 17 (3): 223–43.

Miserandino, Christine. 2003. "The Spoon Theory." http://www.butyoudont looksick.com/articles/written-by-christine/the-spoon-theory/.

Mitchell, David T., and Sharon L. Snyder. 2007. "Jesus Thrown Everything Off Balance: Disability Studies and Contemporary Biblical Exegesis." In *This Abled Body: Rethinking Disability and Biblical Studies*, edited by S. Melcher, H. Avalos, and J. Schipper, 173–83. Atlanta, Ga.: Society of Biblical Literature.

Mitchell, David T., and Sharon L. Snyder. 2015. *Biopolitics of Disability: Neoliberalism, Ablenationalism, and Peripheral Embodiment*. Edited by Sharon L. Snyder. Ann Arbor: University of Michigan Press.

Moscoso, Javier. 2012. *Pain: A Cultural History*. Basingstoke, U.K.: Palgrave Macmillan.

Nagi, Saad Zaghloul. 1970. *Disability and Rehabilitation: Legal, Clinical, and Self-Concepts and Measurements*. Columbus: Ohio State University Press.

Nail, Thomas. 2016. *Theory of the Border*. Oxford: Oxford University Press.

National Center for Health Statistics. 2017. *Health, United States, 2017: With Special Feature on Mortality*. https://www.cdc.gov/nchs/data/hus/hus17.pdf.

Nettleton, Sarah. 2006. "'I Just Want Permission to Be Ill': Towards a Sociology of Medically Unexplained Symptoms." *Social Science and Medicine* 62 (5): 1167–78. https://doi.org/10.1016/j.socscimed.2005.07.030.

Newton, Benjamin J., Jane L. Southall, Jon H. Raphael, Robert L. Ashford, and Karen LeMarchand. 2013. "A Narrative Review of the Impact of Disbelief in Chronic Pain." *Pain Management Nursing* 14 (3): 161–71. https://doi.org/10.1016/j.pmn.2010.09.001.

Nielsen, Kim E. 2012. *A Disability History of the United States*. Revisioning American History. Boston: Beacon Press.

Nietzsche, Friedrich Wilhelm. 1966. *Beyond Good and Evil: Prelude to a Philosophy of the Future*. Translated by Walter Arnold Kaufmann. New York: Vintage Books.

Nietzsche, Friedrich Wilhelm. 1967. *On the Genealogy of Morals: Ecce Homo*. Translated by Walter Arnold Kaufmann. New York: Vintage Books.

Nussbaum, Martha. 2000. *Women and Human Development: The Capabilities Approach*. John Robert Seeley Lectures. Cambridge: Cambridge University Press.

Olivier, Abraham. 2007. *Being in Pain*. Frankfurt am Main, Germany: Lang.

Ortega y Gasset, José. 1957. *Man and People*. 1st ed. New York: W. W. Norton.

Osborn, Jody, and Stuart W. G. Derbyshire. 2010. "Pain Sensation Evoked by Observing Injury in Others." *PAIN* 148 (2): 268–74. https://doi.org/10.1016/j.pain.2009.11.007.

Pantelia, Maria, dir. n.d. *Thesaurus Linguae Graecae*. Irvine: University of California. http://www.tlg.uci.edu/.

Parens, Erik, and Adrienne Asch. 2000. *Prenatal Testing and Disability Rights*. Washington, D.C.: Georgetown University Press.

Parens, Erik. 2015. *Shaping Our Selves: On Technology, Flourishing, and a Habit of Thinking*. Oxford: Oxford University Press.

Parens, Erik. 2017. "Choosing Flourishing: Toward a More 'Binocular' Way of

Thinking about Disability." *Kennedy Institute of Ethics Journal* 27 (2): 135–50. https://doi.org/10.1353/ken.2017.0013.

Parent, C. M. 2002. "Casey Martin's Four-Year Struggle with the PGA Tour." *Sport Lawyers Journal* 9: 57–92.

Pateman, Carole. 1988. *The Sexual Contract*. Stanford, Calif.: Stanford University Press.

Patsavas, Alyson. 2014. "Recovering a Cripistemology of Pain: Leaky Bodies, Connective Tissue, and Feeling Discourse." *Journal of Literary and Cultural Disability Studies* 8 (2): 203–18.

Peña-Guzmán, David, and Joel Michael Reynolds. 2019. "The Harm of Ableism: Medical Error and Epistemic Injustice," *Kennedy Institute of Ethics Journal* 29 (3): 205–42. doi: 10.1353/ken.2019.0023.

Pernick, Martin S. 1985. *A Calculus of Suffering: Pain, Professionalism, and Anesthesia in Nineteenth-Century America*. New York: Columbia University Press.

PGA Tour, Inc. v. Martin, 532 U.S. 661 (2001).

Piepzna-Samarasinha, Leah Lakshmi. 2018. *Care Work: Dreaming Disability Justice*. Vancouver, B.C.: Arsenal Pulp Press.

Pinker, Steven. 2015. "The Moral Imperative for Bioethics." *Boston Globe*, July 31. https://www.bostonglobe.com/opinion/2015/07/31/the-moral -imperative-for-bioethics/JmEkoyzlTAu9oQV76JrK9N/story.html.

Pitcher, George. 1970. "Pain Perception." *Philosophical Review* 79 (3): 368–93.

Plato. 1997. *Complete Works*. Indianapolis, Ind.: Hackett.

Plato. 2002. *Five Dialogues*. Translated by G. M. A. Grube. 2nd ed. Indianapolis, Ind.: Hackett.

Price, Donald D. 2000. "Psychological and Neural Mechanisms of the Affective Dimension of Pain." *Science* 288 (5472): 1769–72. https://doi.org/10.2307/3075424.

Price, Margaret. 2015. "The Bodymind Problem and the Possibilities of Pain." *Hypatia* 30 (1): 268–84.

Puar, Jasbir K. 2013. "The Cost of Getting Better: Ability and Debility." In *The Disability Studies Reader*, edited by Lennard J. Davis. New York: Routledge.

Puar, Jasbir K. 2017. *The Right to Maim: Debility, Capacity, Disability*. Durham, N.C.: Duke University Press.

Ramey, Joshua. 2016. *Politics of Divination*. Reprint ed. New York: Rowman and Littlefield.

Reeve, Donna. 2014. "Psycho-Emotional Disablism and Internalised Oppression." In *Disabling Barriers—Enabling Environments*, edited by J. Swain, S. French, C. Barnes, and C. Thoms, 92–98. London: Sage.

Rey, Roselyne. 1995. *The History of Pain*. Cambridge, Mass.: Harvard University Press.

Reynolds, Joel Michael. 2015. "The Ableism of Quality of Life Judgments in Disorders of Consciousness: Who Bears Epistemic Responsibility?" *American Journal of Bioethics Neuroscience* 7 (1): 59–61.

Reynolds, Joel Michael. 2016a. "Infinite Responsibility in the Bedpan: Response Ethics, Care Ethics, and the Phenomenology of Dependency Work." *Hypatia* 31 (4): 779–94.

Reynolds, Joel Michael. 2016b. "Toward a Critical Theory of Harm: Ableism, Normativity, and Transability (BIID)." *APA Newsletter on Philosophy and Medicine* 16 (1): 37–45.

Reynolds, Joel Michael. 2017a. "'I'd Rather Be Dead than Disabled'—the Ableist Conflation and the Meanings of Disability." *Review of Communication* 17 (3): 149–63.

Reynolds, Joel Michael. 2017b. "Merleau-Ponty, World-Creating Blindness, and the Phenomenology of Non-Normate Bodies." *Chiasmi International* 19: 419–34.

Reynolds, Joel Michael. 2018. "Three Things Clinicians Should Know about Disability." *AMA Journal of Ethics* 20 (12): 1181–87.

Reynolds, Joel Michael. 2019. "Normate." In *50 Concepts for an Intersectional Phenomenology,* edited by Ann Murphy, Gayle Salamon, and Gail Weiss, 243–48. Evanston, Ill.: Northwestern University Press.

Reynolds, Joel Michael. 2021. "Genopower: On Genomics, Disability, and Impairment." *Foucault Studies* 31.

Reynolds, Joel Michael. 2022. "Health and Other Reveries: Homo Curare, Home Faber, and the Realization of Care." In *Normality, Abnormality, and Pathology in Merleau-Ponty,* edited by Talia Welsh and Susan Bredlau, 203–24. New York: SUNY Press.

Reynolds, Joel Michael, and Christine Wieseler, eds. 2022. *The Disability Bioethics Reader.* New York: Routledge.

Rich, Adrienne. 1985. "Notes toward a Politics of Location." In *Women, Feminist Identity, and Society in the 1980's: Selected Papers,* edited by Myriam Díaz-Diocaretz and Iris M. Zavala, 7–22. Amsterdam: Benjamins.

Richardson, Jane C., Bie Nio Ong, and Julius Sim. 2006. "Is Chronic Widespread Pain Biographically Disruptive?" *Social Science and Medicine* 63 (6): 1573–85. https://doi.org/10.1016/j.socscimed.2006.03.040.

Richter, Gerhard, and Theodor W. Adorno. 2002. "Who's Afraid of the Ivory Tower? A Conversation with Theodor W. Adorno." *Monatshefte* 94, no. 1: 10–23. http://www.jstor.org/stable/30161947.

Roberts, Jessica L., and Elizabeth Weeks Leonard. 2016. "What Is (and Isn't) Healthism?" *Georgia Law Review* 50 (3): 833–907.

Rogers, Richard. 2008. *Clinical Assessment of Malingering and Deception.* 3rd ed. New York: Guilford Press.

Rogerson, John. 2004. *Genesis 1–11.* London: T&T Clark International.

Rorty, Richard. 1989. *Contingency, Irony, and Solidarity.* Cambridge: Cambridge University Press.

Rose, Martha L. 2003. *The Staff of Oedipus: Transforming Disability in Ancient Greece.* Ann Arbor: University of Michigan Press.

Rose, Nikolas S. 1999. *Powers of Freedom: Reframing Political Thought*. Cambridge: Cambridge University Press.

Rothaug, J., T. Weiss, and W. Meissner. 2013. "How Simple Can It Get? Measuring Pain with NRS Items or Binary Items." *Clinical Journal of Pain* 29 (3): 224–32. https://doi.org/10.1097/AJP.0b013e31824c5d7a.

Rubin, Gayle. 2012. *Deviations: A Gayle Rubin Reader*. Durham, N.C.: Duke University Press.

Russell, Marta. 2019. *Capitalism and Disability: Selected Writings by Marta Russell*. Edited by Keith Rosenthal. Chicago: Haymarket Books.

Russell, Marta. 2002. *Beyond Ramps: Disability at the End of the Social Contract*. Monroe, Maine: Common Courage Press.

Said, Edward W. 1993. *Culture and Imperialism*. 1st ed. New York: Knopf.

Salamon, Gayle. 2012. "The Phenomenology of Rheumatology: Disability, Merleau-Ponty, and the Fallacy of Maximal Grip." *Hypatia* 27 (2): 243–60. https://doi.org/10.1111/j.1527-2001.2012.01266.x.

Salmon, Peter. 2007. "Conflict, Collusion or Collaboration in Consultations about Medically Unexplained Symptoms: The Need for a Curriculum of Medical Explanation." *Patient Education and Counseling* 67 (3): 246–54. https://doi.org/10.1016/j.pec.2007.03.008.

Samuels, Ellen Jean. 2014. *Fantasies of Identification: Disability, Gender, Race, Cultural Front*. New York: New York University Press.

Sandel, Michael J. 2007. *The Case against Perfection: Ethics in the Age of Genetic Engineering*. Cambridge, Mass.: Belknap Press of Harvard University Press.

Sanders, E. P. 1977. *Paul and Palestinian Judaism: A Comparison of Patterns of Religion*. 1st American ed. Philadelphia: Fortress Press.

Sargent, C. 1984. "Between Death and Shame: Dimensions of Pain in Bariba Culture." *Social Science and Medicine* 19: 1299–1304.

Sartre, Jean-Paul. 1984. *Being and Nothingness: An Essay in Phenomenological Ontology*. Translated by Hazel E. Barnes. New York: Washington Square Press.

Scarry, Elaine. 1985. *The Body in Pain: The Making and Unmaking of the World*. New York: Oxford University Press.

Schürmann, Reiner. 2003. *Broken Hegemonies*. Translated by Reginald Lilly. Studies in Continental Thought. Bloomington: Indiana University Press.

Scully, Jackie Leach. 2008. *Disability Bioethics: Moral Bodies, Moral Difference, Feminist Constructions*. Lanham, Md.: Rowman and Littlefield.

Scuro, Jennifer. 2017. *Addressing Ableism: Philosophical Questions via Disability Studies*. Lanham, Md.: Lexington Books.

Shakespeare, Tom. 2014a. *Disability Rights and Wrongs Revisited*. 2nd ed. London: Routledge.

Shakespeare, Tom. 2014b. "The Social Model of Disability." In *The Disability Studies Reader*, edited by Lennard J. Davis, 214–21. New York: Routledge.

Shakespeare, Tom, and Nicholas Watson. 2001. "The Social Model of Disability: An Outdated Ideology?" In *Exploring Theories and Expanding*

Methodologies: Where We Are and Where We Need to Go, 9–28. London: Emerald Group.

Shalk, Sami. 2018. *Bodyminds Reimagined: (Dis)ability, Race, and Gender in Black Women's Speculative Fiction*. Durham, N.C.: Duke University Press.

Sherry, Mark. 2010. *Disability Hate Crimes: Does Anyone Really Hate Disabled People?* Burlington, Vt.: Ashgate.

Shildrick, Margrit. 1997. *Leaky Bodies and Boundaries: Feminism, Postmodernism and (Bio)Ethics*. London: Routledge.

Shklar, Judith. 1989. "The Liberalism of Fear." In *Liberalism and the Moral Life*, edited by Nancy L. Rosenblum, vi. Cambridge, Mass.: Harvard University Press.

Siebers, Tobin. 2008. *Disability Theory, Corporealities*. Ann Arbor: University of Michigan Press.

Silvers, Anita. 1995. "Reconciling Equality to Difference: Caring (f)or Justice for People with Disabilities." *Hypatia* 10 (1): 30–55. https://doi.org/10.2307/3810457.

Silvers, Anita, and Leslie Pickering Francis. 2005. "Justice through Trust: Disability and the 'Outlier Problem' in Social Contract Theory." *Ethics* 116: 40–76.

Simplican, Stacy Clifford. 2015. *The Capacity Contract: Intellectual Disability and the Question of Citizenship*. Minneapolis: University of Minnesota Press.

Smith, David Livingstone. 2011. *Less than Human: Why We Demean, Enslave, and Exterminate Others*. 1st ed. New York: St. Martin's Press.

Smith, Diane L. 2009. "Disparities in Patient–Physician Communication for Persons with a Disability from the 2006 Medical Expenditure Panel Survey." *Disability and Health Journal* 2 (4): 206–15.

Snyder, A. R., J. T. Parsons, T. C. Valovich McLeod, R. C. Bay, L. A. Michener, and E. L. Sauers. 2008. "Using Disablement Models and Clinical Outcomes Assessment to Enable Evidence-Based Athletic Training Practice, Part I: Disablement Models." *Journal of Athletic Training* 43 (4): 428–36.

Social Security Advisory Board: Schieber, Sylvester & Bilyeu, Dana & Hardy, Dorcas & Katz, Marsha & Kennelly, Barbara & Warshawsky, Mark. 2009. *The Unsustainable Cost of Health Care*. Washington, D.C. https://www.researchgate.net/publication/283347029_The_Unsustainable_Cost_of_Healthcare.

Spivak, Gayatri Chakravorty. 2006. *In Other Worlds: Essays in Cultural Politics*. New York: Routledge, Taylor and Francis Group.

Staton, L. J., Panda M. Chen, Genao J. Kurz, M. Pasanen, A. J. Mechaber, M. Menon, J. O'Rorke, J. Wood, E. Rosenberg, C. Faeslis, T. Carey, D. Calleson, and S. Cykert. 2007. "When Race Matters: Disagreement in Pain Perception between Patients and Their Physicians in Primary Care." *Journal of the National Medical Association* 99 (5): 532–38.

Stevens, Bethany. 2011. "Interrogating Transability: A Catalyst to View Disability as Body Art." *Disability Studies Quarterly* 31 (4). https://dsq-sds.org/article/view/1705/1755.

Stoller, Robert J. 1991. *Pain and Passion: A Psychoanalyst Explores the World of S&M.* New York: Plenum Press.

St. Pierre, Joshua. 2015. "Distending Straight-Masculine Time: A Phenomenology of the Disabled Speaking Body." *Hypatia* 30 (1): 49–65. https://doi.org/10.1111/hypa.12128.

Stramondo, Joseph A. 2016. "Why Bioethics Needs a Disability Moral Psychology." *Hastings Center Report* 46: 22–30. https://doi.org/10.1002/hast.585.

Stramondo, Joseph A. 2020. "Disability and the Damaging Master Narrative of an Open Future." *Hastings Center Report* 50 (S1): S30–36. https://doi.org/10/gg94m4.

Strong, James. 1996. *The New Strong's Exhaustive Concordance of the Bible: With Main Concordance, Appendix to the Main Concordance, Hebrew and Aramaic Dictionary of the Old Testament, Greek Dictionary of the New Testament.* Nashville, Tenn.: T. Nelson.

Strong, Marilee. 1998. *A Bright Red Scream: Self-Mutilation and the Language of Pain.* New York: Viking.

Sullivan, Mark D. 1995. "Pain in Language: From Sentience to Sapience." *Pain Forum* 4 (1): 3–14. https://doi.org/10.1016/S1082-3174(11)80068-1.

Sussman, Marvin B. 1965. *Sociology and Rehabilitation.* Edited by Marvin B. Sussman. Washington, D.C.: American Sociological Association.

Tait, Raymond C., and John T. Chibnall. 2014. "Racial/Ethnic Disparities in the Assessment and Treatment of Pain: Psychosocial Perspectives." *American Psychologist* 69 (2): 131–41. https://doi.org/10.1037/a0035204.

Talley, Colin Lee. 2008. *A History of Multiple Sclerosis, Healing Society—Disease, Medicine, and History.* Westport, Conn.: Praeger.

Tan, S. Y. 2002. "Medicine in Stamps: Moses Maimonides (1135–1204): Rabbi, Philosopher, Physician." *Singapore Medical Journal* 43 (11): 551–53.

Thagard, Paul. 1999. *How Scientists Explain Disease.* Princeton, N.J.: Princeton University Press.

Thernstrom, Melanie. 2010. *The Pain Chronicles: Cures, Myths, Mysteries, Prayers, Diaries, Brain Scans, Healing, and the Science of Suffering.* 1st ed. New York: Farrar, Straus, and Giroux.

Thomas, Carol. 2004. "Developing the Social Relational in the Social Model of Disability: A Theoretical Agenda." In *Implementing the Social Model of Disability: Theory and Research,* edited by C. Barnes and G. Mercer, 32–47. Leeds, U.K.: Disability Press.

Titchkosky, Tanya. 2011. *The Question of Access: Disability, Space, Meaning.* Toronto: University of Toronto Press.

Titchkosky, Tanya, and Rod Michalko. 2012. "The Body as the Problem of Individuality: A Phenomenological Disability Studies Approach." In *Disability and Social Theory: New Developments and Directions,* edited by Dan

Goodley, Bill Hughes, and Lennard J. Davis, 127–42. New York: Palgrave Macmillan.

Toombs, S. Kay. 1992. *The Meaning of Illness: A Phenomenological Account of the Different Perspectives of Physician and Patient, Philosophy and Medicine.* Boston: Kluwer.

Toombs, S. Kay. 1995a. "The Lived Experience of Disability." *Human Studies* 18: 9–23.

Toombs, S. Kay. 1995b. "Sufficient unto the Day: A Life with Multiple Sclerosis." In *Chronic Illness: From Experience to Policy,* edited by S. K. Toombs, D. Barnard, and R. A. Carson, 3–23. Bloomington: Indiana University Press.

Toombs, S. Kay. 1998. "Articulating the Hard Choices: A Practical Role for Philosophy in the Clinical Context." *Human Studies* 21 (1): 49–55.

Toombs, S. Kay. 2001. *Handbook of Phenomenology and Medicine.* Philosophy and Medicine. Boston: Kluwer Academic.

Toombs, S. Kay. 2012. "Personal/Professional Background." *Curriculum Vita.*

Traustadóttir, Rannveig. 2009. "Disability Studies: The Social Model and Legal Developments." In *The UN Convention on the Rights of Persons with Disabilities: European and Scandinavian Perspectives,* International Studies in Human Rights 100, edited by Oddný Mjöll Arnardóttir and Gerard Quinn, 1–16. Leiden, The Netherlands: Martinus Nijhoff.

Tremain, Shelley, ed. 2005. *Foucault and the Government of Disability.* Corporealities. Ann Arbor: University of Michigan Press.

Tremain, Shelley, ed. 2015a. *Foucault and the Government of Disability.* 2nd ed. Ann Arbor: University of Michigan Press.

Tremain, Shelley. 2015b. "This Is What a Historicist and Relativist Feminist Philosophy of Disability Looks Like." *Foucault Studies* 19: 7–42.

Trent, James W. 2017. *Inventing the Feeble Mind: A History of Intellectual Disability in the United States.* 2nd ed. Oxford: Oxford University Press.

Tronto, Joan C. 1993. *Moral Boundaries: A Political Argument for an Ethic of Care.* New York: Routledge.

Verbrugge, L. M., and A. M. Jette. 1994. "The Disablement Process." *Social Science and Medicine* 38 (1): 1–14.

Vlaeyen, J. W. S., and G. Crombez. 1999. "Fear of Movement/(Re)Injury, Avoidance, and Pain Disability in Chronic Low Back Pain Patients." *Manual Therapy* 4 (4): 187–95. https://doi.org/10.1054/math.1999.0199.

Vrancken, Mariet A. E. 1989. "Schools of Thought on Pain." *Social Science and Medicine* 29 (3): 435–44. https://doi.org/10.1016/0277-9536(89)90292-X.

Wailoo, Keith. 2014. *Pain: A Political History.* Baltimore: Johns Hopkins University Press.

Wall, Patrick D. 2000. *Pain: The Science of Suffering.* Maps of the Mind. New York: Columbia University Press.

Wall, Patrick D., Ronald Melzack, S. B. McMahon, and Martin Koltzenburg. 2006. *Wall and Melzack's Textbook of Pain.* 5th ed. Philadelphia: Elsevier/Churchill Livingstone.

Wasserman, David, Adrienne Asch, Jeffrey Blustein, and Daniel Putnam. 2013. *Disability: Definitions, Models, Experience*. Stanford, Calif.: Stanford Encyclopedia of Philosophy.

Wendell, Susan. 1996. *The Rejected Body: Feminist Philosophical Reflections on Disability*. New York: Routledge.

Wendell, Susan. 2001. "Unhealthy Disabled: Treating Chronic Illnesses as Disabilities." *Hypatia* 16 (4): 17–33. https://doi.org/10.1111/j.1527-2001.2001.tb00751.x.

Werner, Anne, Lise Widding Isaksen, and Kirsti Malterud. 2004. "'I Am Not the Kind of Woman Who Complains of Everything': Illness Stories on Self and Shame in Women with Chronic Pain." *Social Science and Medicine* 59 (5): 1035–45. https://doi.org/10.1016/j.socscimed.2003.12.001.

Werner, Anne, and Kirsti Malterud. 2003. "It Is Hard Work Behaving as a Credible Patient: Encounters between Women with Chronic Pain and their Doctors." *Social Science and Medicine* 57 (8): 1409–19. https://doi.org/10.1016/S0277-9536(02)00520-8.

White, Daniel P. 2013. "The Uncontrollable Increase in United States' Disability Rolls and the Inevitable Exhaustion of the United States' Disability System." Honors scholar thesis, University of Connecticut, Storrs.

Willis, Marjorie Canfield. 2006. *Medical Terminology: The Language of Health Care*. 2nd ed. Philadelphia: Lippincott Williams and Wilkins.

Winscom, Jane Cave. 1795. *Poems on Various Subjects, Entertaining, Elegiac and Religious. By Miss Cave, Now Mrs. Winscom. The Fourth Edition, Corrected and Improved, with Many Additional Poems, Never before Published*. Eighteenth Century Collections Online. Bristol, U.K.: Gale Group.

Wittgenstein, Ludwig. 2003. *Philosophical Investigations: The German Text, with a Revised English Translation*. Translated by G. E. M. Anscombe. 3rd ed. Malden, Mass.: Blackwell.

Woolf, Virginia. 1994. *The Essays of Virginia Woolf: Vol. 4. 1925–1928*. Edited by Andrew McNeillie. London: Hogarth Press.

World Health Organization. 2001. *International Classification of Functioning, Disability and Health*. Geneva: World Health Organization.

Young, Iris Marion. 2005. *On Female Body Experience: "Throwing Like a Girl" and Other Essays*. Studies in Feminist Philosophy. New York: Oxford University Press.

Zebrowski, Robin Lynn. 2009. "We Are Plastic: Human Variability and the Myth of the Standard Body." PhD diss., University of Oregon.

Index

ability: as access, 116, 129, 130, 158; to
breathe (*see* oxygen); as care, 116;
as charm, 119; fluidity, 95–96, 102;
as function, 134–135; and moral
worth, 128–29; as relations, 157;
social versus human, 131; transitions, 91–96; variability of, 109,
128, 137. *See also* built environment; disability theory; theory of
personal ability
ability expectations, 65, 92–93, 119,
126. *See also* attentional reconfiguration; chess
ableism: beyond, 155–59; defined, 18,
169n2; imaginary, 117–19; norms,
63
ableist conflation, 4–14, 50–51, 56–57,
93; and dehumanization, 110;
hyperinflation of, 105; origins of,
115–16
Abrahamic traditions: accounts of
disability, 66–71; accounts of pain,
20–25
absence, 117–18
access: ability as, 116, 129, 130, 158;
and attentional reconfiguration,
100–101; and social environment,
107, 110. *See also* built environment
accidental injury. *See* helmet-wearing
activism, 5, 61–65, 71, 76, 154; bioethicists contra, 8; UK versus U.S.,
175n1
Adorno, Theodor, 84
advocating for loved ones, 145

allergies, 102, 140, 142, 181n9
Alzheimer's, 72
ambivalent medicalization, 48
Americans with Disabilities Act, 63,
107, 120
anti-ableist future, 157
arche, 2
Aristotle, 1, 2, 17, 25, 64, 119, 128, 155,
171n18, 176n11
assistive devices, 106
attentional reconfiguration, 99–103
Austin, Alfredo Lopez, 70
autonomy, 118–19, 155
Autonomy Myth, The, 118–19

Barnes, Elizabeth, 108
BDSM, 31, 51
Beauvoir, Simone de, 56, 92, 127
beholdenness, 46–47
Being and Nothingness, 29–32
being-in-the-world, 31, 32, 54, 72, 83,
100, 102, 108, 127
Bell, Christopher M., 78
Bergson, Henri, 115
Bible: cosmogony, 20–23; documentary hypothesis, 20–21; healing
miracles, 68, 69; Pauline theology,
23
binary thinking, 99, 104, 117, 118
bioethics, 7–9
bioreckoning, 47–49
biosocial theories of disability, 75–80
Birth of the Clinic, The, 37
#BlackLivesMatter, 125

welfare state: experience with, 140; resistance to, 120, 133
Wendell, Susan, 5, 78, 139
West, Cornel, 160
Western canon, 1–7, 20–25
"what about you?," 140–43, 146

What Can a Body Do?, 153
wheelchair, 98, 100–107; discrimination, 105; as freedom, 107; heavy versus light, 106–7; use, 98, 100
World Health Organization publication, 77

Joel Michael Reynolds is assistant professor of philosophy and disability studies at Georgetown University, senior research scholar in the Kennedy Institute of Ethics, senior advisor to The Hastings Center, and core faculty in Georgetown's Disability Studies Program. He is the founder and coeditor of *The Journal of Philosophy of Disability* and cofounder as well as coeditor of the book series Oxford Studies in Disability, Ethics, and Society.